161 091122 3

effective lear

Two week
loan

Please return on or before the last
date stamped below.
Charges are made for late return.

WITHDRAWN

IS 239/0799

INFORMATION SERVICES PO BOX 430, CARDIFF CF10 3XT

HIGHER
EDUCATION SUPPLEMENT

KOGAN
PAGE

First published in 2001

Kogan Page Limited
120 Pentonville Road
London N1 9JN
UK

Stylus Publishing Inc.
22883 Quicksilver Drive
Sterling VA 20166 2012
USA

The views expressed in this book are those of the author and are not necessarily the same as those of *The Times Higher Education Supplement*.

British Library Cataloguing in Publication Data

A CIP record for this book is available from the British Library.

ISBN 0 7494 3448 1

Typeset by Saxon Graphics Ltd, Derby
Printed and bound in Great Britain by Clays Ltd, St Ives plc

Contents

About the editors

Dr Bruce Macfarlane is Senior Lecturer in Educational Development at City University, London. He has 13 years' experience as a business and management lecturer in higher education and has also worked in the banking sector and as a teacher in Hong Kong. He has published widely on a range of issues including the business and management curriculum, the teaching of business ethics and aspects of academic practice in higher education. He is an accreditor with the Institute for Learning and Teaching in Higher Education (ILT).

Roger Ottewill is Head of the Centre for Business Education Research at Sheffield Hallam University. He has been engaged in various forms of learner support for over 25 years. His educational research interests include open learning, the nature of vocationalism, cross-cultural capability, the application of communication and information technology, and course evaluation. He has published in a wide variety of academic journals and contributed to international conferences organised by Educational Innovation in Economics and Business (EDINEB).

About the specialist contributors

Dr Ardha Danieli is Lecturer in Qualitative Research Methods and Organisational Analysis in the Industrial Relations and Organisational Behaviour group at Warwick University. She is also Academic Co-ordinator for the Warwick Business School Doctoral Methodology programme. Her research interests include gender and employment, organisational change and the management of identity.

June Fletcher is Head of Master of Business Administration (MBA) programmes at Southampton Business School, Southampton Institute. Her experience of teaching a wide range of qualification and in-company management development programmes is complemented by directorships of a family chemicals firm and a property management company. She is a member of the editorial board of the *Journal of Strategic Change*.

Philippa Gerbic is the Programme Leader of the Bachelor of Business degree at the Auckland University of Technology. She has wide experience in designing, developing and implementing integrated/interdisciplinary programmes in business and has taught commercial law in this context. Her research interests include curriculum development, electronic learning, reflective practice and innovation in business education.

Peter L Jennings is Director of the MBA for Recent Graduates at the University of Southampton, School of Management. He is editor of the *Journal of Small Business and Enterprise Development* and is a Director of the Institute for Small Business Affairs. He is also a member of the editorial board of the *Journal of Strategic Change*.

Karina Jensen is an Online Training Manager at Macromedia, a Web development software company in San Francisco, where she develops and manages e-learning programmes worldwide. Her interest in international business education and new technologies stems from her work at Ecole Nationale des Ponts et Chaussées (ENPC) School of International Management in Paris.

Dr Ranald Macdonald is Associate Head of Academic Development in the Learning and Teaching Institute at Sheffield Hallam University. He is Co-chair of the Staff and Educational Development Association. His research interests are in the areas of student and teacher conceptions and experiences of learning, in particular problem-based learning.

Andrew McConchie is a Senior Lecturer in the Faculty of Business at the Auckland University of Technology and Programme Leader within the Integrated Business Studies department. He has been teaching entrepreneurship and related courses within the department since 1993. His research interests include teamwork, professional practice, new business development and interdisciplinary education.

Andrew Perkins is Principal Lecturer in Marketing at Canterbury Christ Church University College where he is Programme Director of the Marketing degree. He is a member of the Chartered Institute of Marketing and his research interests include customer service, cross-cultural advertising and marketing education.

Dr Alan B Thomas is Senior Lecturer in Sociology and Organisational Behaviour at the Manchester Business School (MBS), University of Manchester. He has been involved with management education for over 25 years and has published numerous books and articles on management education topics. He is a former Director of both the Doctoral and the Executive MBA programmes at MBS. He is a member of the Board of the International Schools of Business Management and a Director of the International Teachers Programme.

Acknowledgements

We are very grateful to Sally Brown at the ILT and Jonathan Simpson at Kogan Page for commissioning us to edit this book. The commission has enabled us to pool our experience and expertise concerning the nature of effective learning and teaching in business and management. Our reflections on this subject have been shaped over many years through interaction with learners and debates with colleagues, especially Laurie Lomas, Kevin Tomlinson, Robert Melville, Rosie Bingham, Claire Capon, Fiona Drew, David Laughton, Peter Long, Christine O'Leary and Ann Wall. To all of those who have helped us in this way, albeit often unwittingly, we owe a considerable debt of thanks.

Learning how to facilitate learning is, of course, a never-ending process and one that depends not simply on personal reflection but also on engagement with others. Thus, it would not have been possible to produce a book of this kind without an input from those who share our concerns.

With this in mind, we are particularly indebted to Jonathan Slack for writing a foreword and to our specialist contributors. Undoubtedly, their chapters, reflecting a variety of different perspectives, enrich the book.

Last, but by no means least, we wish to thank our wives Alice and Valerie for their support and understanding.

Forewords

Effective teaching and learning support impacts positively on student performance, the student experience and the community into which our graduates emerge. This is the first book in a new series endorsed by the Institute for Learning and Teaching (ILT) in partnership with Kogan Page and *The Times Higher Education Supplement*.

Launched in June 1999, the ILT is a fast-growing membership body for all who teach and support learning in higher education in the UK, which aims to enhance the status of teaching, improve the experience of learning and support innovation in higher education. The ILT supports its members in their ongoing professional updating through a range of activities, which include publications, conferences and events and Web-based interactions.

These books are explicitly designed to improve teaching and learning support by drawing on the experience and expertise of subject specialists who are themselves effective teachers. The series provides practical, accessible guides, which are grounded in good practice, draw on relevant pedagogical research and aim to be useful to both new and experienced teachers. The ILT plans to produce 24 books in the series, which will include contributions from colleagues from the 24 UK Learning and Teaching Support Network (LTSN) Subject Centres.

In this book, the editors have brought together the work of UK and international authors committed to sharing good practice within the business and management field in higher education. The subject area is diverse, complex, expanding and central to the missions of many higher education institutions worldwide, all of which makes this book a fitting first volume in the series.

The Minister for Higher Education in the UK, Baroness Tessa Blackstone, speaking at the first National Teaching Fellowships Scheme award ceremony in July 2000, said, 'There is nothing universities do that is more important than teaching.' This book and those that are to follow it recognise the centrality of effective learning and teaching to an excellent higher education system and make a valuable contribution to promoting effective practice.

Sally Brown
Series Editor/Director of Membership Services
Institute for Learning and Teaching

Today, business and management education is big business. In the UK, for example, there are around 100 major business schools, providing learning to over 250,000 students each year in a sector that is worth annually in excess of £1.5 billion. The corporate training sector is also very large and expanding in most countries.

It is therefore encouraging to find, among the large volume of books in the business and management field, normally targeted at students and practising managers, one that is specifically designed for the growing community of business and management educators, trainers and developers.

Given the multidisciplinary nature of business and management and, historically speaking, its comparatively recent arrival into mainstream higher education, it is perhaps not surprising that teachers in the field generally have rather diverse backgrounds and experiences and arrive as tutors and researchers via an array of different routes.

Against this backdrop, therefore, the book provides an invaluable insight into the educational context of business and management by exploring its traditions and tensions together with the particular characteristics of typical learners in the field. All of this helps to reinforce its essentially inclusive nature and the multi-faceted contributions to opportunities for learners and graduating students to demonstrate their acquisition and application of knowledge, understanding and skills.

However, the main focus of the book is about the business and management learning environment and its underlying principles, upon which readers are encouraged to engage as 'reflective practitioners'.

This is highly beneficial given the evident dynamism, internationalism and pace of change in the general business and management arena. Specific areas, including for example international business, business ethics and innovation and entrepreneurship, are all covered in detail and provide illustrative 'good practice' guides in the process.

However, if the momentum and popularity that have characterized this sector to date are to be maintained, and even further advanced, then additional challenges that inevitably lie ahead need to be addressed and acted upon. These are covered as the book draws to a close by the attempt to anticipate the future via a range of scenarios, including for example work-based and online learning.

Finally, consideration is given to the likely impact upon the needs of individual teachers and learning facilitators in this highly important field in terms of their future professional development aspirations.

Jonathan Slack
Chief Executive
Association of Business Schools

Preface

Setting the scene

Over the past few decades business and management as a field of learning and teaching in higher education (HE) has experienced rapid growth and considerable diversification. Moreover, this has been a worldwide phenomenon, with the result that today there can be few countries where there is not a rich array of business and management courses and programmes at all levels of HE which encompass a wide variety of modes of delivery. The learning experiences of contemporary business and management students are many and varied. These range from sub-degree college-based courses to doctoral research-based programmes and from specialist masters courses by open and distance learning, in subjects such as marketing and international business, to corporate programmes delivered in collaboration with educational institutions. At the same time the increasing use of the World Wide Web and the resultant globalization of business and management education is adding a further dimension to these experiences.

Identifying the audience

The main purpose of this book is to serve as a guide for everyone who contributes to the learning experiences of business and management students, regardless of the nature of their contribution. Although it is anticipated that college and university-based teachers and learning facilitators, whether newly appointed or experienced, will constitute the core readership, many others including corporate trainers, information specialists, technical support staff and practising managers, who may be called upon to give guest lectures or act as mentors, should also find something of interest and value in what follows.

Use of the expression 'learning experiences' in this context is intended to underline the variety of influences at work, both planned and unplanned, that can either facilitate or hinder learning. In the field of business and management, effective learning and teaching increasingly depends upon ensuring that these influences are complementary and mutually reinforcing. Thus, everyone who makes a contribution to the learning experiences of business and management students should see themselves as part of a collaborative enterprise dedicated to making connections between the different elements and to providing opportunities for learners not simply to acquire, but also to apply, knowledge and skills.

Moreover, although the editors are based in the UK, the book is intended to meet the needs of business and management educators, wherever they are located geographically. To this end, a number of contributors are from other countries and/or have experience of business and management education in non-UK settings. Efforts have also been made to ensure that the terminology is accessible to all.

Explaining the aim

Throughout the book, the underlying aim of the authors is to assist those committed to the goal of effective learning and teaching in business and management at HE level. Thus, it does not focus on generic aspects of learning and teaching in HE for which there is now a substantial and rapidly expanding literature. Nor is it intended as a direct classroom resource with immediately 'consumable' exercises and activities. There are abundant materials of this nature available. Rather, it seeks to explain the challenges of business and management education and give examples of good practice from experienced facilitators in the field. Hence, it provides a guide for reflective practice and seeks to inspire and encourage educators to develop their own pedagogic principles.

In pursuing their aim, the authors have been guided by a number of considerations, all of which have a particular resonance for business and management.

First, account has been taken of the five areas for which experienced educators who apply for membership of the UK's Institute for Learning and Teaching in Higher Education (ILT) are required to produce evidence. These are:

- teaching and the support of learning;
- contribution to the design and planning of learning activities;
- assessment and giving feedback to students;
- developing effective learning environments and student learning support systems;
- reflective practice and personal development.

Such areas reflect the multifaceted and disparate nature of the contemporary learning environment, which is of particular significance for business and management students. Arguably, the circumstances and settings in which they learn are more varied and diverse than those of learners studying other subjects. With respect to settings, these include campus locations (eg lecture theatres, seminar rooms, computer suites and libraries/learning centres); corporate locations (eg training centres, workplace, meeting rooms); and the home.

Recognition is also given to the professional values that are expected to be evidenced in the behaviour of ILT members. These are:

- a commitment to scholarship in teaching, both generally and within their own subject;
- respect for individual learners and for their development and empowerment;
- a commitment to the development of learning communities, including students, teachers and all those engaged in learning support;
- a commitment to encouraging participation in HE and to equality of educational opportunity;
- a commitment to continued reflection and evaluation and consequent improvement of their own practice.

Clearly such values need to be espoused by all engaged in HE. However, they are particularly apposite for business and management given its popularity and position at the cutting edge of initiatives designed to extend educational opportunity in many countries. Furthermore, in developing learning communities the range and diversity of those engaged in providing learner support is considerable and embraces those in the workplace as well as the academy.

A second consideration concerns a feature of business and management education that can best be described as 'pedagogic pluralism'. Unlike some other subjects, within business and management there is not a dominant pedagogic paradigm (eg lecture/seminar). Indeed, business and management education has been at the forefront of experimentation with many different approaches to learning and teaching, such as action learning, case studies, problem-based learning, groupwork, computer-assisted learning, enterprise projects and dissertations. Thus, there is a great variety of methods from which to choose. In making choices, however, it is important for educators to be guided by the notion of 'fitness for purpose'. For example, while role play and simulations are well suited for developing practical skills and attributes, where the intention is to help learners become more adept at conceptualization, seminar discussions may well prove to be a more effective method.

Third, in the context of this book the use of the terms 'business' and 'management' is intended to be generic in the sense that they embrace the public and voluntary sectors, as well as the private sector. From an educational point of view, many of the challenges faced in creating rewarding, stimulating and effective learning experiences for students are identical regardless of the sector to which the course or programme is geared. Indeed, in many cases, members of the student group may well be mixed in terms of their career aspirations and/or the organisations for which they currently work.

Fourth, within business and management education the need for a multidisciplinary curriculum, incorporating an appropriate mix of disciplines, cross-disciplinary themes, such as ethics or globalization, and interdisciplinary perspectives, involving collaboration between subject areas to facilitate a more integrated approach to learning and understanding, is particularly compelling. This latter imperative can be seen in subject areas, such as business environment, strategic management and innovation and entrepreneurship, and moves towards what in North America is called 'learning across functional silos'. However, the compartmentalization of learning can still occur if steps are not actively taken to counteract such a tendency.

A fifth consideration relates to the concept of 'vocationalism'. Business and management learning is characterized by an economic imperative to a far greater extent than many other subjects. Indeed, responding to the needs of business is one of the prime motivators of educators in this sphere. However, while recognizing the vocational orientation of business and management education, the importance of subscribing to a comprehensive view of vocationalism cannot be overstated. Such a view sees vocationalism as embracing not simply the acquisition of knowledge and skills required for immediate employment purposes but also the development of intellectual qualities and critical faculties needed for career advancement; the generation of creative and innovative responses to business problems; and active citizenship.

Sixth, within the book is a heavy emphasis on practice, albeit underpinned by theory. This is in keeping with the vocational and applied nature of business and management education and the extensive use of experiential learning in business and management courses and programmes. Hence, much of the guidance stresses the importance of facilitating the application of knowledge and skills, not simply their acquisition, and of relating learning experiences to business practice through simulation and replication.

Finally, steps have been taken to accommodate the social, ethical and international role of business within business and management education. Increasing recognition of this presents particular challenges for business and management educators that have to be faced if learners are to appreciate that business functions and managerial activities are not simply value-free, technical matters and increasingly require a high degree of cross-cultural sensitivity.

Outlining the structure

The first two chapters of the book, constituting Part A, are designed to set the scene. Chapter 1 provides a summary of some of the key developments in business and management education and some of the unresolved tensions that lie at its heart. Whatever the particular contribution of readers to the learning experience of business and management students and their area(s) of specialism, it is important to be able to relate to some of these ongoing debates. The premise of Chapter 2 is that the facilitation of effective learning depends partly upon knowing something about the relevant life experiences, motivations and aspirations of students. It is also important to see learners as a resource, bringing to their learning encounters with educators and peers something of value. This means treating them as active participants and partners in the process of learning and not simply as passive recipients of what is being taught.

Part B covers all the key components of learning environments and support systems:

- the educational challenges that face those who contribute to learning and teaching (Chapter 3);
- the aims, objectives and learning outcomes that inform curriculum design (Chapter 4);
- the learning, teaching and assessment activities that characterize the student learning experience (Chapter 5);
- integration and the potential for cross-fertilization (Chapter 6);
- reflective practice and evaluation on the part of educators (Chapter 7).

In exploring the issues associated with each of these components particular attention is given to the distinctive needs of business and management students. The agenda is also set for Part C.

The seven chapters that make up Part C each focus on a subject area central to the business and management curriculum. Since business and management is now a very broad and diverse sphere of learning and teaching, this has involved some difficult choices. However, it is felt that the resulting selection does provide something for everyone engaged in supporting the learning of business and management students at every level from sub-degree to doctoral. It incorporates a mix of more established subject areas, such as organisational behaviour and marketing, and emerging areas, such as innovation and entrepreneurship. Specialist spheres of learning and teaching in their own right, such as information technology, finance, economics and languages, are only covered to the extent that they impinge on the learning experience of business and management students in understanding the nature of organisational life and the external business environment. This is not because they are unimportant. It is simply due to limitations of space and the need to retain a clear focus for the book.

The role of the Part C chapters is to provide those who can identify with one or more of the subject areas, in whatever capacity, with ideas and guidance for securing more effective learning and teaching. Although distinctive in style and perspective, within each the prime constituents of the learning environment and support systems can be found. It is strongly recommended that before dipping into one of the Part C chapters, the contents of Parts A and B are studied closely. These should help to put the detailed guidance into context.

The final two chapters, which comprise Part D, are there to underline the importance of recognizing that the development of effective learning environments is not a once-and-for-all activity. This involves facing up to the rapid changes affecting the way students will learn in HE in the future as a result of global and technological trends. It also means a commitment to reflective practice where experimentation and evaluation should be very much in evidence. Likewise, modification of practice in the light of feedback and reflection, as well as changing business needs and demands, should be a permanent feature of educational activity. In this way, curriculum and professional development can go hand in hand.

Meeting the challenge

Contributing to the learning of others is both challenging and rewarding. It is also a highly visible activity. Thus, in a sphere of learning and teaching like business and management, mismatches between what is being taught and the performance and behaviour of those providing learner support are likely to be very apparent with potentially serious consequences for learning. For example, encouraging learners to adopt the attributes of a reflective practitioner or exhorting the virtues of teamwork are unlikely to 'cut much ice' if it is patently obvious that those contributing to these aspects of their learning experience do not 'practise what they preach'. In business and management education, it is particularly important to be 'businesslike' in one's approach and to serve as a role model for students to emulate, thereby contributing to the credibility of the whole enterprise. This book, in its modest way, is designed to help those who wish to improve the effectiveness of their contribution to the learning experiences of others.

Part A

Business and management education in context

The purpose of the first two chapters is partly scene setting and partly guidance. They set the scene by highlighting some of the principal traditions and trends in the development of business and management education worldwide; a number of the tensions that lie at the heart of the business and management curriculum; and the backgrounds and motivations of those studying aspects of business and management. Knowledge of this kind should assist those engaged in the facilitation of learning to contextualize their contribution. It should also inform their approach by encouraging them to consider, for example, the vocational relevance of their aims and objectives.

Specific guidance includes suggestions for:

- dealing with student expectations and the motivational challenges to which they can give rise;
- managing the differences in learning style that are likely to exist in most groups of students;
- utilizing the prior experiences and concerns of learners in the design of learning activities;
- helping students maximize the potential of their learning time;
- treating students as a resource rather than as 'empty vessels waiting to be filled'.

While the guidance is by no means comprehensive it provides a basis for further exploration of the issues involved. In addition, it reinforces the crucial principle of effective learning and teaching, namely that of always putting the learner first.

1

Traditions and tensions

Bruce Macfarlane and Roger Ottewill

Introduction

Business and management education is booming. It straddles the globe and is one of the largest components of HE provision in many countries, regardless of their pedagogic and business traditions. In Australia, the Netherlands, Spain, the United States and the UK there are more business and management graduates than in any other subject area. Canada and the United States alone produce over half a million business and management graduates each year (unpublished OECD figures).

While the structure and format of the courses and programmes that comprise business and management education may vary with respect to content and delivery methods there is sufficient commonality to justify their treatment as a single entity. Such commonality derives from a shared concern with different facets of organisational life and the interaction of organisations with their external environments in all the complexity that this implies. It also arises from a willingness amongst many business and management educators to experiment and innovate in learning, teaching and assessment.

In this chapter it is intended to:

- outline the origins, growth, range and current scale of provision of business and management education in HE;
- highlight some of the tensions concerning the aims of the business and management curriculum as a whole;
- consider the perspectives of some of the key stakeholders.

In subsequent chapters, some of these topics will be re-examined from the perspective of the various subject areas that constitute the business and management curriculum. Here the emphasis is very much on business and management education as a whole.

Origins and subsequent growth

Although the rapid expansion of business and management education is a relatively recent phenomenon, its origins can be traced back to the late 19th century. Business and management courses in HE were pioneered in the United States. The first modern business school was endowed by Joseph Wharton, a Philadelphia financier and manufacturer, in the latter part of the 19th century. Others soon followed, among which the Harvard Business School, founded in 1908, is probably the world's most famous. By 1911 there were 30 similar business schools in operation in the United States as most prestigious universities began to introduce business programmes (Barry, 1989).

With a few exceptions, such as the Hautes Etudes Commerciales in Paris, known as HEC, business and management education in Europe did not begin to take off until after the Second World War. The Institute of Management Development based in Lausanne, Switzerland dates back to 1946 while the European Institute of Business Administration, otherwise known as INSEAD, was established in Paris in 1958. US business schools, particularly Harvard, were highly influential in the establishment of European, and later Asian, schools with teaching routines often shaped by the Harvard case study method developed during the 1920s. The Asian Institute of Management set up in Manila in 1968 is an example of this phenomenon (Crainer and Dearlove, 1998).

There is a considerable contrast between the well-established role of business and management studies in US universities since the early part of the 20th century and their development in the UK. Although other European countries developed higher-level, prestigious technical and vocational institutions, such as the *grandes écoles* in France and the *technische Hochschulen* in Germany, the UK lagged behind. According to Wiener (1980) this was due to an anti-industrial bias rooted in Victorian society and the tradition of the manager as a 'gentleman amateur'. Before the Second World War, there were a limited number of Bachelor of Commerce degree programmes offered at Birmingham, Liverpool and Edinburgh universities although these were quite general in nature. Two institutions, Manchester College of Science and Technology (now the University of Manchester) and the London School of Economics and Political Science also offered postgraduate management programmes in the 1930s.

This *ad hoc* pattern of development in the UK continued after the Second World War. Growth was inspired, at least in part, by US management methods, observed during the war, and spurred on by the need to raise productivity (Barry, 1989). The Diploma in Management Studies (DMS) was launched in 1949 by the newly formed British Institute of Management. During the 1950s the bulk of management education provision was to be found in technical colleges outside the university system (Barry, 1989). Despite the growth of the DMS, there was only limited interest in postgraduate management education in UK universities. It is significant that this slack was, to some extent, taken up by large companies that established their own internal management centres and by independent management providers, such as the Administrative Staff College (now called Henley) and Ashridge Management College.

While the tradition of the manager as a 'gentleman amateur' held back the development of business and management education in the UK, in the early 1960s its position and place in HE was re-evaluated by the Robbins Report (Robbins, 1963). Influenced by evidence that business and management should be taught predominantly at the postgraduate level, the report recommended the establishment of two major business schools, which the later Franks Report (1963) determined should be in London and Manchester respectively. The development of business and management education at undergraduate level was left to the polytechnic sector to pioneer (Laughton and Ottewill, 1998). In so doing, it was guided by the recommendations of the Crick Report (Department of Education and Science, 1964). This identified a traditional disciplinary base for degrees in business consisting of economics, sociology and mathematics with some introduction to law and accounting. Departments of economics often acted as a 'midwife' for the new degrees (Healey, 1993). Indeed, it is significant that in many countries, such as the United States and Germany, business and management education emerged from the study of economics (Grambsch, 1981; Pieper, 1990).

Thus, particularly in Europe, the business and management curriculum is a comparative newcomer to HE. Further impetus was provided, particularly in the UK, by reports into the condition of management education, which linked poor national economic performance with the lack of qualified managers (Constable and McCormack, 1987; Handy, 1987). The Management Charter Initiative (Watson, 1993) and other developments, sometimes labelled the 'new vocationalism', aimed to improve national standards of management competence (Laughton and Ottewill, 1998).

Scale and nature of current provision

In recent decades business and management education has come a long way. The rapid growth in student numbers is representative of global HE trends. An increasing proportion of provision is vocational and market-led, with students from developing nations in Asia and Africa contributing to this trend. In Britain, for example, business, management and accountancy have displaced science, engineering and public administration as the most popular subject area among overseas students (Scott, 1998). In keeping with the increasing flexibility of educational provision, business and management programmes are delivered full and part time in traditional university and college-based settings; via online and distance learning; and within the corporate classroom.

In many parts of the world a key role in the provision of business and management education is played by business schools. These include elite, research-based schools with leading Master of Business Administration (MBA) programmes; schools with a market niche in a specialist area of post-experience management education; and more generalist providers offering courses at both undergraduate and postgraduate level. Such providers network with each other through bodies, such as the American Assembly of Collegiate Schools of Business, which boasts a membership of 600 US educational institutions and a further 140 worldwide; the Australian/New Zealand Academy of Management; and the Association of Indian Management Schools. In the UK the Association of Business Schools acts on behalf of over 100 educational providers. The European Foundation for Management Development, based in Brussels, brings together business school and corporate members from over 40 countries.

Educational institutions have never been the sole provider of business and management education. Corporations act as significant contributors to this provision (Scott, 1995). Moreover, the emergence of the knowledge economy means that corporate learning is now the key strategic motor of growth in the developed world (Conceicao and Heitor, 1999). Global businesses now consider learning, especially in business and management, vital in establishing and maintaining competitive advantage rather than as an irksome cost. The global executive education market alone has been calculated to be worth more than US $12 billion (Crainer and Dearlove, 1998). The knowledge-based economy is driving many organisations to establish their own corporate 'university' or advanced education and training facility, often in collaboration with leading business schools. Intel University, Polaroid Leadership Institute and Shell Learning Center in the United States, together with British Aerospace Virtual University, Cable and Wireless College and Unipart 'U' in the UK, are all examples of this growing phenomenon. Competition between business schools and corporate providers is also increasing, especially as more sophisticated virtual learning environments are created via Internet access.

At the international level, dialogue between business and management educators associated with both educational and corporate providers is fostered by bodies including the European Foundation for Management Development, the British Academy of Management and EDINEB (Educational Innovation in Economics and Business). This latter organisation, founded in the early 1990s, is run from Maastricht University in the Netherlands.

With respect to business and management qualifications, at postgraduate level the MBA, pioneered in the United States in the 1960s, is now the world's most popular. European business schools currently produce 20,000 MBA graduates per year although four times this number graduate from business schools in the United States alone (Association of MBAs, 2000). Alongside the MBA, there exists a broad range of other postgraduate qualifications, such as the increasingly well-respected Doctorate of Business Administration. Likewise, at undergraduate level, there is a variety of qualifications, with the business studies degree, traditionally incorporating a work experience year, being the most popular and well established in the UK. However, with an increasing proportion of business now taking place online, degrees in e-business and e-commerce are beginning to emerge. Not surprisingly, numbers on undergraduate courses are significantly higher than those studying for postgraduate qualifications, both in Europe and the United States. Moreover, at undergraduate level, the popularity of business and management relative to other subject areas is demonstrated by the fact that, in the UK, approximately one in eight students is currently on a first degree course in a business and management-related area (Higher Education Statistics Agency, 2000).

However, defining the parameters of business and management provision for statistical purposes is an almost impossible task given the vast range of programmes that might potentially be included in any definition. For example, business and management programmes in their broadest sense could be said to embrace areas such as tourism and hospitality, and specialist qualifications in subjects like marketing. At the same time, many academic subjects now include a 'business' or 'management' element where, until relatively recently, this has been absent. This is particularly the case with respect to the preparation of learners for public sector professions such as nursing, social work and public administration.

A kindred issue concerns the relationship between 'business' education and 'management' education. While they may be linked for statistical purposes, over the years attempts have been made to develop a logical distinction between them (eg Robbins, 1963). In practice, however, the intellectual coherence of such a divide is hard to sustain, especially given the fact that managerial responsibilities in modern organisations are no longer restricted to a traditional cadre of the elite few. Nonetheless, the existence of such a debate is indicative of the tensions that exist both within the business and management teaching community and in the relationship between business and management education and the wider HE community of which it is an integral part.

Tensions within the curriculum

An initial tension concerns the knowledge-base of business and management education, which is mainly drawn from an eclectic mix of more traditional disciplines such as economics, sociology, psychology and mathematics. Marketing (Chapter 13), for example, a key component in the modern business curriculum, derives much of its knowledge-base from the latter three of these disciplines. The derivative and vocational nature of knowledge in business and management has led critics to argue that the study of business is a spurious discipline with a dubious claim to academic legitimacy. Moreover, business lecturers are often assumed (wrongly) to act as uncritical apostles of capitalist values (Macfarlane, 1997a; and see box on page 8). Thus, the sceptical attitude of the academic community both in Europe and the United States partly explains why business schools have developed in semi-detached isolation from parent institutions and why, in particular, business and management education in the UK was pioneered outside the traditional university sector in technical colleges and polytechnics.

Mammon and the academy

'Some universities still doubt whether industrial management provides the scope for students to participate in the advancement of knowledge and the pursuit of truth.'
(R W Revans, quoted by Barry, 1989: 61)

'Such [business and management] departments are in fact simply training schools for management, and live off the fruits from other trees of knowledge. While there can be no objection to such schools in their proper place, it is quite unclear why they should exist in universities, or why people working in them should enjoy the specific academic freedom which involves their having tenure. Those who live by the market should die... by the market.'
(O'Hear, 1988: 14)

'Business is educationally suspect because it is not a discipline. It does not have much to do with the disinterested pursuit of knowledge, which I see as the function of a university. The syllabus is an agglomeration of several disciplines, and the student may not get an adequate grounding in any of them. The departments tend to be so large, and so closely linked to industry, that they threaten to be a Trojan horse inside the university.'
(A professor of English, quoted by Bain, 1990: 13)

Another tension arises from the fact that, despite attempts at integration, business and management educators still largely specialize in the teaching of discrete areas of the curriculum such as economics, marketing (Chapter 13), quantitative methods, information technology, organisational behaviour (Chapter 9) and strategic management (Chapter 12). The academic community of business scholars and educators naturally reflects this diverse knowledge-base. Staff are recruited and promoted on the basis of their subject expertise and associated scholarly activity. This can mean that educators tend to be more committed to the claims of their academic 'tribe' (Becher, 1989) rather than the broader aims of the business and management curriculum (Macfarlane, 1998). Moreover, on both sides of the Atlantic, educators tend to be career academics rather than facilitators with considerable business experience (Simon, 1976; Macfarlane, 1997b), with some specializing in subject areas that are largely quantitative (or 'hard') in nature and others in areas that are principally qualitative (or 'soft'). Mulligan (1987) refers to this division in terms of two 'cultures' within business and management, one science-based and the other humanities-based. To obviate argument, an implicit balance is often struck within the curriculum between science-based (or 'hard') elements and humanities-based (or 'soft') aspects.

However, this balance often hides a more deep-rooted tension. A long-running controversy, particularly within management education, concerns the extent to which the curriculum presents the role of the manager as a neutral technician. According to a range of critics (eg Roberts, 1996), the curriculum overemphasizes the teaching of analytical techniques at the expense of debating the tensions and uncertainties of management practice. Management is presented, in other words, as a 'science' rather than an 'art', applying quantitative approaches to social processes rather than developing a range of 'softer' skills. It is claimed, for example, that the teaching of innovation and creativity within the curriculum has been suppressed owing to the dominance of technical rationality (Rickards, 1999).

Other ongoing tensions within the business and management curriculum need to be understood in the context of debates concerning the purpose of education, and especially that of HE. Educational goals are often expressed in terms of well-worn dualities, having the effect of polarizing debate. One side of this debate is represented by the notion of knowledge for its own sake where the love of learning is the primary motivational factor. This is a classic definition of a liberal education in which the aim is purely 'intrinsic'. On the other side of the debate the purpose of learning is to serve the extrinsic needs of society and the economy. The term 'vocationalism' is often associated with knowledge as a means for achieving these (largely economic) ends. In some respects, this traditional divide expressed in terms of liberal education versus vocationalism, or intrinsic versus extrinsic aims, sets up an oversimplified dichotomy. Debates concerning the aims of a business and management education are a microcosm of this broader discourse.

The purpose of a business and management curriculum is often conceived in terms of preparing students with the skills and knowledge needed to participate in some form of business activity. From this perspective, a business and management education is a study 'for' business with the essentially practical or vocational purpose of equipping learners for the needs of commerce, industry and public services. However, the purpose of a business and management education may also be conceived in wider terms as a study 'about' the nature of business activity. This is concerned more broadly with the analysis of the role of business in society deploying sociological, economic, philosophical and other perspectives. While a study 'for' business seeks to produce learners ready to begin, or continue to build on, a business career, a study 'about' business seeks to provide learners with a critical understanding of business as a social phenomenon. This particular dichotomy, first expressed by Tolley (1983), has often been discussed in the context of undergraduate business education in the UK (Brown and Harrison, 1980; Boys, 1988; Silver and Brennan, 1988; Macfarlane, 1994). Other writers concerned with the aims of a management education have produced a relatively similar conceptual dichotomy (see box below). Simon (1976) directly discusses the conflicting traditions of 'liberal' and 'utilitarian' (or vocational) education in the context of US business schools. From a European standpoint, Grey and French (1996) distinguish between 'managerialist' and 'critical' perspectives with regard to the management curriculum. A 'managerialist' perspective is equated with teaching students a set of techniques and skills that will be subsequently applied in the workplace, while a 'critical' perspective is about understanding management as a social, political and moral practice. A similar dichotomy is elaborated by Kallinikos (1996).

Expressions of dual aims in business and management education

- a study 'for' and a study 'about' business (Tolley, 1983);
- 'managerialist' and 'critical' perspectives (Grey and French, 1996);
- 'utilitarian' and 'liberal' education (Simon, 1976);
- management as an 'ensemble of techniques' and an 'overall world orientation' (Kallinikos, 1996).

Most writers on the aims of business and management argue that a study 'for' business tends to dominate the curriculum (eg Brown and Harrison, 1980; Boys 1988; Grey and French, 1996). In reality, however, most courses of study incorporate aims from across the spectrum including both applied knowledge and skills and a critical evaluation of business as a social activity. Even though tensions remain within individual subject areas (see Chapters 9 and 10), there is increasing recognition that a business and management education can accommodate both perspectives, producing what Silver and Brennan (1988) have termed a 'liberal vocationalism'.

Moreover, there are pressures reshaping the nature of 'vocationalism'. Modern business organisations are better served by business graduates with the ability to think critically and independently in post-Fordist economies where human–capital has become crucial to competitiveness. These fundamental changes in economic infrastructure and the structure of occupations are leading many writers to develop broader definitions of vocationalism that incorporate principles drawn from a liberal education (eg Jamieson, 1993; Williams, 1994; Ottewill and Wall, 2000). Practically, this means that most courses of study will aim to provide learners with a body of (useful) knowledge but will also seek to develop intellectual skills of criticism and analysis in the process.

Where then does this leave the development of 'business skills' and attitudes? Most business and management programmes still provide learners with opportunities for acquiring largely technical, work-related skills in areas such as information technology, communication and presentation in addition to knowledge elements. However, there is controversy regarding the degree of prominence to which programmes should seek to 'mould' learners with the personal and social attitudes favoured by business organisations (Lloyd, 1996). Examples include flexibility, negotiation and persuasion, creativity and team working as well as a positive attitude to both change and entrepreneurial risk (see Chapters 11 and 14). These personal and social skills go well beyond the traditional and largely technical. Including an emphasis on the development of such skills within a programme would represent a much closer orientation towards an education 'for' business.

To some extent this and the other tensions highlighted above reflect the differing perspectives of those interests that have a significant stake in business and management education. It is the interplay between these perspectives that contributes to the enrichment of the curriculum as well as the potential contradictions.

Stakeholder perspectives

The nature of business and management education and its future development are closely connected with both the particular context of national educational policy and the power of various stakeholders. Within policy frameworks determined by national governments, the specific aims of the curriculum are shaped by the relative influence of a range of mediating agents, including business and management educators, employers, professional bodies and learners (Laughton and Ottewill, 1998).

Increased state intervention in HE is a global trend although this has had a variable effect on the political and organisational management of universities. The impact of so-called 'new managerialism' has been greater in the UK than Italy, for example (Braun and Merrien, 1999). In the UK, contemporary developments suggest that the state, via the power of funding bodies and the Quality Assurance Agency for HE, will play an increasingly significant role in influencing the aims of the curriculum. In other words, it will act more like a 'hands-on' customer than a 'hands-off' trustee of the HE system (Scott, 1995). Specifically, this has led to the development of a set of 'benchmarks' for the HE curriculum at undergraduate level, including business and management provision (Quality Assurance Agency, 2000).

Within the parameters of national education policy, a particular issue for business and management educators is the extent to which they should tailor the curriculum to meet the current, perceived needs of employers and the wider business community or rely on their own judgement as to the requirements of learners. While employing organisations may represent a key stakeholder group, their requirements may be subject to frequent changes owing to economic and industrial factors that have led to the rise and fall of many management 'fads'. Moreover, given the replacement of 'organisation man' with 'portfolio man', educators need to consider what is in the best, long-term interest of learners and ensure that the education provided is a solid foundation for flexibility in terms of career changes.

Nonetheless, employers and the wider business community remain key stakeholders with respect to the business and management curriculum. Having said that, their involvement and influence in the design of programmes does vary according to the exact nature of the provision. At one end of the scale, employing organisations may have only limited interest and involvement with general degrees in business studies (Silver and Brennan, 1988). Such degrees are unrelated to any specific occupational or professional context with a 'diffuse' rather than 'specific' relationship with employment opportunities (Brennan, 1985). By contrast, degree studies in specialist business disciplines, such as human resource management and accountancy, are related more closely to a particular professional context. Certain other business degrees, including those in retail management and risk management, reflect a very specific occupational orientation leading to strong connections with relevant employers. Indeed, at the far end of the 'specific' scale, some management education provision is directly tailored to meet the needs of a single employer. Business schools are increasingly competing to offer so-called 'collaborative', 'custom' or 'in-house' management programmes (Crainer and Dearlove, 1998; Macfarlane, 2000). Such programmes often play an integral role as part of an organisational change initiative. Here, it is often the case of 'he who pays the piper calls the tune'.

It is clear that the needs of employers have changed dramatically since the 1960s as many traditional industrial occupations, characterized by limited autonomy and clearly defined work roles, have been swept away. A new, more knowledge-based business environment has led organisations to develop smaller federal structures that are more responsive to customer needs. This, in turn, has led to employers demanding a different type of employee to fill ambiguous, increasingly complex and constantly shifting work roles. As indicated earlier, the narrow vocationalism developed in the 1960s for technical education no longer meets the needs of modern business organisations (Scott, 1995). This has led some commentators to argue that employers may now be defining the notion of workplace competence in terms of older, elite forms of liberal education (Ainley, 1994).

There is an attendant concern that some employers, although espousing commitment to business and management education, tend to recruit from the more established academic disciplines. This may be prompted partly by perceptions that business and management has a weak academic reputation (Bain, 1990). It may also be a phenomenon particularly associated with the UK where, historically, nepotism and the 'gentleman amateur' tradition, mentioned earlier, have played a more significant role in management careers than formal business and management qualifications (Barry, 1989). This has led to claims that employers are 'janus-faced', arguing on the one hand in favour of business and management qualifications tailored to their needs but, in practice, preferring to recruit non-business graduates from older universities.

The challenge of resolving the potentially conflicting interests of stakeholders has been likened to requiring the wisdom of Solomon (Evan and Freeman, 1988). Clearly, however, developing at least an understanding of, and sensitivity towards, contrasting stakeholder interests is particularly important in the context of business and management education where a broader range of legitimate interests may exist than in other, less vocationally relevant areas of study.

Conclusion

Whatever the future holds for business and management education, these are undoubtedly exciting and challenging times. While it is likely that demand will stay buoyant, diversification and increased heterogeneity, in response to the expectations of various key stakeholders, will almost certainly remain significant trends with respect to provision.

As previously indicated, the involvement of institutional stakeholders in the development and, to some extent, the design and delivery of courses and programmes is a key feature of business and management education and one that distinguishes it from many other subject areas. It also places additional pressure on educators, who are faced with reconciling the demands of the business community with the requirements of their own agenda. At the same time, it is incumbent upon them to ensure that the needs of the other important stakeholder group, namely learners, are not overlooked or marginalized. Their characteristics, concerns and needs are the subject of the next chapter.

References

Ainley, P (1994) *Degrees of Difference: Higher education in the 1990s*, Lawrence and Wishart, London

Association of MBAs [accessed 14 March 2000] [Online] http://www.mba.org.uk/

Bain, G (1990) A vocational vortex, *The Times Higher Education Supplement*, 23 February, p 13

Barry, B (1989) Management education in Great Britain, in *Management Education: An international survey*, ed W Byrt, pp 57–77, Routledge, London

Becher, T (1989) *Academic Tribes and Territories*, Open University Press/Society for Research into Higher Education, Buckingham

Boys, C (1988) Business studies, in *Higher Education and the Preparation for Work*, ed C J Boys et al, pp 111–22, Jessica Kingsley, London

Braun, D and Merrien, F X (1999) *Towards a New Model of Governance for Universities? A comparative view*, Jessica Kingsley, London

Brennan, J (1985) Preparing students for employment, *Studies in Higher Education*, **10** (2), pp 151–61

Brown, D and Harrison, M (1980) The demand for relevance and the role of sociology in business studies degrees, *Journal of Further and Higher Education*, **4** (3), pp 54–61

Conceicao, P and Heitor, M (1999) On the role of the university in the knowledge economy, *Science and Public Policy*, **26** (1), pp 37–51

Constable, J and McCormack, R (1987) *The Making of British Managers*, Confederation of British Industry/British Institute of Management, London

Crainer, S and Dearlove, D (1998) *Gravy Training: Inside the shadowy world of business schools*, Capstone, Oxford

Department of Education and Science (1964) *A Higher Award in Business Studies: Report of the advisory sub-committee on a higher award in business studies (The Crick Report)*, HMSO, Swindon

Evan, W M and Freeman, R E (1988) A stakeholder theory of the modern corporation: Kantian capitalism, in *Ethical Theory and Business*, ed T L Beauchamp and N E Bowie, pp 254–66, Prentice Hall, Englewood Cliffs, NJ

Franks, Rt Hon Lord (1963) *British Business Schools*, HMSO, London

Grambsch, P V (1981) Business administration, in *The Modern American College*, ed A W Chickering, pp 473–86, Jossey-Bass, San Francisco

Grey, C and French, R (1996) Rethinking management education: an introduction, in *Rethinking Management Education*, ed R French and C Grey, pp 1–16, Sage, London

Handy, C B (1987) *The Making of Managers: A report on management education training and development in the United States, West Germany, France, Japan and the UK*, Manpower Services Commission/National Economic Development Council/ British Institute of Management, London

Healey, N M (1993) What role for economics in business and management education?, *Journal of Further and Higher Education*, **17** (3), pp 34–39

Higher Education Statistics Agency (2000) *Students in Higher Education Institutions*, HESA, Cheltenham

Jamieson, I (1993) The rise and fall of the work-related curriculum, in *The Work-Related Curriculum: Challenging the vocational imperative*, ed J J Wellington, pp 200–17, Kogan Page, London

Kallinikos, J (1996) Mapping the intellectual terrain of management education, in *Rethinking Management Education*, ed R French and C Grey, pp 36–53, Sage, London

Laughton, D and Ottewill, R (1998) Values and norms in British undergraduate business education: implications for the student experience, *Journal of European Business Education*, **8** (1), pp 51–61

Lloyd, J (1996) Learning business studies, *Economics and Business Education*, **4** (2), pp 77–80

Macfarlane, B (1994) Issues concerning the development of undergraduate business curriculum in UK higher education, *Journal of European Business Education*, **4** (1), pp 1–14

Macfarlane, B (1997a) The business studies first degree: institutional trends and the pedagogic context, *Teaching in Higher Education*, **2** (1), pp 45–57

Macfarlane B (1997b) In search of an identity: lecturer perspectives of the business studies degree, *Journal of Vocational Education and Training*, **49**, pp 5–20

Macfarlane, B (1998) Refugees, nomads and tourists: an anatomy of business and management lecturers in higher education, *Journal of European Business Education*, **7** (2), pp 37–44

Macfarlane, B (2000) Inside the corporate classroom, *Teaching in Higher Education*, **5** (1), pp 51–60

Mulligan, T (1987) The two cultures in business education, *Academy of Management Review*, **12** (4), pp 593–99

O'Hear, A (1988) Academic freedom and the university, in *Academic Freedom and Responsibility*, ed M Tight, pp 6–16, Open University Press, Milton Keynes

Ottewill, R and Wall, A (2000) Vocationalism and relevance in higher education, *Journal of Vocational Education and Training*, **52** (3), pp 521–34

Pieper, R (1990) The history of business administration and management education in the two Germanies – a comparative approach, *The International Journal of Human Resource Management*, **1** (2), pp 211–29

Quality Assurance Agency [accessed 2000] *Benchmark Statement for General Business and Management*, [Online] http://www.qaa.ac.uk/crntwork/benchmark/business.pdf

Rickards, T (1999) *Creativity and the Management of Change*, Blackwell, Oxford

Robbins, Lord (1963) *Higher Education: Report of the committee appointed by the Prime Minister under the chairmanship of Lord Robbins 1961–1963*, HMSO, London

Roberts, J (1996) Management education and the limits of technical rationality: the conditions and consequences of management practice, in *Rethinking Management Education*, ed R French and C Grey, pp 54–75, Sage, London

Scott, P (1995) *The Meanings of Mass Higher Education*, Society for Research into Higher Education/Open University Press, Buckingham

Scott, P (1998) Massification, internationalization and globalization, in *The Globalization of Higher Education*, ed P Scott, pp 108–29, Society for Research into Higher Education/Open University Press, Buckingham

Silver, H and Brennan, J (1988) *Liberal Vocationalism*, Methuen, London

Simon, H A (1976) *Administrative Behavior*, Collier-Macmillan, New York

Tolley, G (1983) Foreword, in *The Hidden Curriculum in Business Studies: Proceedings of a conference on values in business education*, ed D Graves, p 5, Higher Education Foundation, Chichester

Watson, S R (1993) The place for universities in management education, *Journal of General Management*, **19** (2), pp 14–41

Wiener, M (1980) *English Culture and the Decline of the Industrial Spirit 1850–1919*, Penguin, Harmondsworth

Williams, K (1994) Vocationalism and liberal education: exploring the tensions, *Journal of Philosophy of Education*, **28** (1), pp 89–98

2

Understanding learners

Roger Ottewill and Bruce Macfarlane

Introduction

It is tempting to begin this chapter by claiming that there is no such thing as a typical business and management student. Such a claim could be justified by pointing to the proliferation of business and management courses and programmes, mentioned in Chapter 1. One consequence of this development has been a rapidly expanding community of learners that is becoming increasingly diverse in its composition. Whether in terms of age, maturity, gender, ethnicity, social class, ability, personality traits, self-worth, preferred learning style, prior education, previous life and employment experiences, and time available for their studies and other commitments, there is now enormous variation amongst business and management students and this applies across the globe. Moreover, although courses and programmes are often geared towards distinctive segments of this learning community, on any particular course or programme there can still be a very varied mix of students.

One thing, however, that most of these learners are likely to have in common, whatever their level or background, is that their prime motivation in studying is very probably economic. In other words, their learning in the sphere of business and management is prompted primarily by the desire to improve their employment prospects, whether in terms of a first job or subsequent career advancement, or to perform their current job more effectively. Indeed, research into the expectations of learners has indicated that they share an essentially pragmatic rationale, in the sense that they regard a business and management education as instrumental to their future career (Graves, 1983; Horner, 1983; Roberts, 1996). More specifically, in the terminology of Ashcroft and Foreman-

Peck (1994), the primary educational orientations of most business and management students are likely to be intrinsically or extrinsically vocational (see Table 2.1).

Table 2.1 Vocational educational orientations

Interest	Aim	Primary Concern
Intrinsic	Training	Relevance of course to future career
Extrinsic	Qualification	Recognition of value of qualification

In these circumstances, 'love of the subject' as a motivating factor is likely to have a lower priority. While it is to be hoped that learners also have a considerable interest in the substance of what they are studying, this cannot be taken for granted. At the same time, learners can be critical of those subject areas that they do not perceive as being particularly useful to their future careers (Coates and Koerner, 1996; and see Chapters 9 and 10). As Lloyd argues, in commenting on the role of micro-economics within business degrees, 'students are more critical and less patient of material with less than direct relevance to career development and/or (business) application' (1996: 169). Consequently, those contributing to the learning experiences of business and management students do face particular challenges with respect to motivation, which may well be greater in kind than those encountered in non-vocational areas. As previously indicated, a deep love of the subject on the part of learners, as in fields such as history (Booth, 1997), cannot be assumed.

In this chapter, it is intended to consider, in general terms, the implications of the varied backgrounds of business and management students for the development of learning environments and student support systems; and the motivational challenges faced by those engaged in learner support. Such an objective has been prompted by the belief that effective learning and teaching depends, at least in part, in working with 'the grain of the students' for whom one is responsible. Thus, it is important to devote attention to finding out something about them. At the same time, this process can be used to establish what learners can offer in terms of the resources that they bring to their studies.

Backgrounds of business and management students

Given the increasing diversity of business and management students, it is incumbent upon those responsible for supporting their learning to take this into account in the design of learning activities. Here a particularly important consideration is the nature and extent of their learning experiences to date and their acquaintanceship with prevailing pedagogic practice, coupled with their direct experience of the content of the programme. With respect to the former, past assumptions concerning learner familiarity with various approaches to learning and teaching are now far less likely to be valid. This is because in the UK and elsewhere, those engaged in business and management education have been affected by moves towards what is known as 'widening access', which involves opening up HE to those with possibly limited prior academic learning (Morris, Newman and Stringer, 1993). While their life experiences may, to some extent, compensate for their unfamiliarity with pedagogic matters, for educators there is clearly a need to establish precisely the expectations of their students regarding learning, teaching and assessment and to use this intelligence to inform the content of their learning and teaching strategies, regardless of the level and/or nature of the course or programme.

Even where students have considerable experience of academic learning it is still a good idea to spend some time determining the nature of this experience and how it might shape their expectations of what is to come. Similarly, discovering what relevant knowledge students bring with them to their studies and how they acquired it can be built into the process of helping learners explore how they learn (Race and Brown, 1993). Adult learners, in particular, have a rich resource of experiences on which to base further learning (Knowles and Associates, 1984).

Students as a resource

Seeing students as a resource, in the sense that they bring to their studies experiences that can be utilized to enhance both their own learning and that of their peers, is an important pedagogic principle. It is also one that has a particular relevance in the context of business and management. This is because of the pervasiveness of business and management and the variety of roles from which these experiences emanate. Such roles can be conceptualized in terms of various stakeholder perspectives, including those of consumer, service user or client, investor or borrower, work experience student and actual or potential employee.

On courses and programmes incorporating an element of face-to-face learning and teaching, the best opportunity for identifying aspects of these roles that are of particular relevance for learning and teaching is likely to be during a pre-course meeting or an induction session. Various methods can be used for this purpose. Three are highlighted here. The first is a questionnaire specially designed to identify experiences that relate directly to the subject matter of the course or programme. If prepared with care, questionnaires can serve as a means of demonstrating the value of reflection in the learning process as well as helping facilitators recognize potential contributions. Some sample questions are shown in the box on page 19. For distance learners, 'online' facilities can be used to achieve similar ends.

A second method is to use a buzz session, in which learners in small groups help each other, through discussion, to highlight experiences that they think might be of relevance. Each group then reports back on its findings to the class as a whole for further consideration. At a suitable point, those responsible for facilitating the

Questions to identify relevant experiences and encourage reflection on the part of learners

- Provide an example of a situation where you have had a judgement made about your suitability for a job or course or the quality of your work. What methods and criteria were used in making the judgement? To what extent do you think they were suitable and fair?
- Have you ever contributed to the induction of a new employee? If so, what form did your contribution take? How might the new employee have rated the quality of your contribution?
- Think of a voluntary organisation with which you have been involved. What was the nature of your involvement (eg fund raising, working with members/clients, administration, making use of services provided)? Identify the aims and objectives of the organisation. To what extent do you think they are being achieved?
- In what circumstances have you ever made a complaint? What was the cause of the complaint? How was it handled? What criteria would you use to evaluate the handling of complaints?
- Would you describe yourself as a line manager? List three reasons for your answer.
- Have you ever made use of the services of an independent financial adviser? If so, to what extent did you follow his/her advice? Has it proved to be sound advice?
- Think of a TV advertisement that has recently attracted your attention. What makes it so memorable?
- Select an example of a skill you have been developing as part of your educational experience. In what ways could it be transferred to a business setting? What evidence would you use to demonstrate your competence in this skill during the selection process for a job or work experience attachment?

learning process can indicate linkages between the experiences and the curriculum.

A final method involves using oneself or a colleague as an 'expert witness'. Learners are asked to identify an aspect of their prior experience for the 'expert witness' to relate to the aims of the course or programme.

It needs to be stressed, however, that all these methods are only starting points for learning and that subsequent use should be made of the information generated to ensure the credibility of the exercise. At the same time, it is important to recognize the dangers inherent in such an approach and to take steps to counteract them. One, in particular, is that the emphasis on experience may give the impression that this alone is sufficient for learning. While experiential learning has its place, at some point learners need help and support in relating their experiences to broader and more theoretical perspectives. Assisting learners to relate theory and practice is a crucial task facing all business and management educators (see Chapters 3, 9 and 12).

As well as using students' experiences in the world at large as a resource, a similar approach can be adopted towards their engagement with the learning process. Mazen, Jones and Sergenian (2000), for example, describe how they use weekly student reflections on the content of each class as well as the performance of the educator to transform it into a 'learning organisation', that is 'an organisation which facilitates the learning of all its members and continuously transforms itself' (Pedler, Burgoyne and Boydell, 1991). Despite some conceptual and practical ambiguities, given the attention that the concept of the learning organisation has received in the business and management literature (eg Argyris and Schon, 1978, 1996; Coopey, 1995), applying it to academic life is to be commended. However, as Mazen and his colleagues explain (2000), such an innovation is not for the faint-hearted, since it is characterized by uncertainty and vulnerability for both students and learning facilitators. These are elements of what Vince (1996) calls the emotional component of learning and their importance is not to be underestimated. Nonetheless, if one is committed to the principle of personal growth in learning and teaching, it is inevitable that at some stage emotions associated with risk taking will have to be confronted.

Whatever the backgrounds of learners, their mode of study, or the method used to find out about them, it is clearly essential to determine beforehand what is relevant and to focus on that, initially at least. Relevance will depend on a variety of factors including:

- the purpose of the intended learning, both skill and knowledge-based;
- potential linkages between the learning and the prior experiences of the learners;
- an understanding of the cultural influences on learners (see Chapters 11 and 13);
- familiarity with the approaches to learning and teaching that are to be used.

Time allocated for the purpose of getting to know learners and 'what makes them tick' is likely to pay dividends later especially if the knowledge gained is utilized in the design of learning activities. The potential of, for example, a case study, role play, simulation or seminar discussion is more likely to be fully realized if it is configured in such a way that it relates to the backgrounds and direct concerns of the learners and enables them to draw upon and apply their prior engagement with the subject matter. Examples of what this can mean in practice are shown in the box below.

Working with 'the grain of the students' in this way does not mean, of course, that nothing new should be attempted, but simply that it is a sound principle to start with the familiar and only move on to the less familiar and unfamiliar once trust, confidence and a sound relationship with learners have been established. At the same time, account needs to be taken of student learning styles.

Utilizing the prior experiences and concerns of learners in the design of learning activities

- At the beginning of a business skills programme students identify some-thing they can do that they feel would be useful in a business setting. Consideration is then given to how they acquired their skill with a view to demonstrating the importance of motivation, practising, feedback and reflection in the learning process.
- Two students with direct experience of staff appraisal play the roles of appraiser and appraisee in a simulated interview, which other students watch, subsequently discussing the issues that arise.
- Students carry out a cash flow/financial planning exercise, which incorpo-rates some of their financial concerns and experiences, with the aim of introducing them to more general concepts and principles.
- Learners gather information about a particular company, product or public service from sources with which they are familiar (eg teletext, Internet, popular newspapers), as opposed to more academic sources, and evaluate its worth and reliability.
- Students list the factors that have influenced their decision-making in respect of products, services or employment, which are then considered in relation to more general/theoretical approaches to decision-making.
- Learners from a variety of cultural backgrounds share their prior experiences of customer service with a view to enhancing cross-cultural understanding.

Preferred learning styles

Research has shown that there is considerable variation in preferred learning styles (Honey and Mumford, 1992). There are also clear benefits that business and management students can derive from locating and evaluating their own preferred learning style (Holden and McGrath, 1992). Moreover, on many business and management programmes the variety of aims implies the need for flexibility in style. For example, aims that relate to skill acquisition and development are most likely to be achieved through the adoption of a style where the emphasis is on learning from direct experience and/or practical application. By contrast, more theoretically based aims require a more cerebral style.

Much of the discussion around learning styles tends to be informed by Kolb's well-known learning cycle of experiencing, evaluating, conceptualizing and experimenting (1981, 1983). Drawing on Kolb's work, Honey and Mumford (1992) have identified four types of learner based on where each prefers to enter the learning cycle (see Table 2.2).

Whether this or another schema is used, such as the contrast drawn between serialist and holist learning styles (Pask, 1976), given the differences, uniformity of

Table 2.2   The four types of learner (based on Honey and Mumford, 1992)

Style	Stage in the Cycle	Learn Best	Learn Least	Possible Learning Activities
Activist	experiencing	lots of new tasks to experience and new problems to confront	passive learning that involves a great deal of reading	role plays simulations educational games
Reflector	evaluating	plenty of thinking time between new tasks/problems to facilitate; evaluation	too many new tasks/problems	learning logs case studies in-tray exercises educational visits
Theorist	conceptualizing	seeing how task/problem relates to the whole and being directed to the theoretical background	being required to undertake tasks and tackle problems before getting to grips with the theoretical underpinning	reading discussion groups guided study
Pragmatist	experimenting	putting theoretical ideas into practice	unable to see practical relevance of theory	experiments demonstrations action learning

provision in terms of learning activities and student support may not be appropriate. At the very least they need to be configured in such a way that differences in preferred style can be accommodated. Clearly with limited resources the extent to which this can be done will be curtailed. Nonetheless, by incorporating a variety of learning activities into a programme there should be opportunities for learners 'to play to their strengths'. Uniformity of learning and assessment activities is likely to disadvantage some students. It may also make their motivation that much more difficult, owing to the mismatch between their preferred learning style and the learning activities that predominate. Less preferred styles though need to be identified and worked on. Holden and McGrath (1992) illustrate how a business student with a preferred 'activist' style was able to use this self-knowledge to draw up a personal development plan to strengthen her *least* preferred learning style in a variety of ways. By giving due weight to learning styles there is scope for not only enhancing the performance of students but also for strengthening their motivation to learn.

Motivational challenges

Student motivation should be a matter of intense concern to all who contribute to the learning of others. Ultimately, the quality of learning will depend more on the extent to which motivational needs are met than anything else. Thus, in the case of business and management, given the strong economic orientation of most students, mentioned earlier, the relevance of what is being learnt and how it is being learnt with respect to the 'world of work' is a key consideration. However, it is very easy in these circumstances to be seduced into adopting an extremely narrow view of what is vocational, based exclusively on a 'for' business approach (see Chapter 1), thereby reinforcing the instrumentality of students. In other words, if something is not perceived as being of immediate practical value in the workplace it is dismissed as being irrelevant, a problem alluded to in Part C by a number of chapter authors (see Chapters 9 and 10). At the same time, educators are faced with the temptation of transmitting knowledge in a predigestible and immediately usable form (Roberts, 1996). However, responding to the instrumentality of students in this way is damaging and can easily undermine the whole process of learning, in which a variety of goals of an academic and personal kind should be equally valued. Moreover, this is likely to encourage a 'surface' as opposed to a 'deep' approach to learning (Marton and Saljo, 1976).

A surface approach to learning is characterized by students reducing what is to be learnt to a series of unconnected facts, which have to be memorized and repro-duced later, with the intention of meeting the assessment requirements with the minimum of effort. By contrast, in adopting a deep approach learners try to make sense of what is being learnt, seeking to integrate and make connections between concepts and learning activities. Biggs (1999) and others contend that it is the orientation of educators in structuring the learning environment, together with the preference or predilection of learners for a particular approach, that deter-mines whether a deep or surface approach is adopted. 'Encouraging the need-to-know, instilling curiosity, building on students' prior knowledge are all things that teachers can attempt to do; and conversely, they are things that poor teaching can discourage. There are many things the teacher can do to encourage deep learning' (Biggs, 1999: 17). Arguably a deep approach to learning equates more closely to the broader view of vocationalism highlighted in Chapter 1.

Thus, part of the motivational challenge for business and management educators involves helping students appreciate that pursuit of a deep approach to their learning requires them to see that vocationalism is more than simply training for a particular job. In so doing, inevitably a balance has to be struck between, on the one hand, a study 'for' business and, on the other, a study 'about' business (see Chapter 1). The latter involves stimulating interest by constantly posing the 'why' as well as the 'who', 'what', 'when' and 'how' questions; requiring learners to identify and evaluate alternatives to received wisdom; raising issues that not only impact upon the business world but extend well beyond the day-to-day aspects of working life; and getting learners to reflect on the processes and not simply the substance of learning. Encouraging learners to think critically 'about' business not only resonates with a deep approach to learning but also reflects a key distinguishing characteristic of a 'higher' education as defined by Barnett (1990) and others. Moreover, there is evidence that many business and management educators identify strongly with such goals (Macfarlane, 1997).

Another motivational challenge arises in situations where learners are studying for negative rather than positive reasons. For example, on 'in-house' and collaborative corporate programmes, participants can often be motivated more by job insecurity or the 'need to be seen to be doing it' than by promotion prospects or a genuine commitment to lifelong learning (Macfarlane, 2000). In other words, some programme members see themselves as conscripts rather than willing participants. With the diffusion of management throughout organisations and the consequent need to develop skills and to extend one's knowledge this is increasingly likely to be the case.

Generally speaking, when faced with disgruntled and resentful learners it is probably best to meet the challenge 'head on'. By getting them to identify and articulate their frustrations and concerns at the beginning of the course and responding to them with respect and reasoned argument based on their needs, as opposed to those of the organisation, it should be possible to ease the situation. At the same time there is the value to be derived from the cathartic effect of learners giving vent to their feelings and by linking this to the process of learning, since as mentioned earlier this is as much an emotional as a cerebral activity (Pask, 1976). For example, it can be used to encourage and legitimize their contributions throughout the course of study. Ignoring any resentment or acting as an apologist for the organisation running the course is only likely to make matters worse.

Since the motivation of employees has attracted a great deal of attention from organisation theorists and specialists in human resource management, business and management educators have at their disposal many insights that can be utilized in seeking to motivate learners. Elton (1996), for example, has demonstrated how Herzberg's motivation at work theory can be applied to student learning. The more educators can learn about student motivation and the factors that affect it the better.

Utilization of learning time

Arguably one of the greatest challenges facing learners and those responsible for facilitating their learning is that of time management. For most business and management students, learning has to compete with many other commitments on their limited time. While this is most evident where students are studying on a part-time basis, it would be wrong to assume that this is not an issue for full-time students. All students, regardless of their mode of study, incur an 'opportunity cost'. In other words, in devoting time to their learning they forgo the other uses to which the time could be put, such as recreation and paid employment. Many learners are acutely aware of the problems involved in striking an appropriate balance between meeting the demands of their course and securing their financial position through paid employment.

This goes some way to explaining why learners are becoming more instrumental in their approach, with the result that there needs to be a clear link between the required learning and various 'sticks' and 'carrots'. Consequently, for those facilitating learning it is necessary, not simply to make students aware of the time commitment and provide them with help in developing their time management skills, but also to devise their learning, teaching and assessment strategies in such a way that all the components are mutually reinforcing and that there are explicit connections between them (see Chapter 5). Likewise, realistic estimates of the time involved in undertaking particular activities need to be made. Ultimately a balance has to be struck between those learning and assessment activities that are essential, given the diversity of aims and preferred learning styles, and the time available for study. In so doing, however, it is important to avoid reinforcing what has been termed 'strategic' learning (Entwistle, 1992). 'Strategic' students (Kneale, 1997) are those who approach learning purely on the basis of the assessment requirements of the course and seek to obtain the highest possible grades for the least amount of effort. This is an undesirable phenomenon because such learners are reluctant to engage fully with the subject, seek out an in-depth understanding of concepts or participate adequately in non-assessed learning activities. Given the instrumentality of many business and management learners it is likely that a 'strategic' approach will not be uncommon. Finding ways of coping or even trying to counteract this tendency should be a high priority for educators.

While the foregoing are difficult tasks, if tackled creatively and with the full participation of students, they can provide a learning experience of particular relevance in the field of business and management. They provide a means of illustrating not only the concept of 'opportunity cost' mentioned earlier and the calculations and trade-offs that lie at the heart of many business and public sector decisions, but also the 'short-termism' inherent in a purely 'strategic' approach to learning.

In showing students how to get the most from the time available to them, it is also a good idea to encourage them to be opportunistic in their learning. During a programme there are likely to be many occasions, in going about their daily business, when they encounter something of relevance to their studies. This is especially the case in business and management given its ubiquity. If these opportunities are missed or ignored then learners are not making the best use of the time at their disposal. Helping learners to recognize them and to exploit their potential for learning should be given a high priority since it might enable them to 'kill two birds with one stone' and thereby double the output from the time involved. It might be thought that such a principle can only be applied on 'in-house' corporate programmes or courses where most or all of the learners are working full time. In fact, with a little imagination all learners, regardless of their employment situation, can benefit if they are encouraged to do so.

At one level, being opportunistic might simply mean relating something that happens in another context (eg while shopping, watching television, reading a newspaper, talking to a colleague) to a concept, model or theory of relevance to a course of study. In other words, it is a way of generating examples or illustrations that can be added to those provided in the literature or by educators. These, of course, can be shared with fellow learners in seminars, workshops or online conferences. Learners can also be encouraged to think of situations encountered as potential case study material, which could be written up for assessment purposes (see Chapter 5). Asking students to keep a learning log in which they reflect on the link between their workplace and/or other experiences and academic study is a further means of achieving this synergy (see Chapter 10).

At another level, being opportunistic might mean taking advantage of a situation where one can contribute to the learning of others. As is often pointed out, the best way to confirm that one has learnt something is to pass it on to someone else (eg Biggs, 1999). Opportunities for doing so can take a variety of forms, some of which relate to the substance of learning and others to the processes. In either case, there are gains both for students who are facilitating the learning of others and for those whose learning is being supported. Some examples are provided in Table 2.3.

Table 2.3 Ways in which business and management learners can support the learning of others

Method	What Is Involved
Mentoring	helping individual learners to reflect on their practice and apply their learning to tasks in the workplace or elsewhere
Coaching	instructing learners, generally on a one-to-one basis, in a skill or technique
Demonstrating	showing learners, often on a group basis, how a particular procedure or system operates
Supervising	overseeing a project undertaken to enhance learning
Buddying	providing those who have just started a course of study with support and encouragement based on prior personal experience of what is involved
Expediting	creating conditions within which learning can flourish by negotiating access to facilities and resources for learners that might not otherwise be available to them
Expounding	serving on a panel of 'experts'

Conclusion

Underlying this chapter is the belief that for learning in business and management to be effective the relationship between learners and educators needs to be grounded in the principle of partnership. In other words, learners need to see themselves as active participants in the process of learning as opposed to passive recipients. Because many students have been socialized into a model of learning that tends to emphasize the expertise of the educator and the relative ignorance, and consequent passivity, of the learner, it is the responsibility of those engaged in the support of learning to open up the possibility of a more equal relationship. What this means in practice is taking steps to empower the learner with respect not only to the substance, but also to the process of learning. Thus, the contents of the chapters that follow, focusing as they do on the processes of learning, teaching and assessment, may be seen as a potential resource for students as well as those contributing to their learning.

References

Argyris, C and Schon, D (1978) *Organizational Learning: A theory of action perspective*, Addison Wesley, Reading, MA

Argyris, C and Schon, D (1996) *Organizational Learning II: Theory, method and practice*, Addison Wesley, Wokingham

Ashcroft, K and Foreman-Peck, L (1994) *Managing Teaching and Learning in Further and Higher Education*, Falmer Press, London

Barnett, R (1990) *The Idea of Higher Education*, Society for Research into Higher Education/Open University Press, Buckingham

Biggs, J (1999) *Teaching for Quality Learning at University*, Society for Research into Higher Education/Open University Press, Buckingham

Booth, A (1997) Listening to students: experiences and expectations in the transition to a history degree, *Studies in Higher Education*, **22** (2), pp 205–20

Coates, N and Koerner, R (1996) How market oriented are business studies degrees?, *Journal of Marketing Management*, **12**, pp 455–75

Coopey, J (1995) The learning organization, power, politics and ideology, *Management Learning*, **26** (2), pp 193–213

Elton, L (1996) Strategies to enhance student motivation: a conceptual analysis, *Studies in Higher Education*, **21** (1), pp 57–68

Entwistle, N (1992) *The Impact of Teaching on Learning Outcomes in Higher Education: A literature review*, Committee of Vice-Chancellors and Principals of the Universities of the United Kingdom, Sheffield

Graves, D (1983) Values in business studies – an overview, in *The Hidden Curriculum in Business Studies*, ed D Graves, pp 7–15, Higher Education Foundation, Chichester

Holden, R and McGrath, J (1992) Shadowing for self development, *Journal of Further and Higher Education*, **16** (2), pp 40–49

Honey, A and Mumford, P (1992) *A Manual of Learning Styles*, P Mumford, Maidenhead

Horner, D (1983) Expectations of the student, in *The Hidden Curriculum in Business Studies*, ed D Graves, pp 15–19, Higher Education Foundation, Chichester

Kneale, P (1997) The rise of the 'strategic student': how can we adapt to cope?, in *Facing Up to Radical Changes in Universities and Colleges*, ed S Armstrong, G Thompson and S Brown, pp 119–30, Kogan Page/SEDA, London

Knowles, M and Associates (1984) *Andragogy in Action*, Gulf Publishing Co, Houston

Kolb, D (1981) Learning styles and disciplinary differences, in *The Modern American College*, ed A W Chickering *et al*, pp 232–55, Jossey-Bass, San Francisco

Kolb, D (1983) *Experimental Learning: Experience as the source of learning and development*, Prentice Hall, New York

Lloyd, J (1996) The contribution of micro-economics at the undergraduate level, with particular reference to business programmes, *Economics and Business Education*, **4** (4), pp 168–70

Macfarlane, B (1997) The business studies first degree: institutional trends and the pedagogic context, *Teaching in Higher Education*, **2** (1), pp 45–57

Macfarlane, B (2000) Inside the corporate classroom, *Teaching in Higher Education*, **5** (1), pp 51–60

Marton, F and Saljo, R (1976) On qualitative differences in learning, *British Journal of Educational Psychology*, **46**, pp 4–11

Mazen, A, Jones, M and Sergenian, G (2000) Transforming the class into a learning organization, *Management Learning*, **31** (2), pp 147–61

Morris, D, Newman, J and Stringer, B (1993) Widening access to business education: some results from BA Business Administration at Coventry University, *Journal of Access Studies*, **8**, pp 82–95

Pask, G (1976) Learning styles and strategies, *British Journal of Educational Psychology*, **46**, pp 4–11

Pedler, M, Burgoyne, J and Boydell, T (1991) *The Learning Company: A strategy for sustainable development*, McGraw-Hill, Maidenhead

Race, P and Brown, S (1993) *500 Tips for Tutors*, Kogan Page, London

Roberts, J (1996) Management education and the limits of technical rationality: the conditions and consequences of management practice, in *Rethinking Management Education*, ed R French and C Grey, pp 54–75, Sage, London

Vince, R (1996) Experiential management education as the practice of change, in *Rethinking Management Education*, ed R French and C Grey, pp 111–31, Sage, London

Part B

Preparing the agenda – the learning environment

The chapters constituting this part of the book deal with generic issues concerning the business and management curriculum as a whole. In so doing, they are designed to set the agenda for the seven chapters that make up Part C. They contain an explanation of the thinking behind the structure for each of the Part C chapters and indicate what educators need to take into account in planning, preparing, implementing and evaluating mechanisms for learner support. Whatever the level or mode of study, consideration has to be given to a wide variety of matters, particularly where it is necessary to produce a fully developed learning and teaching strategy and to undertake a thorough appraisal motivated by the desire to secure 'continuous quality improvement' in the student learning environment and support systems.

Regardless of the substance of each subject area within business and management, such matters include those relating to:

- the educational challenges faced in facilitating effective learning;
- the specification of aims, objectives and learning outcomes;
- the design of activities for effective learning, teaching and assessment;
- means of securing an integrated learning experience;
- the encouragement of reflective practice and evaluation of the student experience.

Systematic consideration of these aspects should help to secure a strategy that is robust and capable of delivering effective learning and teaching and subsequently to ensure a rigorous appraisal of the learning experience.

3

Educational challenges

Roger Ottewill and Bruce Macfarlane

Introduction

Making a contribution to the effective learning of others is a challenging as well as an exhilarating experience. In the case of business and management education, some of the challenges are common to the curriculum as a whole, including those concerning the motivation and commitment of learners that were discussed in Chapter 2. Alongside these more generic challenges there are others that are specific to particular subject areas and a number that cross subject boundaries. Such challenges emanate from either the context within which that part of the curriculum has evolved or the forces that are driving its development. Thus, before looking in more detail at the challenges, some attention is given to the contemporary context and drivers in business and management education.

Contemporary context and drivers

As discussed in Chapter 1, business and management education is characterized by its eclecticism. Consequently, in facing up to educational challenges and making decisions about the form and content of learning, teaching and assessment strategies and activities, it is especially important to have some understanding and appreciation of the particular context and the drivers involved. Whether these should be shared with learners is a moot point. The stance adopted here, however, is that, wherever possible, explicitness and transparency are to be encouraged, since this is in keeping with a commitment to learner empowerment. In other words, the more learners are made aware of the background to not only what they are learning but also how they are expected to learn, the greater the potential for a shared understanding between learners and educators.

For some subject areas that lie at the heart of the curriculum, such as strategic management (Chapter 12), the context and drivers are directly related to trends within the mainstream of business and management education. Of particular importance in this respect are the tensions between education 'about' business and education 'for' business (see Chapter 1) and between course design based on the principles of separate and distinctive subject areas, known in the UK as unitization or modularization, and that based on the principle of integration (Chapter 6).

For other subject areas, such as business environment (Chapter 8) and business organisation (Chapter 9), the context and drivers are more disparate and extend well beyond business and management into other disciplinary areas. This can be clearly seen in the case of the business environment, which enjoys what can best be described as a symbiotic relationship with the disciplines of economics, law, sociology, politics and other social sciences. In the case of business organisation, there is a similar relationship with subjects such as sociology and psychology.

In addition to the academic world, for every subject area much of the context comprises, and many of the drivers derive from, the 'real' world of business and management. While traditional academic subjects tend to rely on knowledge produced in a primarily disciplinary, cognitive milieu, knowledge in applied areas, like business and management, is shaped via a broader transdisciplinary social and economic context (Gibbons et al, 1994). Thus, developments within the external environment of businesses and the problems they confront, as well as organisational procedures and practices, play a central part in shaping the substance and form of learning. It is important to recognize that these developments, problems, procedures and practices are often subject to a process of mediation in which various agencies, including academic institutions, play a part (Laughton and Ottewill, 1998). Thus, the resultant learning experiences do not necessarily replicate in full what is happening in the 'real' world. Instead, they are often a mediated version reflecting current educational fashion and/or politico-academic trends and a desire on the part of members of the academic community to resist transient influences from the 'real' world and provide a business and management education of lasting value (Macfarlane, 1997).

In drawing this kind of analysis to the attention of learners it is important to proceed with a degree of caution. While at early stages of their studies it might prove to be a distraction, at later stages, even on undergraduate programmes, a strong case can be made for doing so. This rests not only on the principle of empowerment mentioned earlier, but also on the premise that learning experiences are enriched through the process of metacognition (also recommended in Chapter 14). Such a process involves consideration of the reasons why particular topics are being studied and the extent to which they mirror 'reality'. In addition, it can be used to confront learners with issues of pedagogy, thereby introducing them to the discourse they need in order to participate more fully in the shaping of their learning environment. Engaging learners in a dialogue concerning the values and norms that permeate this environment makes an important contribution to the development of learning communities.

For those responsible for learner support, an awareness of the context and drivers, together with the process of mediation, should help to counteract any potentially negative influences. For example, in subject areas, such as the business environment (see Chapter 8), with strong links to long-established disciplines on which specialist courses are based, there is always a danger that the learning activities for business and management students will not be sufficiently differentiated from those designed for students specializing in these disciplines. Similar concerns arise in areas like statistics and accountancy, where delivery methods can be overly influenced by the traditions of the subject. In other words, too little account is taken of the distinctive needs of business and management students and all they receive is a 'watered-down' version of a disciplinary-based course, with insufficient emphasis on application. This is an ever-present danger, given that most educators tend to identify more strongly with their discipline than with business and management as a coherent field of study (see Chapter 1). Also, as pointed out in several of the Part C chapters, disciplinary specialists may be called on to teach broadly multidisciplinary subject areas, placing considerable demands on the knowledge-base of educators (see Chapters 8, 9, 13 and 14).

Familiarity with the context and drivers might also help where it is necessary to provide a rationale or explanation for a particular approach or stance. Faced with questions from various stakeholders, including learners, employers and educational agencies, concerning delivery methods as well as subject matter, appropriate responses might well need to include references to those factors that have shaped the curriculum. In short, knowledge of the context and drivers should enable educators to rise more effectively to the educational challenges faced in every subject area.

The sources of challenge

Awareness of the challenges is a crucial first step towards surmounting them. In other words, 'to be forewarned is to be forearmed'. Knowing something about the potential challenges, including their source and nature, should help to indicate where it is necessary for those engaged in the facilitation of learning to concentrate their energies.

In business and management, the sources from which challenges arise are many and varied. An underlying source of challenge is pedagogic tradition. In the pursuit of effective learning and teaching, it is easy to be 'blown off course' by the strong educational conventions that exist within the different subject areas that make up the business and management curriculum and provide most educators with their academic point of reference. Such conventions can exert a powerful and, arguably, pernicious influence over approaches to learning, teaching and assessment. For example, in the more disciplinary-based areas (eg economics) seminars and unseen essay-style examination questions still tend to predominate. By contrast, in more overtly vocational areas (eg marketing, human resource management) and integrative areas (eg business environment, strategic management) problem-based learning and case studies are far more in evidence. While traditions in pedagogy have a value, there is a danger that they become straitjackets and inhibit experimentation and innovation.

Here, the challenge is to break free from such traditions in order to seek more effective and creative ways of engaging with the changing mix of learners and responding to the evolving requirements of employers. More specifically, the motivation might be a recognition of the need to accommodate a wider variety of learning styles (see Chapter 2) or an awareness of some of the limitations of certain modes of teaching. While the shortcomings of lectures are well documented (eg Bligh, 1998; Ottewill and Jennings, 1998), they remain a central feature of learning and teaching strategies for many parts of the business and management curriculum, especially with large groups of learners. While they can make a contribution, given their limitations in stimulating student-centred learning, it might be felt that they ought to be used more sparingly or with a greater degree of inventiveness. Incorporating short problem-solving exercises and/or getting students to work with partial or incomplete handouts are well-established means of breaking up a lecture and reinforcing learning points. Equally, in challenging pedagogic traditions it can be argued that learners should be provided, as a matter of course, with a justification for the use of particular methods, including lectures, as well as an explanation of their role and purpose. Learners should also be made aware of their responsibilities in respect of any particular method.

In seeking to challenge the pedagogic traditions of their subject area, business and management educators often need some support and encouragement. To an extent, this can come through collaboration with colleagues from different academic backgrounds (see Chapter 13). Increasingly, however, they can look to the units and centres that institutions of HE are establishing to stimulate innovation in learning, teaching and assessment. Through the sponsorship of research, demonstration projects, networking initiatives and other methods, such units are playing an increasingly important role in facilitating the emergence of educational communities that cut across established disciplinary boundaries. For cross-disciplinary fields like business and management, this is an extremely welcome development. Moreover, it should help to sustain those subject areas within business and management, like business environment (Chapter 8), strategic management (Chapter 12) and innovation and entrepreneurship (Chapter 14), that seek to provide students with a broad view of particular issues and topics by integrating a variety of disciplinary perspectives. While such an aim is highly desirable, it does require educators to be conscious of the need to balance 'breadth' with 'depth' (see Chapters 8 and 9 for discussion of this issue).

A more specific source of challenge is learner perceptions of the degree of difficulty of different subject areas. Such perceptions can be reinforced, sometimes inadvertently, by educators. While learning in every subject area can present some students with problems, certain areas are often perceived as more demanding than others. In the UK, for example, subject areas with a quantitative orientation generally present learners with more difficulties than those without. As reported by Dent and North (1996), some of those responsible for teaching economics on business and management programmes believe that students struggle with the statistical aspects because of deficiencies in their prior mathematics education. However, drawing attention to the difficulties may damage the confidence of learners, with the result that they underperform, thus giving rise to a self-fulfilling prophecy. Moreover, in many instances, such perceptions of difficulty can misrepresent the demands of those subject areas that are deemed to be relatively straightforward and this can have similarly disastrous consequences if learners are lulled into a false sense of security. As pointed out in Chapter 13, for example, marketing is sometimes regarded as a 'soft' subject area even though there are significant quantitative elements within the curriculum.

Regardless of their accuracy, perceptions are important and need to be addressed in the structuring of learning environments and the design of learning activities. Supplementary instruction (SI) schemes serve as a means of addressing some of these concerns. Using more advanced students to provide less experienced learners with additional support can formalize existing peer relationships and generate advantages to all parties. SI schemes have been widely used in the United States and have also been adopted in the UK to improve the performance of first year management accounting students (Carman and Beveridge, 1997). Whatever methods are used, clearly a balance needs to be struck between encouragement and reassurance, on the one hand, and making students aware of the demands they face, on the other. Ideally, learner support should focus on those parts of the course that, on the basis of past experience, cause learners the greatest difficulty.

A further source of educational challenge is again the subject matter but this time its perceived relevance from a vocational point of view. As pointed out in Chapters 1 and 2, some components of the business and management curriculum, such as marketing and business skills, are seen by employers and learners as self-evidently vocational, with the result that those engaged in learner support do not have to give very much attention to, or expend any energy on, justifying what they are doing. By contrast, in other subject areas, such as organisational behaviour (Chapter 9) and business ethics (Chapter 10), learners are often highly sceptical of what is being covered from a vocational point of view (Coates and Koerner, 1996). While this scepticism may arise from a very narrow-minded view as to what constitutes vocationalism, it still needs to be addressed as a precursor to effective learning and teaching. This is not necessarily an easy task and needs to be handled with care. Failure in this respect can result in a reinforcement of prejudice as opposed to its reduction. Here, what has been referred to in Chapter 2 as working with 'the grain of the learners' is particularly important. This means, in effect, ensuring that the discussion of vocational relevance incorporates examples and illustrations to which learners can readily relate and helps them acquire a broader perspective on the nature of vocationalism. Part of this involves sensitivity to the learners' cultural context by using examples and illustrations to which they can relate. The dominance of US-based textbooks and case studies in business and management education is a particular challenge here (see Chapters 10, 12 and 13).

Arguably, attention should also be given to issues of relevance in those subject areas that are perceived as self-evidently vocational. This is because there can often be a significant mismatch between what is actually taught and what is happening in the 'world of work'. Furthermore, even in subjects like accountancy, learners can still express scepticism about their relevance and hold negative preconceptions. For example, accountancy and accountants are 'boring' (Fisher and Murphy, 1995; Lucas, 1998). Having to justify, on a regular basis, the inclusion of every component of the curriculum in broad vocational terms helps to maintain a degree of compatibility between the student learning experience and the exigencies of business.

The availability and appropriateness of resources for learning and teaching purposes are also a source of educational challenge. For business and management education as a whole there is no shortage of suitable material (see Chapter 5). However, this can result in information overload and a feeling of being overwhelmed. Moreover, given the speed and frequency with which new and reworked material becomes available, it is essential for educators to develop strategies for keeping up to date. With this in mind, it is important to allocate time for sifting through some of what is available in order to ensure that learners are presented with contemporary material and to seek help from others, such as information specialists, so that the burden is shared. Having said that, while contemporaneity is a necessity in many spheres of business and management education, a purely a-historical approach is to be eschewed. As Horn (1981) and others have argued, the historical dimension should not be ignored since there is much that can be learnt from the experiences of the past. Indeed, business history represents an important area of interest amongst some business and management educators.

In establishing the availability of material, both contemporary and historical, and its suitability and relevance, it should be noted that at the level of individual subject areas the situation is variable. In some areas what is available may provide learners with a distorted or incomplete view. For example, there tend to be more case studies relating to private sector enterprises than to the public or voluntary sector, and these tend to be large multinationals rather than small and medium-sized enterprises, with the result that insufficient attention is given, in general, to the latter (see Chapters 8, 9 and 10). Moreover, many case studies tend to focus on strategic-level decisions as opposed to those levels to which learners can more easily relate and at which they are more likely to be employed or secure employment on completion of their course (see Chapters 10 and 12). Thus, they may be deemed less suitable than case studies that incorporate more day-to-day and down-to-earth scenarios. It also needs to be borne in mind that case studies are just one means of facilitating active learning within business and management. The

Harvard case study method should not be used to the exclusion of other effective tools such as problem-based learning assignments (see Chapter 8), business games or role plays (see Chapter 10), simulations (see Chapters 11 and 13) or enterprise projects (see Chapter 14).

A final source of educational challenge harks back to Chapter 2. In view of the enormous diversity of learners on business and management programmes, particularly in terms of their prior and current experience of business and organisational life, facilitation of learning in some subject areas is likely to be tougher than in others or with some groups of students than others. Clearly, in those subject areas where there is very heavy emphasis on application of theory, concepts and principles, such as business organisation (Chapter 9), business ethics (Chapter 10) and strategic management (Chapter 12), progress will probably be faster with those learners who possess the relevant work experience than with those who do not. In general, although experienced managers can express scepticism as to the value of theory (see Chapter 9), learners familiar with the workplace tend to find it easier to make the link between theory and business practice. This is one of the main reasons why many undergraduate programmes incorporate a period of supervised work experience (Day *et al*, 1982; Hollinshead *et al*, 1983).

Notwithstanding arrangements of this kind, there is still considerable variation in the nature and extent of student familiarity with the workplace and as a result approaches to learning and teaching have to be fine-tuned. Where learners have little or no knowledge, greater emphasis may well have to be placed on raising awareness and less on application and the aims modified accordingly. However, a considerable amount can be achieved by means of simulations, case studies and, where possible, using the organisation responsible for the learning environment as a source of illustrative material. Casting learners in the role of customers/consumers is another tool (see Chapters 8 and 10). On programmes with a work experience component, it is clearly important to take account of whether a contribution to student learning occurs before or after the period of employment and design activities accordingly.

While the challenges outlined above can appear daunting they should be viewed positively. In terms of a SWOT (ie strengths, weaknesses, opportunities, threats) analysis they should be seen, ideally, as opportunities not as threats. By this means they serve as a stimulus for creativity and the development of imaginative responses that enrich the learning experience of students and provide a deep sense of satisfaction for the innovator. Viewing the challenges in negative terms can be counter-productive. At best, it might engender a spirit of resignation and at worst, paranoia. In both cases this can lead to paralysis and a diminishing of the quality of the student learning experience.

Conclusion

When responding to the challenges, regardless of their source, it is important to remember that this is not a once-and-for-all exercise. Changes in the context and configuration of the drivers as well as the composition of groups of learners can mean that a response that works on one occasion might be less successful the next. Thus, challenges need to be closely monitored with a view to ensuring that responses are adjusted to take account of any significant change. Here flexibility of outlook and approach, based on the principles of reflective practice (see Chapter 7), is the key. Simply rolling forward a standard set of learning activities year on year should not be regarded as an option.

References

Bligh, D (1998) *What's the Use of Lectures?*, Intellect Books, Exeter

Carman, R and Beveridge, I (1997) Improvements in performance on a first year management accounting module – using SI to help students succeed, *Journal of European Business Education*, **6** (2), pp 47–71

Coates, N F and Koerner, R E (1996) How market oriented are business studies degrees?, *Journal of Marketing Management* **12**, pp 455–75

Day, J *et al* (1982) The role of industrial training in the business studies sandwich degree, *Business Education*, Summer, pp 105–22

Dent, C and North, N (1996) Educational issues amongst HE economics educators: a survey, *Economics and Business Education*, **4** (2), pp 58–64

Fisher, R and Murphy, V (1995) A pariah profession? Some student perceptions of accounting and accountancy, *Studies in Higher Education*, **20** (1), pp 45–58

Gibbons, M *et al* (1994) *The New Production of Knowledge*, Sage, London

Hollinshead, B *et al* (1983) *Supervised Work Experience in Education Programmes*, CNAA, London

Horn, C (1981) The case for history in business studies courses, *Business Education*, Autumn, pp 169–74

Laughton, D and Ottewill, R (1998) Values and norms in British undergraduate education: implications for the student experience, *Journal of European Business Education*, **8** (1), pp 51–61

Lucas, U (1998) *'Accounting for the world' and the 'world of accountancy': phenomenographic research in accounting education*, Paper presented at Higher Education Close-Up: An International Conference, University of Central Lancashire, Preston, 6–8 July

Macfarlane, B (1997) The business studies first degree: institutional trends and the pedagogic context, *Teaching in Higher Education*, **2** (1), pp 45–57

Ottewill, R and Jennings, P (1998) Open learning versus lecturing, in *Educational Innovation in Economics and Business III: Innovative practices in business education*, ed R Milter, J Stinson and W Gijselaers, pp 267–82, Kluwer Academic Publishers, Dordrecht

4

Aims, objectives and learning outcomes

Roger Ottewill and Bruce Macfarlane

Introduction

Being clear about what one is seeking to achieve is a key business principle at every level within an organisation, from that of the individual employee to that of the boardroom or executive group. Without aims and objectives it is less likely that progress will be made, tasks completed and efficiencies secured. Similarly in the design of a learning environment the need for transparency and clarity over intentions is vital. Increasingly in HE, these are being expressed in terms of aims, objectives and learning outcomes. Although controversial in certain quarters and demanding to put into practice (especially when seeking to distinguish between learning at different levels) aims, objectives and learning outcomes have become a well-established feature of the discourse of HE (eg Boore, 1993; Boulton-Lewis, 1995; D'Andrea, 1999).

The primary purpose of aims, objectives and learning outcomes is to 'concentrate the minds' of those responsible for designing learning experiences and to serve as a means of communicating intentions to other stakeholders, especially students. Aims and objectives are generally written from the perspective of educators and indicate what they are seeking to achieve. In the language of strategic planning, aims express the broader, longer-term goals, that is the mission of the enterprise. Objectives are more detailed and, in an educational setting, indicate where educators need to direct their efforts if their intentions are to be realized. By contrast, learning outcomes express what learners should know, understand or be able to do by the end of a course of study or learning activity. In each case, they are intended to inject a sense of purpose into the learning process and to provide a benchmark for assessing effectiveness. For many of the subject areas that constitute the business and management curriculum, they also serve to illustrate the value of applying business principles to the processes of learning and teaching.

Moreover, learning outcomes, in particular, are a means whereby business and management educators can clearly indicate to employers the potential capabilities of students. There is a danger, though, that educators will focus too narrowly on learning outcomes that concentrate on subject knowledge. Given the vocational remit of business and management education, it is important that learning outcomes also relate to skills and, more controversially, attitudes and values.

Aims and objectives

At first sight, determining the aims and objectives for a course of study or for one or more learning activities may seem relatively straightforward. Such a view, however, is oversimplistic, since it fails to take into account a number of complicating factors. Foremost amongst these is the tension surrounding the aims of HE, in general, and business and management education, in particular, to which attention was drawn in Chapter 1. As pointed out, at the heart of this tension is the dualism inherent in the notion of education 'for' business, on the one hand, and education 'about' business, on the other. This tension is evident not only at the macro level but also at the micro, as illustrated in the differing perspectives of authors in Part C of this book. Those contributing chapters on the business environment (Chapter 8), business organi-sation (Chapter 9) and business ethics (Chapter 10) regard their aim as principally getting students to learn 'about' business. By contrast, the authors of the interna-tional business (Chapter 11), strategic management (Chapter 12), marketing (Chapter 13) and innovation and entrepreneurship (Chapter 14) chapters, define their purpose as mainly providing an education 'for' business. However, these are essentially differences of emphasis and it is important to recognize the danger of seeing certain subject areas and activities as purely applied or purely critical. For example, activities such as case studies are often seen as essentially applied, while essay writing is regarded as essentially critical. Ideally, educators should consider the extent to which they can pursue aims and objectives that relate to both applied knowledge and a critical evaluation of business as a social activity.

There is, of course, less need for educators to do this where they are contributing to a coherently designed programme in which different aims and objectives are clearly allocated to subjects and activities and the full range is covered by this means. Quite often, however, this is not the case and it is therefore incumbent upon those responsible for a subject area or activity to ensure that in specifying aims and objectives notions of mutual exclusivity are eschewed. Only in this way will learners appreciate the importance of securing a balanced view that incorporates both applied and critical perspectives.

Taking this analysis a stage further, the issue of balance is compounded by what many commentators see as the triple, as opposed to dual, aims of HE. Bligh,

Thomas and McNay (1999), for example, in drawing upon Bloom's (1956, 1964) taxonomy, distinguish between cognitive and affective aims and adaptable occupational skills. At the heart of cognitive aims are 'knowledge, perception and thought'. Affective aims relate to 'attitudes, emotions, motivation, values and interpersonal skills based upon feelings for others', while occupational skills are developed through the application of cognition and affect (Bligh, Thomas and McNay, 1999: 7). Moreover, Bligh and his colleagues argue that such aims are of benefit both to the individual learner and to the community at large. This framework is applied to business and management education in Table 4.1. It provides an example of each type of aim from the perspective of those who make a contribution to the learning of others.

Table 4.1 Benefits of HE aims applied to business and management education

Aim	Learner	Community
Affective	assisting learners to become customer-focused	encouraging learners to respect the rights and interests of all sections of society
Cognitive	contributing to learners' understanding of the business environment	enabling learners to become wealth-creating agents to the benefit of society
Adaptable Occupational	supporting learners in the design of a spreadsheet	facilitating the development of oral communication and presentation skills

Once again, it is incumbent on course designers to consider how best to incorporate these aims into the curriculum and to ensure an appropriate balance between them. Naturally, there are differences of emphasis between contributing subject areas. In terms of affective objectives, for example, some areas of the curriculum are more concerned with developing the personal attitudes of students such as tolerance of disagreement (see Chapter 10), others with cross-cultural awareness (see Chapter 11) and others with flexibility (see Chapter 14). With respect to adaptable skills, some areas of the curriculum tend to focus on developing decision-making abilities (see Chapter 12), others on research skills (see Chapter 8) and others on numeracy (see Chapter 13).

Another complicating factor relates to the language used in specifying aims and objectives. On the one hand, it needs to be clear and concise with the meanings attached to key terms and concepts being shared, as far as possible, by all concerned. On the other hand, the language needs to accommodate differences in level as well as the nuances associated with different facets of cognition, emotional integrity and skill development. In finding suitable terminology, recourse is often made to Bloom's taxonomy (1956, 1964), mentioned earlier. This distinguishes, in ascending order of complexity, between knowledge, comprehension, application, analysis, synthesis and evaluation. While this is extremely helpful, care still needs to be taken with terms, such as analysis, that are capable of being interpreted in a variety of ways.

While aims and objectives play an important part in creating an element of certainty needed for effective learning and teaching, they should not be treated as immutable. Indeed, their value is enhanced if they are regularly revisited with a view to adjusting them to take account of what has been learnt through teacher and learner support and of changes in the context of HE, in general, and business and management education, in particular. In other words, they serve as a framework for reflection and evaluation (see Chapter 7). They also provide the starting point for the specification of learning outcomes.

Learning outcomes

Ideally learning outcomes should be clear, relevant, challenging and achievable. In seeking to articulate outcomes that reflect these attributes, educators are compelled to consider their aspirations for learning more systematically and explicitly than has traditionally been the case in HE and focus on the changes in learners that they anticipate will result from particular learning experiences. Once specified, outcomes provide learners with a yardstick for assessing their progress; contributors to their learning with a basis for aligning their input with the intentions of those responsible for enumerating the outcomes; and other interested parties, such as employers and funding agencies, with a benchmark against which to judge the quality of the learning and whether or not it represents value for money. In addition, they help to highlight any outcomes from learning that were not anticipated, thereby contributing to any subsequent appraisal of the learning process.

While learning outcomes tend to be written for a course of study, the same principle can be applied to individual learning activities, such as an essay, role play or case study. Indeed, there is a great deal to be gained from ensuring that learners are aware of the anticipated outcome(s) associated with each component of their learning experience. At the very least, it demonstrates that it has been planned in a coherent and purposeful manner. This is often a great help to learners with limited time at their disposal (see Chapter 2) and those requiring reassurance regarding the nature of the enterprise on which they are engaged. However, it is clearly important to ensure that planning does not stultify the learning process and undermine the potential for the achievement of unanticipated but valuable learning outcomes, such as an enhanced appreciation of the importance of collaboration or the value of coaching.

Because of their current popularity in many education systems, there is now a variety of schemas for categorizing different types of learning outcome. Otter (1992), for example, distinguishes between subject-based and personal outcomes and Allan (1996) between subject-based, personal transferable and general academic outcomes. Moreover, in the UK the Quality Assurance Agency for HE now requires all HE courses and programmes to be specified in terms of learning outcomes incorporating knowledge and understanding; cognitive skills; subject-specific, practical or vocational skills; and generic skills.

Not surprisingly, there is a considerable overlap between these schemas and the framework developed by Bligh, Thomas and McNay (1999), which was outlined in the previous section and is used in the Part C chapters as the basis for providing examples of different types of outcome for each of the subject areas covered. By this means it is intended to illustrate the kind of outcome to which learners might aspire and the potential for learning. The examples are not meant to remove from educators the responsibility for devising their own outcomes, since ultimately the best way to learn about learning outcomes is experientially. In other words, far more can be learnt from devising outcomes, even where this is not a formal requirement, than from reading about them.

To assist with this task a number of guidelines can be offered. First, a learning outcome generally comprises three components:

- an active verb or phrase, such as describe or illustrate;
- an object or objects, such as terminology and concepts or particular skills;
- a context or condition, such as a marketing department or the external environment of a business organisation.

Thus, when drafting outcomes it is a good idea to use a tabular format with three columns in order to enhance the explicitness of the process.

Second, it is important to remember that a key role of outcomes is to communicate intentions to others, especially learners. This means trying to put oneself in 'their shoes' with respect to the language used. Thus, clarity and the avoidance of educational jargon are attributes of good-quality outcomes. In addition, outcomes should be neither too broad, which is likely to result in them being ambiguous, nor too narrow, in order to avoid the production of over-detailed and cumbersome lists. They should also be realistic in terms of the time available for learning and teaching. If in doubt, ask someone who is not directly involved to assess and comment on them from the point of view of their clarity, degree of detail and practicality.

Third, outcomes should reflect the changes that educators wish to see in the understanding, skills and attributes, and affective states of learners for whom they have responsibility and who have experienced the learning opportunities that have been created for them. They are not designed to be an alternative version of content-based course descriptions associated with traditional syllabuses, but a set of cognitive and/or behavioural statements. It is also important to avoid the use of evaluative words, such as 'satisfactory', 'good' and 'excellent', since these should be reserved for assessment criteria, which are considered in Chapter 5. Similarly, they should not contain references to learning and teaching methods, such as case studies and seminars, since outcomes are often achievable by a wide variety of means.

Fourth, it is important to ensure that the balance within a set of outcomes between affective, cognitive and adaptable occupational skills accurately reflects the nature of the course or learning activity. It is very easy to overemphasize certain types of outcome and underemphasize others. As implied earlier, outcomes should reflect the desired balance between the occupational skills and knowledge required 'for' business and the affective and cognitive attributes that enable learners to engage in discourse 'about' business.

Fifth, learning outcomes may not all be of equal importance. Hence it is worth taking time to consider whether an outcome is essential or useful or optional. Once determined, their relative importance needs to be communicated to learners to assist them in prioritizing their efforts.

Sixth, consideration needs to be given to the relationship between the outcomes for a specific activity or course of study and those for the students' learning experience as a whole (see Chapter 6). Are they compatible? Do they take account of what is happening elsewhere? Where relevant, are they developmental? In other words, do the outcomes facilitate integration?

Last, like determining aims and objectives, devising outcomes should not be seen as a once-and-for-all task. It is an iterative process both at the initial draft stage and subsequently. To assist with the iteration it is desirable to involve others, including learners, practising managers, information specialists and technical support staff. They can be used as sounding boards and as inquisitors. Constant attention should be given to developments, such as technological innovations, changes in business practice, alterations to other parts of the curriculum and changes in the student mix, that may have implications for the continued relevance of the outcomes.

Conclusion

If devised with integrity and rigour, aims, objectives and learning outcomes can play a key role in the planning, implementation and evaluation of student learning experiences. Moreover, as indicated earlier, they have the added value of demonstrating how business practices can be incorporated into the learning environment. They should be used to drive the selection of appropriate learning, teaching and assessment methods (Chapter 5), to highlight relationships between the varied contributions to the learning experiences of students (Chapter 6) and to generate some of the questions for reflection on practice (Chapter 7). In short, they should be seen as the springboard from which to make progress in many of the other spheres that contribute to the effective learning and teaching of business and management students.

References

Allan, J (1996) Learning outcomes in higher education, *Studies in Higher Education*, **21** (1), pp 93–108

Bligh, D, Thomas, H and McNay, I (1999) *Understanding Higher Education*, Intellect Books, Exeter

Bloom, B (ed) (1956) *Taxonomy of Educational Objectives, vol I: Cognitive domain*, McKay, New York

Bloom, B (ed) (1964) *Taxonomy of Educational Objectives, vol II: Affective domain*, McKay, New York

Boore, J (1993) Teaching standards from quality circles, in *Quality Assurance for University Teaching*, ed R Ellis, pp 194–210, Society for Research into Higher Education/Open University Press, Buckingham

Boulton-Lewis, G (1995) The SOLO taxonomy as a means of shaping and assessing learning in higher education, *Higher Education Research and Development*, **14** (2), pp 143–54

D'Andrea, V-m (1999) Organizing teaching and learning: outcomes-based planning, in *A Handbook for Teaching and Learning in Higher Education*, ed H Fry, S Ketteridge and S Marshall, pp 41–57, Kogan Page, London

Otter, S (1992) *Learning Outcomes in Higher Education*, UDACE, London

5

Learning, teaching and assessment activities

Roger Ottewill and Bruce Macfarlane

Introduction

Inherent in this chapter is the belief that, for business and management students at every level, learning, teaching and assessment should be planned in a co-ordinated manner rather than as a series of discrete activities. Assessment should lie at the heart of what current business jargon might describe as a 'joined-up' approach to education (Knight, 1995), instead of being an afterthought. Moreover, the design of learning, teaching and assessment activities should be driven by aims, objectives and learning outcomes, not the conventions of particular subject areas. Within the parameters of the curriculum, experimentation and innovation are to be encouraged. In this way, courses and programmes are less likely to become stale and routinized and there is a clear demonstration of some of the qualities that ought to characterize business and management learners. While recognizing that the room for manoeuvre is frequently restricted by limited resources and rigid timetables, a bigger constraint is often the inclination to 'play safe'. A willingness to experiment has more to do with a supportive academic culture than the availability of suitable facilities (see Chapter 16). Provided there are sound justifications for departing from the norm, there is much to be gained and little to lose from educators being creative. Moreover, being prepared to experiment and innovate are characteristics of a reflective practitioner (see Chapter 7).

To experiment and innovate effectively, it is necessary to be aware of the range of resources and the variety of methods at one's disposal. Increasingly, these are being shaped by developments in the field of communication and information technology (CIT). As a result, learning, teaching and assessment strategies for many courses and programmes combine electronic resources and methods with those based on more traditional technologies.

Resources

As highlighted in Chapter 3, the availability of resources for business and management education has rapidly increased in recent years. This applies both to resources specifically produced for educational purposes and to those intended for other purposes that can be readily adapted for learning, teaching and assessment. However, such an 'abundance of riches' does throw up a range of issues.

Looking first at dedicated resources, an issue arises from the magnitude and diversity of provision. Although there are variations between subject areas, choices have to be made from the various types of resource shown in the box below.

Types of learning and teaching resource

- journals;
- books and associated guides for educators;
- lecture notes and handouts;
- Web sites;
- open learning materials;
- case studies;
- videos and films;
- audiotapes;
- role plays;
- prior experiences of learners;
- computer simulations;
- visiting speakers.

Boxes containing specific examples of paper-based and electronic resources are provided in each of the Part C chapters.

In dealing with the proliferation of resources, a key issue for educators concerns the guidance that should be given to learners to help them access and utilize what is available. Too much guidance can undermine the notion of 'reading' for a qualification and the encouragement of learner autonomy. However, too little guidance can result in learners feeling abandoned by those responsible for supporting their learning and unable to 'see the wood for the trees'. There is a need to give careful consideration to the form and content of what is provided to learners to assist them to get the most from resources in the time at their disposal. Such support should reflect the aims, objectives and learning outcomes. As a result, the degree of detail is likely to vary from subject area to subject area and from level to level. Unless the provision of support is addressed in an overt and systematic manner, there is a danger that traditional practices, such as the provision of rapidly lengthening reading lists, will simply be rolled forward, regardless of suitability.

As to other more generic resources, there is a formidable volume and diversity available to those engaged in business and management education. Current issues in business and management receive saturation coverage, of varying degrees of sophistication and objectivity, from all the mass media including newspapers, magazines, TV, radio and the Internet. Also, most organisations, in public, private and voluntary sectors, produce documents for public consumption and may be willing to provide paper-based or electronic information, for learning, teaching and assessment purposes. These include company reports, Web sites, mission statements, codes of conduct and personnel policies. Given their undoubted relevance, much use can be made of this type of material in planning and designing learning activities.

While exploitation of these sources is to be encouraged, it is worth injecting a note of caution. Their overuse, coupled with a failure to make clear to learners their limitations, can result in them being put on a par with dedicated academic resources. *In extremis*, learners might come to rely on them to the exclusion of all other resources, including academic ones. Increasingly, learners see non-academic resources, particularly Web sites of organisations, as the sole source of learning material, regardless of their function, purpose and quality. Clearly, for the vast majority of courses and programmes, this is an undesirable development.

Since organisations understand the strategic value of knowledge and the public relations advantages of good communication, learners need to be cautioned against the uncritical use of corporate publications and material and an over-reliance on 'in-house' material. Ideally, they should learn how to discriminate between resources and to use material from a variety of sources in a complementary manner. Moreover, effective learning and teaching demands that students develop their critical faculties with respect to the purpose, as well as the substance, of the material to which they are exposed and the sources that they are required to tap as an integral part of their learning experience. To reinforce this point, it is important to note Jefferies and Hussain's cautionary remark about electronic resources: 'The World Wide Web is anarchic – there are no quality controls over the data that are presented' (1998: 365). There are, however, some Web facilities, such as the 'Internet detective' (http://www.netskills.ac.uk/tonicng/cgi/sesame?detective), to which learners can be directed to help them become more discriminating users of the Internet.

Moreover, in response to the wealth of business material, both academic and generic, there is now an increasing number of specialist databases and Web sites dedicated to the identification of useful sources of information (see Table 5.1).

Many of these sites are fee-based services, to which learning centres and libraries may or may not subscribe. However, a number do provide free access.

Given their increasing importance, effective utilization of dedicated resources, such as databases and Web sites, should be a key learning outcome for all business and management courses and programmes. At the same time, learners need to

Table 5.1 Specialist databases and Web sites for the identification of useful sources of information (prepared by Alison Ward, Information Specialist, Sheffield Hallam University)

Title	Address	Maintained By	Indicative Contents
ABI/Inform via ProQuest Direct	http://www.umi.com/proquest	Bell & Howell	mostly full text articles from over 1,000 international business and management journals
Anbar	http://www.anbar.com	Anbar Electronic Intelligence	references and abstracts of articles from 450 management journals
Biz/ed*	http://www.bized.ac.uk	Institute for Learning and Research Technology, University of Bristol	catalogue of internet sites for students and some business teaching materials
Business Information Sources on the Internet*	http://www.dis/strath/ac/uk/business	Sheila Webber at University of Strathclyde	guide to business internet sites
Emerald	http://www.emerald-library.com	MCB University Press	full text articles from 130 academic management journals published by MCB University Press
European Case Clearing House	http://www.ecch.cranfield.ac.uk	ECCH, Cranfield University University	over 14,000 titles from the case study collections of leading business schools throughout the world
FAME (Financial Analysis Made Easy)	http://www.bvdep.com/products/fame/overview.htm	Bureau van Dijk	financial data on UK companies
Global Market Information DataBase	http://212.240.205.5/	Euromonitor	worldwide data on consumer market sizes and country parameters, plus forecasts and marketing profiles of selected sectors in the UK, USA, France and Germany

Table 5.1 *contd*

Title	Address	Maintained By	Indicative Contents
Northcote★	http://www.northcote.co.uk	Northcote Internet Ltd	annual reports of over 800 companies and information on share prices
LEXIS–NEXIS Executive	nttp://www.lexis-nexis.co.uk/	LEXIS–NEXIS Group	full text news and company information on share prices
Mintel	http://www.mintel.co.ul	Mintel	full text market research reports
Worldclass Supersite★	http://web.idirect.com/~tiger/supersit.htm	Mike Kuiack and associates	lists and provides commentaries on 1,025 top business sites from 95 countries

★ = free access sites

become adept at drawing upon material from many different sources so as not to simply rely on those that are most readily accessible.

Methods

Today there is no shortage of learning, teaching and assessment methods from which to choose those most suited to facilitating the pursuit of one or more learning outcomes. In addition, there is an extensive literature covering most of these methods. Some examples are provided in Table 5.2.

Surprisingly, despite this availability of guidance and, in some contexts, strong encouragement to experiment, many of those engaged in the support of learning are, as indicated in Chapter 3, remarkably conventional in their choice of method. For example, Ballantyne, Bain and Packer (1999) report that lectures and tutorials are the most common types of teaching in most subjects, including business, and, according to Orpen (2000), lectures and tutorials remain the most common means of teaching management. In part, this is due to the educational traditions in particular subject areas. It is also due to learning facilitators getting 'stuck in a rut' in the way they deploy a particular method. Thus, while case studies are widely popular among business and management educators (see Chapters 9, 10, 11 and 12) and have a history dating back to before the First World War (Orpen, 2000), their use can easily fall into a routinized pattern. However, according to Booth *et al* (2000), case studies are a means of facilitating both the development of skills, via an emphasis on decision-making, and conceptual development, through exploration of the complexity and ambiguity provided by the case – they are an effective means of achieving a variety of learning outcomes. Thus, there is much to be gained, in terms of enhanced student achievement and motivation, from using case studies. Their value can be strengthened through the adoption of innovative strategies (see box below).

Innovative strategies for case studies

- Introduce more 'live' elements into case studies, such as business visits and the involvement of employers or other stakeholders in briefings and/or assessment.
- Ask learners to take responsibility for updating case study material or ask them to write a different account of the case from the perspective of a key stakeholder.
- Use fewer case studies during a course or programme and revisit these on several occasions to promote deeper understanding of the complexity of the context and allow for the application of a broader range of theoretical principles or perspectives.
- Design role plays that draw on clearly defined case study characters, such as managers, employees or customers.

Other barriers to educational innovation include the rigidities of timetables, which are often based on standardized assumptions about methods (eg lecture slots always being one hour in length); the desire to conform to 'conservative' learner expectations; semesterization; and dividing the curriculum into a series of self-contained components, a process referred to earlier as unitization or modularization. These barriers also inhibit attempts to secure a more appropriate balance between diagnostic, formative and summative assessment. Diagnostic assessment is usually undertaken at the beginning of a course and consists of identifying the learning needs of students through, for example, a numeracy test or a short essay to detect abilities with respect to writing style and referencing. Formative assessment is any assessment that takes place during a course of study, where learners are provided with constructive feedback on their progress and advice on how they can improve. Marks or grades provide students with a 'reality check'. Summative assessment often occurs at the conclusion of a course and marks/grades are used to 'measure' the overall performance of students. Owing, in part, to the trend toward short duration courses, greater attention is generally given to summative assessment than the other two forms, often to the detriment of effective learning (Rust, 2000). At the same time, moves towards group-based assessment, on the grounds that it replicates more closely the nature of working life, are often circumscribed because of the individual basis of most academic awards (Macfarlane, 1998).

At a personal level, innovation can be inhibited by the reward structures within HE. In most parts of the world, academic careers in HE have traditionally been shaped and rewarded on the basis of excellence in subject-related research rather than the development and application of innovative approaches to learning and teaching (see Chapter 16).

For those who do wish to innovate, it is relatively rare to find guidance on the application of particular methods that is subject-specific. Much literature on learning and teaching is generic (see Table 5.2). Moreover, within the literature a distinction is often made between learning methods, teaching methods and assessment methods, thereby discouraging a creative mixing of methods across the divides. As implied earlier, however, here it is felt that most methods are sufficiently flexible to be used for learning or teaching or assessment or any combination of these. This can be illustrated by reference to oral presentations, which in recent years have become increasingly popular in the field of HE, in general, and business and management, in particular. Through the preparation and delivery of oral presentations, students can learn a great deal about not only the subject matter of the presentation but also the processes of research and oral communication. Presentations are often undertaken on a team basis, with the result that groupwork skills can also be developed. In this way, oral presentations provide an excellent means of experiential learning. They can also serve as a method of learner support. Anyone involved in advising the presenter(s) on the information gathering and/or communication aspects and giving feedback on the performance is clearly providing a taught input to the experience. This can take a variety of forms from a

Table 5.2 Learning, teaching and assessment methods and their literature

Method	Books and Articles
case studies	Council for National Academic Awards (1992) Heath (1998) Orpen (2000) Booth *et al* (2000)
role plays and simulations	Milroy (1982) Dorn (1989)
learning journals	Moon (1999)
seminars, tutorials and discussion groups	Habeshaw, Habeshaw and Gibbs (1992) Brookfield and Preskill (1999) Tiberius (1999) Jaques (2000)
lectures and oral presentations	Behr (1988) Gibbs, Habeshaw and Habeshaw (1992) Bligh (1998)
projects, dissertations and theses	Orpen (1993) Henry (1994) Lewis and Habeshaw (1997) Ryan and Zuber-Skerritt (1999) Smith and Gilby (1999)
groupwork	Reynolds (1994) Thorley and Gregory (1994) Parsons and Drew (1996)
study guides and open learning materials	Race (1998)
personal tutoring	Wheeler and Birtle (1993)
problem-based learning	Boud (1995) Boud and Feletti (1997) Savin-Brown (1999)
mentoring	Mullen and Lick (1999)
action learning	McGill and Beaty (1992)
learning contracts	Stephenson and Laycock (1993)
business games	Gardner (1995) Hickman (1995) Newstrom (1996) Saunders (1995)

formal lecture on what constitutes good practice in the giving of an oral presentation to attending a rehearsal and offering suggestions as to how the presentation could be improved. Oral presentations can also be used for assessment purposes. Depending upon the principles underlying the assessment strategy, presentations can be either informally or formally assessed. Where the assessment is informal it might be carried out for diagnostic or formative purposes. In the case of formal assessment, the main purpose is likely to be summative.

Assessment should always be planned as an integral component of the learning and teaching strategy and should never be simply an afterthought. Thus, it is both valuable and desirable to combine assessment with learning and teaching as a single activity. If viewed creatively, assessment can be deployed as a mechanism linking different parts of the student learning experience. In so doing, it is essential to ensure that assessment is compatible with learning outcomes (Chapter 4) and the reasons for assessing a particular task (see box below).

Some reasons for assessment

- to diagnose individual learning needs;
- to contribute to the extrinsic motivation of students;
- to serve as a mechanism for experiential learning;
- to provide feedback to assist students with their learning;
- to monitor progress over time;
- to establish the effectiveness of learner support;
- to judge understanding of a theoretical concept.

Given the varied nature of learning outcomes and different reasons for assessment, the choice of methods from the great variety outlined in the literature (see box below), should be based on the key business principle of 'fitness for purpose'.

Sources of guidance on methods of assessment

- Brindley and Scoffield (1998);
- Brown, Bull and Race (1999);
- Brown and Glasner (1999);
- Heywood (2000);
- Morgan and O'Reilly (1999).

It is also in keeping with good practice that learners know in advance of undertaking an assessed task not only the associated learning outcomes and their significance but also the criteria that are going to be used as the basis for judging their performance. Such assessment criteria need to be related directly to the relevant learning outcomes and clearly distinguish between different levels of performance. They should also be the focus of feedback on performance.

Depending on circumstances, there might well be a case for making the design of assessment tasks and the specification of criteria a collaborative exercise. On occasions there is much to be gained, in terms of mutual learning and enrichment of the end product, from involving others, including colleagues responsible for other components of the student learning experience, practising managers, information specialists, technical staff and even students, in the assessment process. Again, in seeking to apply this principle it is very easy to feel inhibited by pedagogic tradition and possibly peer pressure and to stick with the familiar (eg essays for business economics and accounting exercises for business finance). While doing so might result in less bother, it is hardly in keeping with breadth and variety of learning outcomes, teamwork, student empowerment and transparency within the learning, teaching and assessment that one should be seeking to facilitate. Likewise, one might fail to recognize and/or appreciate the opportunities that are being opened up with the increasing application of CIT in HE.

Communication and information technology

Clearly, in considering which learning, teaching and assessment methods to adopt, awareness of the contribution that CIT can make is becoming increasingly important. On many business and management courses and programmes there has been a considerable amount of experimentation designed to exploit the potential of CD ROMs, computer-assisted learning, the Internet, e-mail and video conferencing in the facilitation of learning (Gamble, 1998; Polegato, 1999). In part, this has been motivated by the desire of educators to enrich the learning environment by incorporating elements of CIT; in part, by an appreciation of the impact that CIT is having on the world of business and management and the need for learners to develop their information retrieval, processing and management skills and competencies; and, in part, by managers who see CIT as offering a way of delivering learning more efficiently. Moreover, in some parts of the world with geographically dispersed populations, CIT is seen as a means of greatly enhancing the quality of distance education.

If used wisely and creatively, CIT can also make a valuable contribution to assessment. By providing learners with challenging online objective tests, of varying degrees of sophistication (eg right/wrong, multiple choice, multiple completion, short answer), and appropriate feedback on performance, diagnostic, formative and summative assessment can be facilitated and associated learning reinforced. If desirable, privacy and confidentiality can be maintained and learners can take the tests as often as necessary to reach the required standard. Moreover, after the initial investment of time and energy, utilizing CIT in this way reduces the burden on educators with respect to marking and giving feedback.

Interest in the utilization of technology for educational purposes is also reflected in the increasing number of specialist journals in this field (see box below).

Journals specializing in CIT and education (including HE)

- Association of Learning Technology Journal (ALT-J);
- Education and Information Technology;
- Innovations in Education and Training International (some editions);
- Interactive Educational Multimedia;
- Internet Research.

Many HE conferences, organised by bodies such as EDINEB, the ILT and the Society for Research into Higher Education are devoted in whole or in part to issues concerning the application of CIT in learning, teaching and assessment.

While recognizing the significance of CIT, it is necessary to inject two cautionary notes. First, it is essential to be clear about the aims, objectives and learning outcomes for a particular course or learning activity before considering whether or not CIT can make a contribution to their achievement. In other words, educational practice should be driven by the requirements of learners not by the desire to utilize a particular technology at all costs. Second, on most business and management courses, interpersonal skill development is every bit as important as the acquisition of technological skills, and consequently the human dimension in learning support systems should be neither overlooked nor downgraded (Harris, Ottewill and Palmer, 2000).

In the chapters devoted to particular subject areas, the attention given to CIT is variable and reflects, to some extent, the degree to which it has penetrated educational practice. Developments in this field, however, do need to be kept under constant review with the expansion of virtual institutions of HE and increasing emphasis on e-learning.

Conclusion

Finding one's way around the plethora of resources and methods that can be used for learning, teaching and assessment purposes is not for the faint-hearted. Effective learning and teaching requires that it be tackled in a rigorous and orderly manner. Information and technology specialists play an increasingly central role in facilitating student learning in HE. Seeking help from them is to be commended in terms of both enhancing the richness of what is offered to learners and facilitating collaboration across professional boundaries (Ottewill and Hudson, 1997).

References

Ballantyne, R, Bain, J and Packer, J (1999) Researching university teaching in Australia: themes and issues in academics' reflections, *Studies in Higher Education*, **24** (2), pp 237–57

Behr, A (1988) Exploring the lecture method: an empirical study, *Studies in Higher Education*, **13**, pp 189–99

Bligh, D (1998) *What's the Use of Lectures?*, Intellect Books, Exeter

Booth, C *et al* (2000) The use of the case method in large and diverse undergraduate business programmes: problem and issues, *The International Journal of Management Education*, **1** (1), pp 62–75

Boud, D (1995) *Enhancing Learning through Self Assessment*, Kogan Page, London

Boud, D and Feletti, G (eds) (1997) *The Challenge of Problem-Based Learning*, 2nd edn, Kogan Page, London

Brindley, C and Scoffield, S (1998) Peer assessment in undergraduate programmes, *Teaching in Higher Education*, **3** (1), pp 79–89

Brookfield, S and Preskill, S (1999) *Discussion as a Way of Teaching: Tools and techniques*, Society for Research into Higher Education/Open University Press, Buckingham

Brown, S, Bull, J and Race, P (1999) *Computer-Assisted Assessment in Higher Education*, Kogan Page, London

Brown, S and Glasner, A (1999) *Assessment Matters in Higher Education*, Society for Research into Higher Education/Open University Press, Buckingham

Council for National Academic Awards (1992) *Case Studies in Student-Centred Learning*, CNAA, London

Dorn, D (1989) Simulation games: one more tool on the pedagogical shelf, *Teaching Sociology*, **17**, pp 1–18

Gamble, P (1998) Low cost multi-media for distance learning, in *Educational Innovation in Economics and Business III: Innovative practices in business education*, ed R Milter, J Stinson and W Gijselaers, pp 315–30, Kluwer Academic Publishers, Dordrecht

Gardner, R (1995) *Games for Business and Economics*, Wiley, Chichester

Gibbs, G, Habeshaw, S and Habeshaw, T (1992) *53 Interesting Things to Do in Your Lectures*, 4th edn, Technical and Educational Services Ltd, Bristol

Habeshaw, S, Habeshaw, T and Gibbs, G (1992) *53 Interesting Things to Do in Your Seminars and Tutorials*, 4th edn, Technical and Educational Services Ltd, Bristol

Harris, N, Ottewill, R and Palmer, A (2000) Promoting the human element in resource based learning for undergraduate business education programmes, in *Educational Innovation in Economics and Business V: Business education in the changing workplace*, ed L Borghans *et al*, pp 291–306, Kluwer Academic Publishers, Dordrecht

Heath, J (1998) *Teaching and Writing Case Studies: A practical guide*, European Case Clearing House, Bedford

Henry, J (1994) *Teaching Through Projects*, Kogan Page, London

Heywood, J (2000) *Assessment in Higher Education: Student learning, teaching programmes and institutions*, 3rd edn, Jessica Kingsley, London

Hickman, C R (1995) *The Productivity Game: An interactive business game where you make or break the company*, Prentice Hall, London

Jaques, D (2000) *Learning in Groups: A handbook for improving group working*, Kogan Page, London

Jefferies, P and Hussain, F (1998) Using the internet as a teaching resource, *Education and Training*, **40** (8), pp 359–65

Knight, P (ed) (1995) *Assessment for Learning in Higher Education*, Kogan Page, London

Lewis, V and Habeshaw, S (1997) *53 Interesting Ways to Supervise Student Projects*, Technical and Educational Services Ltd, Bristol

Macfarlane, B (1998) Degree classifications: time to bite the bullet, *Teaching in Higher Education*, **3** (3), pp 401–05

McGill, I and Beaty, L (1992) *Action Learning*, Kogan Page, London

Milroy, E (1982) *Role-Play: A practical guide*, Aberdeen University Press, Aberdeen

Moon, J (1999) *Learning Journals: A handbook for academics, students and professional development*, Kogan Page, London

Morgan, C and O'Reilly, M (1999) *Assessing Open and Distance Learners*, Kogan Page, London

Mullen, C and Lick, D (1999) *New Directions in Mentoring: Creating a culture of synergy*, Falmer Press, London

Newstrom, J W (1996) *The Big Book of Business Games: Icebreakers, creativity exercises and meeting energizers*, McGraw-Hill, London

Orpen, C (1993) On the practical nature of management research, *Journal of European Business Education*, **3** (1), pp 79–84

Orpen, C (2000) Reconsidering the case-study method of teaching management, *Journal of European Business Education*, **9** (2), pp 56–64

Ottewill, R and Hudson, A (1997) Electronic information resource use: implications for teaching and library staff, *Association of Learning Technology Journal*, **5** (2), pp 31–41

Parsons, D and Drew, S (1996) Designing group work to enhance learning: key elements, *Teaching in Higher Education*, **1** (1), pp 65–80

Polegato, R (1999) From bits and bytes to bunches: learning how to place world wide web information in context, in *Educational Innovation in Economics and Business IV: Learning in a changing environment*, ed J Hommes *et al*, pp 163–74, Kluwer Academic Publishers, Dordrecht

Race, P (1998) *500 Tips for Open and Flexible Learning*, Kogan Page, London

Reynolds, M (1994) *Groupwork in Education and Training*, Kogan Page, London

Rust, C (2000) An opinion piece: a possible student-centred assessment solution to some of the current problems of modular degree programmes, *Active Learning in Higher Education*, **1** (2), pp 126–31

Ryan, Y and Zuber-Skerritt, O (1999) *Supervising Postgraduates from Non-English Speaking Backgrounds*, Society for Research into Higher Education/Open University Press, Buckingham

Saunders, D (ed) (1995) *Games and Simulations for Business*, Kogan Page, London

Savin-Brown, M (1999) *Problem-Based Learning in Higher Education: Untold stories*, Society for Research into Higher Education/Open University Press, Buckingham

Smith, A and Gilby, J (1999) *Supervising Students on Industrial-Based Projects: Issues in postgraduate supervision, teaching and management No 4*, Society for Research into Higher Education/Times Higher Education Supplement, London

Stephenson, J and Laycock, M (eds) (1993) *Using Learning Contracts in Higher Education*, Kogan Page, London

Thorley, L and Gregory, R (eds) (1994) *Using Group-Based Learning in Higher Education*, Kogan Page, London

Tiberius, R (1999) *Small Group Teaching: A trouble shooting guide*, Kogan Page, London

Wheeler, S and Birtle, J (1993) *A Handbook for Personal Tutors*, Society for Research into Higher Education/Open University Press, Buckingham

6

Integration

Bruce Macfarlane and Roger Ottewill

Introduction

While it is axiomatic that learning never takes place in a complete vacuum, in practice it is difficult to ensure that learners appreciate and actively look for opportunities to make connections between related components of the curriculum. In view of the diverse and varied nature of the business and management curriculum, it is unlikely that students, at any level, will recognize linkages between their learning experiences and understand the potential for cross-fertilization without help and support. In other words, integration depends on a proactive stance by those responsible for the support of learning at the course design, delivery and appraisal stages. On courses and programmes where components are treated as 'stand-alone', for design and credit accumulation purposes, the need for countervailing measures through the delivery process is even greater. This is particularly important in the field of business and management given the interrelatedness of many of the learning outcomes, covering subject areas such as business environment (Chapter 8) and strategic management (Chapter 12), and the multiplicity of opportunities for the reinforcement of learning.

Depending upon the design features of the student learning experience, various steps can be taken to secure a degree of horizontal and/or vertical integration. Horizontal integration involves making connections between subject areas that comprise the curriculum at one level of attainment or year, while vertical integration is about building understanding over the duration of a programme. An example of horizontal integration might be the sharing of a case study by two or more courses dealing with different components of the curriculum where knowledge boundaries clearly overlap. Such integration might be facilitated further by team teaching.Vertical integration can occur, for instance, where a lower level introductory course in marketing serves as a building block for higher-level courses either in specialized aspects of marketing (eg retail marketing) or in strategic management.

In this chapter some of the problems associated with meeting the demands of integration are explored, together with strategies for securing a degree of horizontal and vertical integration. Ultimately, successful integration of the student learning experience depends upon a recognition by those contributing to the learning that they are engaged in a truly collaborative enterprise.

The context of integration

Educators in business and management have a particular responsibility for ensuring that student learning is a holistic rather than piecemeal experience, given the often eclectic, disciplinary-based nature of the curriculum. In one year alone, subject areas as disparate as marketing, economics, quantitative methods, law, business organisation and accountancy often form the basis of study. Moreover, the business and management curriculum brings together both more established academic disciplines (eg psychology and economics) and functional specialisms (eg marketing and human resource management). Indeed, areas of study can be approached from either a disciplinary or a more functional basis with the contrasting emphasis between accountancy and finance a case in point. Such eclecticism of the curriculum places particular demands on business and management students, in terms of both the breadth of knowledge required and understanding how the jigsaw of the curriculum fits together.Thus, educators should, at the very least, not only stimulate interest in that part of the student learning experience for which they have direct responsibility but also identify other parts of the curriculum where there is potential for mutual reinforcement.

While some business and management programmes, particularly at postgraduate level, are delivered, either in whole or in part, in a fully integrated manner (eg Perotti *et al*, 1998), the teaching of business and management still takes place predominantly in functional (or disciplinary) 'silos'. Indeed, modularization of the HE curriculum in the UK (see Chapters 3 and 5) and elsewhere is reinforcing this tendency.While being able to 'pick 'n mix' modules or subject areas may provide students with greater choice it may also be producing a less coherent learning experience. At the same time, a multidisciplinary, as opposed to interdisciplinary, approach to the curriculum can further obfuscate matters for learners, leaving them without an adequate understanding of the 'bigger picture' and key issues of concern to the business world (see Chapter 8).

Providing learners with an understanding via horizontal integration is, perhaps, the most challenging since students, especially in their early years of study, may possess limited knowledge on which to build a cross-disciplinary grasp of business and management. If insufficient attention is paid to this though, learners may struggle to see how the curriculum fits together throughout their studies. Reassuring learners that an integrative understanding will mysteriously occur at some future point in their studies is an abdication of responsibility in this respect. To a large extent, students are attracted to studying business and management because it holds out the promise of providing them with a practical understanding of the 'real' world in a holistic manner (Hidasi and Wilkinson, 1994) and educators have an obligation to meet this expectation as far as possible.

Integration strategies

There is a range of strategies for securing a high degree of integration within a business and management programme. One means of achieving this goal is via emphasis on the natural overlap of knowledge domains within the curriculum. All business and management subject areas offer opportunities to make links with other parts of the curriculum. Indeed, each of the chapters in Part C of this book provides guidance on such links. A popular means of securing horizontal integration is via the identification of certain cross-curricular themes, such as business social responsibility, globalization or the development of business skills, around which the whole or part of a year/level of study is structured. Where this applies, educators need to demonstrate how their contribution, in terms of subject matter and/or learning, teaching and assessment, relates to the core theme(s). Alternatively, these integrative themes can provide the basis for separate courses with inputs from a variety of learning facilitators. It is vital, however, that where this strategy is adopted a conscious effort is made to afford such courses equality of status with other aspects of the curriculum. Otherwise, there is an inherent danger that a course in, for example, business skills will be perceived by students as peripheral, rather than at the heart of learning (Stephens *et al*, 1998).

Turning to vertical integration, one approach involves using strategic management (see Chapter 12) for this purpose. It is frequently claimed that strategic management plays a key role as the capstone integrator of business and management programmes at both undergraduate and postgraduate level (Talbot, 1993; Gammie, 1995; Monks, 1995). This is particularly evident in programmes organised traditionally on the basis of a series of discrete disciplinary or functional courses. Strategic management is said to create a context that draws on the knowledge-base of a range of subjects covered at earlier stages in a programme of study to provide an understanding of the competitive environment (Macfarlane and Perkins, 1999). Clearly, an understanding of, *inter alia*, marketing, accounting principles, organisational behaviour and economics plays an important part in aiding learners to analyse and evaluate the competitive position of organisations. Opportunities also exist within these subject areas to develop key skills, such as decision-making. However, the effective integration of such knowledge and skill inputs through the medium of strategic management is asking a great deal of both educators and learners. While a group of practising managers may understand the context of strategic decision-making, it is doubtful whether less mature learners with limited work experience will be adequately equipped to do so (Macfarlane and Perkins, 1999). This casts doubt on whether a strategic management course is sufficient to secure a degree of vertical integration for less experienced learners.

Integration, of course, is not just about facilitating linkages between different aspects of the substance of what is being studied. It is also about designing the learning environment in such a way that students can transfer experiences in one part of the course or programme to another and build on them as they progress through different levels of study. This is particularly important where at higher levels they are expected to undertake projects and/or assignments that involve the application of a wide variety of previously honed skills and competencies and to utilize knowledge gained at earlier stages of their studies. While such projects and/or assignments can take a variety of forms, many are essentially an example of problem-based learning or the problem method defined by Ellington and Harris as 'a method of instruction in which learning is stimulated by confronting the student with a series of challenging situations that require solution' (1986: 133). Moreover, they offer the prospect of securing some of the benefits of experiential learning. From the point of view of integration it is significant that for Stinson and Milter (1996) one of the key requirements for successful problem-based learning is that learning outcomes should be holistic and unconstrained by narrow disciplinary boundaries. Thus, problem-based learning is tailor-made for a multidisciplinary area like business environment (see Chapter 8).

On an increasing number of business and management programmes, particularly at postgraduate level, it is becoming common for students to undertake projects commissioned by companies and other organisations (eg Ball, 1995; Winn, 1995; Munro and Preece, 1998; Laughton and Ottewill, 1998). These can be regarded as a form of 'live' case study (see Chapter 5) where a group of learners are introduced to a current business problem by a manager and asked to work creatively, often in groups, on designing solutions, which are assessed in conjunction with the organisation's representatives. Here there is an expectation that students will tackle the problem by pooling their resources and propose a solution that is genuinely integrative.

Likewise, business enterprise projects have been used as an integrative mechanism (eg Macfarlane and Tomlinson, 1993; Monks, 1995; and see Chapter 14). By contrast with commissioned projects, these are basically simulations. For such projects, learners, again normally working in teams, are asked to produce a business plan for a new commercial venture. In so doing, they are required to give consideration to the marketing, financial and legal aspects of a business 'start-up', together with relevant local economic and social conditions. In addition to gaining a 'joined-up' picture of how to combine these knowledge elements in any proposal, learners also develop important skills like team working, negotiation, networking and oral presentation (where this is an assessment requirement) and come to appreciate elements of professional practice. Some see such projects as a means of promoting entrepreneurial or risk-taking attitudes (see Chapter 14), which are of particular importance given the decline of secure lifelong career opportunities (Monks, 1995). It is crucial though that learners understand the harsh realities and risks associated with business start-ups as well as the variety of skills and knowledge that need to be applied if they are to be successful. Paradoxically, students may be less attracted by the prospect of taking entrepreneurial risk via self-employment as a result of such projects (Macfarlane and Tomlinson, 1993). This result should not necessarily be interpreted as a failure since a vicarious insight into the world of enterprise may sober immature expectations and leave learners better equipped to cope in the 'real' world. In simulating this reality, as far as possible, involvement from members of the business and enterprise community, such as bankers, entrepreneurs and venture capitalists, is extremely advantageous. Involving bankers, for instance, in the interviewing of learners about their business plan simulates the reality of seeking financial backing (Macfarlane and Tomlinson, 1993). Moreover, failure to expose students to critical questioning from members of the business community can adversely affect the credibility of such projects (Lloyd, 1996).

Arguably, commissioned and business enterprise projects are unlikely to realize their potential for integration if they are the only integrative mechanism within a course or programme. Learners 'need to be prepared for the integrative aspects of the project through planned and regular exposure to simulations and case studies which are genuinely cross-curricula' (Laughton and Ottewill, 1998: 98–99).

Alongside projects can be set the dissertations and theses that are a key element in the learning environment of business and management programmes at many levels. While these are often more conceptual in their orientation, in reality it is often hard to detect where projects end and dissertations begin. This is because, whatever the precise requirements, there is an expectation on the part of those responsible for supervising and assessing them that students will draw upon a wide variety of skills and knowledge from many different sources. Dissertations, like projects, usually have a problem-based focus that demands an integrated understanding of management as a body of knowledge (Orpen, 1995).

Case studies (see Chapter 5) also serve as an effective means of integrating understanding of business knowledge in a problem-based context. They act as an integrating device in a variety of ways. Well-written case studies invariably provide a rich description of the complex reality of organisational life, creating for readers a 'joined-up' picture of business practice coupled with an insight into the challenges of decision-making. Designing solutions to problems or questions posed will often demand the deployment of a broad knowledge-base rather than applying narrowly focused and/or purely technical solutions removed from the realities of organisational politics together with social, ethical and environmental constraints.

A final strategy for integration is the work placement or co-operative education as it is known in North America and elsewhere. Indeed, for many business and management students, particularly those with little or no previous business experience, placement is the key design feature of their learning environment. In many parts of Europe work placements have become an established feature of a business and management education although national practice varies considerably (Stokes, 1993). In the UK, four-year 'sandwich' degrees in business studies, incorporating either one 12-month or two 6-month placements, have been available since the 1960s. The integrative benefits of this form of work experience are well documented and prominently include the relating of knowledge acquired in academic study to the 'real' world by enabling learners to link theory with practice during, and following completion of, the placement (Kitson, 1993) and the honing of work-related skills initially developed in an academic environment. Where learners are able to take advantage of work placement opportunities in another country there is the added benefit of developing both language skills and cross-cultural awareness (see Chapter 11).

While it is conventional wisdom that work experience helps learners gain a more rounded and integrated understanding of business, some critics have long expressed doubts about the management, quality and benefits of placements (Preece and Flood Page, 1974; Appleton, 1981; Kitson, 1993). For example, the integrative value of placements is undermined when learners spend too much time 'performing low grade tasks at a minimal wage' (Lloyd, 1996: 78). Although this may be a dose of the 'real' world, the educational value of poor-quality placements is dubious.

The success of work placements and their effectiveness in terms of both horizontal and vertical integration will depend on how they are negotiated, managed and valued within a programme. Rather than leaving it to employing organisations to determine the nature of the placement, mutual agreement about the learning outcomes of work experience is vital. One option is for learners to pursue a specific project, negotiated in advance between learners, educators and employers. Another is to require students to produce a report for assessment purposes in which they evaluate their placement experience from a variety of perspectives, such as their studies prior to embarking on the placement and skills developed and knowledge acquired during the placement. However, if the integrative potential of placements is to be fully realized, thought also needs to be given to how the work experiences of learners will be utilized when they return to full-time study. For many, placement serves as a source of potential dissertation topics and, indeed, this is often required or encouraged, thereby enhancing its integrative value. A less common practice involves utilizing students who have undertaken placement as a resource (see Chapter 2), with educators drawing upon student experiences to illustrate theories and concepts being considered in subject areas such as human resource management and strategic management. Of course, in order to do this effectively it is necessary for educators to have some way of logging these experiences and to have a strong commitment to placement even if they are not directly involved.

Notwithstanding the emphasis on strategies, effective integration depends as much upon the commitment of educators as strategic intent. This means that, if integrative strategies are to be successfully implemented, educators must clearly demonstrate that they are aware of ways in which their contribution to the student learning experience relates to, and is complemented by, that of others. To paraphrase, those responsible for the support of learning should never see themselves 'as an island'. This is absolutely crucial in the sphere of business and management education.

Conclusion

One of the abiding criticisms of the business and management curriculum is that it is a nebulous clustering of discrete academic disciplines (Barnett, 1990). To counter this claim effectively it is vital that serious attention be paid to providing students with an integrated learning experience. There are significant barriers in achieving this objective not least of which is the breadth of knowledge demanded from facilitators of learning. There is a significant risk that an espoused commitment to an integrating theme, for example, will become little more than lip-service, ignored in practice owing to strong, but narrowly focused, disciplinary interests. Where integrative aspects are limited to one-off projects they are unlikely to release the full potential for learning and can be complex and time-consuming for educators to manage. Thus, there is a need for an 'integrative ethos' to permeate course and programme design (Laughton and Ottewill, 1998). Where adopted with commitment and care, integrative approaches can play a key role in pursuing the aim of deep, rather than surface, learning (see Chapter 2). Such approaches can also prove immensely rewarding and enjoyable for students and facilitators alike through the provision of a coherent and learner-centred experience.

References

Appleton, D (1981) How should business studies degree courses cope with a decline in the availability of sandwich placements?, *Business Education*, **4** (1), pp 19–25

Ball, S (1995) Enriching student learning through innovative real-life exercises, *Education and Training*, **37** (4), pp 18–25

Barnett, R (1990) *The Idea of Higher Education*, Open University Press/Society for Research into Higher Education, Buckingham

Ellington, H and Harris, D (1986) *Dictionary of Instructional Technology*, Nichols, New York

Gammie, B (1995) Undergraduate management education: an analysis of rationale and methodology, *International Journal of Educational Management*, **9** (4), pp 34–40

Hidasi, J and Wilkinson, R (1994) The relevance of cultural awareness to understanding and effectiveness in the teaching of business studies and management, *Economia*, Winter, pp 48–53

Kitson, A (1993) The business studies sandwich degree: a critique, *The Vocational Aspect of Education*, **45** (2), pp 123–33

Laughton, D and Ottewill, R (1998) Laying foundations for effective learning from commissioned projects in business education, *Education and Training*, **40** (2/3), pp 95–101

Lloyd, J (1996) Learning business studies, *Economics and Business Education*, 4 (2), pp 77–80

Macfarlane, B and Perkins, A (1999) Reconceptualising corporate strategy in business and management education, *Education and Training*, 41 (1), pp 20–26

Macfarlane, B and Tomlinson, K (1993) Managing and assessing student enterprise projects, *Education and Training*, 35 (3), pp 33–36

Monks, K (1995) Combining academic rigour and transferable skills: a business degree for the 1990s, *Education and Training*, 37 (1), pp 17–21

Munro, H and Preece, S (1998) Students as facilitators in the internationalization of small business, *Journal of Teaching in International Business*, 9 (4), pp 1–20

Orpen, C (1995) The relevance of management research, *Journal of European Business Education*, 5 (1), pp 1–11

Perotti, V *et al* (1998) Business 20/20: Ohio university's integrated business core, in *Educational Innovation in Economics and Business III: Innovative practices in business education*, ed R Milter, J Stinson and W Gijselaers, pp 169–88, Kluwer Academic Publishers, Dordrecht

Preece, D and Flood Page, C (1974) Sandwich course undergraduates and industrial experience, *The Vocational Aspect of Education*, 16, pp 95–104

Stephens, J *et al* (1998) Exploring business skills: an innovative approach to promoting lifelong learning, *Journal of Further and Higher Education*, 22 (3), pp 329–41

Stinson, J and Milter, R (1996) Problem-based learning in business education: curriculum design and implementation issues, *New Directions in Teaching and Learning*, 68, pp 33–42

Stokes, P (1993) The European industrial placement environment: a United Kingdom perspective, *Journal of European Business Education*, 3 (1), pp 85–101

Talbot, C (1993) Twin peaks? MBAs and the competence movement – a tale of two courses, *Management Education and Development*, 24 (4), pp 330–46

Winn, S (1995) Learning by doing: teaching research methods through student participation in a commissioned research project, *Studies in Higher Education*, 20 (9), pp 203–14

7

Reflection and evaluation

Bruce Macfarlane and Roger Ottewill

Introduction

In the spheres of business life and professional development generally, the notion of the reflective practitioner, associated particularly with the work of Schon (1983, 1987), has come to exert a powerful influence, and rightly so. Consequently, it is not surprising that reflective practice is now seen as a crucial ingredient for the development of learning facilitators in HE. Indeed, the UK's ILT requires applicants for membership to demonstrate their commitment to reflection through the provision of concrete examples and, in the light of these, improvements in their practice. It is seen as a key instrument in the drive towards encouraging greater creativity and innovation in learning and teaching in HE.

At the same time, it is recognized that there is a close relationship between reflection and evaluation. In many respects they are two sides of the same coin, with both being triggered by a desire to enhance the quality and effectiveness of the student learning experience. Reflection, however, is more introspective and is associated with connotations of meditation and contemplation, while evaluation is more outward-looking with an emphasis on action and procedure. That said, it is difficult to conceive of a situation in which reflective practice is not supported by an array of techniques that facilitate evaluation. These include staff appraisal schemes, course evaluation surveys, staff–student consultative committees, employer liaison groups and peer support reviews (Bingham and Ottewill, 2001).

Clearly, reflective practice and evaluation are relevant to all engaged in learner support within HE. They are not the private preserve of any one branch of the academic community. There are, however, particular ways in which they can be put into practice in the context of providing a business and management education. Therefore, although consideration is given to the general principles of reflective practice and to methods of evaluation in this chapter, it does not seek to replicate the generic literature available (eg Brockbank and McGill, 1998; Forsyth, Jolliffe and Stevens, 1999).

Moreover, in demonstrating how educators can be reflective about their practice, many of the suggestions are equally applicable to learners. They need to be encouraged to reflect and evaluate as a preparation for, or as a feature of their existing, professional life. Indeed, it is widely recognized that the habits of reflective practice, resulting in proactive and adaptable employees, are highly valued by employers (eg Stephens *et al*, 1998; Fitzgibbon and McCarthy, 1999). With this in mind, it is a salient point for business and management educators to remember that they may well be extolling the virtues of reflection and evaluation, thereby enabling learners to be more responsive to stakeholder needs, especially those of the customer, in the workplace. This mantra will ring hollow, however, if they fail to demonstrate such qualities in an educational context. Thus, business and management educators have a particular responsibility to be role models in striving to improve on their practice.

Taking this a step further, by relating the general principles of reflection and evaluation to pedagogic practice, educators can make a useful contribution to learner empowerment. Arguably, this is of greater consequence for business and management students, than for those on other courses, as they develop the attributes required to progress in today's turbulent and rapidly changing business world.

The nature of reflection

The language of reflective practice has attracted the serious interest of professionals working in a wide variety of contexts, including teacher education (Reid and Parker, 1995), nursing (United Kingdom Central Council, 1986) and spheres of business and management, such as accountancy (Velayutham and Perera, 1993). In HE, reflective practice involves developing the habit of thinking about learner support and teaching in a critical and systematic way with a view to improving the quality and effectiveness of student learning. It is a means of enriching the understanding of both learners and educators in business and management. Indeed, it makes educators into learners, thereby blurring the traditional distinction between teacher and learner and stimulating the development of a genuine learning community. Thus, perhaps an apt slogan is: 'We are all learners now.'

Schon (1983) argues that technical rationality has traditionally been the dominant model of professional education, driving out what he terms education for artistry. He contends that professional education, premised on technical rationality, is poor at dealing with the 'intermediate zones of practice – uncertainty, uniqueness, and value conflict' (Schon, 1987: 6). In identifying the need for learners to be properly prepared for the professions, Schon emphasizes the importance of reflecting on problems arising from a practical context. Using a practicum – or 'virtual' world – as a basis for student reflection is thus essential. This enables learners to cope better with a more 'messy' professional reality. The centrality of reflection in professional learning has been developed further by a number of other influential writers including Kolb (1984) and Pedler (1992).

Parallels to Schon's concerns about technical rationality can be found within debates about the business and management curriculum. A number of business and management writers and educators, for example, argue that the orthodox view of management as a rational and 'scientific' process tends to obscure an understanding of a more 'messy' social reality (eg Rickards, 1999; and see Chapter 1). An emphasis on preparing learners 'for' business in this latter way fits with Schon's promotion of an education for 'artistry' where practitioners are adept at coping with situations of uncertainty, uniqueness and conflict (Schon, 1987). Indeed, part of the rationale for using case studies with business and management students is that it helps to prepare them better for the 'messy' reality of business life (Orpen, 2000). At a more general level, there is also a parallel between the notion of reflective practice and the desire of many modern businesses to become 'learning organisations', entering into a process of self-examination and continuous improvement (see Chapter 2).

For educators, reflective practice is an important philosophy because it acts as a powerful means of sustaining the interest, enjoyment and excitement of everyday teaching. Without reflection leading to innovation in, and modifications to, educational practice, learner support can rapidly become a repetitive and frustrating experience. It is important to keep asking hard questions about the effectiveness of learning, teaching and assessment activities.

In reflecting upon reflection, particularly in the context of business and management education, a key issue concerns the reasons for reflection. They may be intrinsic or extrinsic or a combination of both. Ideally, the prime motivation should come from within. Just as the drive for improvements in managerial performance requires a degree of introspection on the part of managers for success, so those responsible for the support of learning need to be equally keen to ponder how they can enhance the quality of what they provide learners. However, reflection is not simply a matter of personal predilection. It is also stimulated by external factors, which include formal procedural requirements, such as staff development review and staff appraisal schemes, sometimes linked to performance-related pay.

Whatever the reasons for reflection, there is a need to consider which approaches to adopt. Consideration also has to be given to how these might be linked to the various methods of evaluation that are available.

Approaches to reflection

Reflective practice can take a variety of forms. Some of these stem from personal commitment while others are associated with the demands of accountability.

Undoubtedly, practitioners committed to their own continuous professional development will seek out opportunities for reflection and may adopt a variety of approaches.

Despite the introspective nature of reflection, it need not be a solitary pursuit. In other words, it can involve sharing experiences and concerns with others to whom one can readily relate. Moreover, while informality might be seen as a key ingredient for reflection, formality is by no means precluded. Thus, approaches can be either personal or collaborative and either informal or formal. Some examples are provided in Figure 7.1.

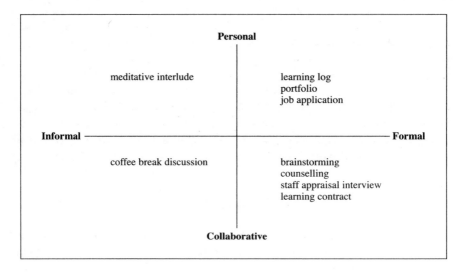

Figure 7.1 Approaches to reflection

What has been described in the figure as a 'meditative interlude' is likely to be one of the most commonly experienced forms of reflection. Nothing is planned; it simply happens that a combination of circumstances results in an educator thinking about an aspect of pedagogy in a relatively unstructured and sometimes creative manner. Such a circumstance, for example, may occur after a less-than-successful teaching session when it is important to analyse what went wrong. When this happens it is often useful to jot down any ideas that might be useful for future reference.

A more, and very popular, formal approach to reflection, at the personal level, is to track one's experiences systematically via a learning log. Honey and Mumford (1986, 1989) recommend the use of learning logs as a means of recording and reflecting on learning experiences and completing a 'learning cycle' (see Table 2.2). Using real experiences is seen as a means of helping professionals to 'learn how to learn'. A learning log is an obvious way for educators to track the development of their professional practice by reflecting on and seeking to make continuous improvements with respect to their teaching and assessment routines. It can be thought of as a kind of personal diary of innovation containing stories of both success and failure. As indicated in Chapter 10, reflective learning logs can also be used as a learning and assessment tool with students.

For many educators, personal reflection is of only limited value and needs to be supplemented with more collaborative approaches, which can often provide the stimuli needed for effective reflection. Such approaches can be formal, such as brainstorming and counselling, or informal, and may be facilitated through a mentoring scheme (see Chapter 16).

While the approaches highlighted in Figure 7.1 are generic and can be applied to any subject area, there are two aspects that are of particular significance for business and management. First, as has been emphasized elsewhere, in demonstrating their commitment to reflective practice, business and management educators are not only contributing to their own development but also setting an example for their students to follow. Second, the substance of the reflection is likely to be more diverse given the eclectic and strongly vocational character of business and management education. For example, the expectation that a business and management education will have vocational relevance and help learners understand the link between theory and practice places a particular onus on educators to reflect on the extent to which they are in touch with business and/or professional practice. Thus, there might well be a need to discuss aspects of learning, teaching and assessment with representatives from the business world to ensure that reflection is appropriately focused.

As already indicated, reflection is closely associated with evaluation. They are mutually reinforcing and it is often difficult to identify where one ends and another begins. Here they have been treated separately, but this is mainly for presentational purposes.

Approaches to evaluation

Evaluation should be seen as far more than an optional, bolt-on extra. It should lie at the heart of a learning, teaching and assessment strategy. To ensure that this is the case and that evaluation is more than mere tokenism, a number of concerns need to be addressed overtly and systematically.

An initial concern is who should be involved in the evaluation process. While on many HE programmes learners are routinely asked to help evaluate the quality of provision with a view to making continuous improvement, business and management education has responsibilities to a wider range of stakeholders, particularly employers, sponsors and professional bodies. Since vocational relevance is a key aim, there is an expectation that employers will play a role in the evaluation process as the direct 'consumers' of business students. Alumni may also be involved as a further means of determining the appropriateness of provision (Coates and

Koerner, 1996). Although contributions from employers and alumni may be difficult to organise, it is well worth the effort since inclusivity is vital to the credibility of a business and management education. In addition, their contributions together with those of learners and educators cultivate a sense of ownership that is a vital ingredient of effective learning and teaching. Fostering an inclusive process is also important since it is hard for customers to evaluate the quality of any professional service, even after it has been received. Strategic learners (see Chapter 2), for example, may give a higher evaluation 'score' to an educator who has made fewer demands on their time and intellect. Studies have shown that grading leniency and undemanding workloads can bias student evaluations (Brodie, 1998). Involvement of all stakeholders, including educators, produces a more valid triangulation of views, which helps to guard against this possibility.

While inclusivity is vital, a second concern is the stage at which students (and other stakeholders) become involved in the evaluation process. Typically, this involvement does not begin until a course or programme has got well under way or even finished. However, if the aim is to focus on the needs of the 'customer', in parallel with those business organisations committed to embedding service quality, it is important to understand the expectations of learners from the outset. While some educators find the analogy uncomfortable, students are key customers or clients. This marketing reality does not mean, however, that 'the customer is always right' regardless of the professional judgement of the educator (Scott, 1999). What it does imply is that there is a need for a mutual understanding of expectations leading to a harmonization of what each party will demand of the other. Practically, this could take the form of getting students to help design the evaluation criteria for a course or, more formally, entering into a learning partnership agreement (see box on page 73).

Another approach is to conduct multiple evaluations as the course progresses. This helps educators maintain contact with reality and build up knowledge as to what is actually happening as learners engage with the subject matter and participate in learning activities (Flash, Tzenis and Waller, 1995). However, frequent evaluations are time-consuming and potentially disruptive. They also run the risk of raising expectations that can only be met if educators are prepared to be completely frank and open about the feedback they receive and to adjust content and delivery methods accordingly, where this can be justified.

A third concern is the choice of evaluation instruments. These can range from traditional surveys, through focus groups, to consultative forums of various kinds. All have their strengths and weaknesses; hence it is important to use a 'battery of techniques' rather than relying on just one instrument of evaluation, such as student questionnaires (King *et al*, 1999). This increases the validity and reliability of the process.

What should be covered in an evaluation exercise is a fourth concern. This is likely to vary considerably depending upon the nature of the learning outcomes and the constituents of the student learning experience. To help set the parameters, for each subject area in Part C there is an indicative list of questions suitable

---

A learning partnership agreement

Tutors will:

- make sure that classes start and end on time (and give notice of any unavoidable changes);
- promote a participative and student-centred learning environment;
- give comprehensive guidance with respect to course content, learning and assessment activities, assessment criteria and further resources;
- encourage students to play a central role in the evaluation process;
- provide access to advice, information and counselling on any educational or personal matter;
- respect differences in the learning community with regard to race, gender, disability, sexuality, religion and culture;
- give feedback on assignments;
- return assignments within the period agreed.

Students will:

- take responsibility for their learning by attending regularly and punctually, participating fully in learning activities, making active use of learning resources and completing assignments on time;
- work co-operatively with both tutors and fellow students;
- seek tutorial help where required while respecting the fact that tutors have other commitments (ie such as research and administrative responsibilities);
- respect differences in the learning community with regard to race, gender, disability, sexuality, religion and culture;
- let tutors know if they feel that the service promised has not been provided;
- abide by the rules and regulations of the institution.

---

for individual or collective use. These can also serve as the starting point for generating a list that reflects the distinctive and unique features of a particular course. Indeed, formulating the questions for course evaluation purposes is a key element of the process of reflection and there is much to be gained from wrestling with this task, either alone or in consultation with colleagues.

A final concern, and arguably the most challenging aspect of evaluation, is 'closing the loop' or, in other words, ensuring that the results of evaluation are acted upon (see Figure 7.2). 'Closing the loop' is critical in producing a learning cycle that can be used to sustain continuous evaluation and increase student confidence in the process. Where formative evaluation is undertaken during a course, there is the possibility of making real and immediately actionable adjustments to practice. Summative evaluation, at the end of a course, provides the basis for cyclical improvements, which are most likely to benefit future learners.

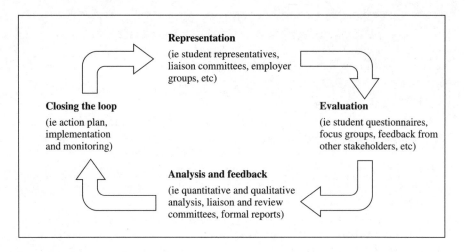

Figure 7.2 The evaluation loop

The importance of demonstrating that evaluation, whether formative or summative, really does lead to improvements in the learning environment cannot be overstated.

Conclusion

Traditionally, reflection upon, and evaluation of, pedagogic practice in HE has had a low priority. This is because career prospects have been shaped more by the quality of research outputs than by competence in learner support (see Chapter 16). There have been few rewards for innovative and creative approaches to teaching that result from taking reflection and evaluation seriously. In the UK, the Dearing Report, for example, found that just 3 per cent of academic staff in HE believed the system rewarded excellence in teaching (National Committee of Inquiry into Higher Education, 1997). Although this culture is gradually changing with the spread of schemes for rewarding excellence in teaching and innovative practice on both sides of the Atlantic, prompted, in part, by pressure from government and students demanding higher standards of practice as educational 'consumers', significant barriers remain in place. Not least of these is the natural reticence of learners to be used as the 'guinea pigs' in experimental approaches to learning and teaching. Creating novel and challenging learning and assessment activities can result in a hostile reaction from students used to a more conventional classroom environment (November, 1997). This may, in turn, be connected with a disposition among some strategic students (Kneale, 1997) to remain disengaged from deep learning.

Notwithstanding these barriers, continuous reflection and a systematic and enthusiastic approach to evaluation involving a variety of stakeholders and leading to actionable results are to be encouraged, not least because without them experimentation and innovation are less likely. Moreover, they are an essential ingredient for ensuring the effectiveness of learning and for sustaining the joy of teaching. Because of the major contribution of reflective practice to effective learning and teaching, it receives further consideration in the final chapter on professional development.

References

Bingham, R and Ottewill, R (2001) Whatever happened to peer review? Revitalising the contribution of tutors to course evaluation, *Quality Assurance in Education*, **9** (1), pp 32–39

Brockbank, A and McGill, I (1998) *Facilitating Reflective Learning in Higher Education*, Society for Research into Higher Education/Open University Press, Buckingham

Brodie, D A (1998) Do students report that easy professors are excellent teachers?, *Canadian Journal of Higher Education*, **28** (1), pp 1–20

Coates, N and Koerner, R (1996) How market oriented are business studies degrees?, *Journal of Marketing Management*, **12,** pp 455–75

Fitzgibbon, K and McCarthy, P (1999) Action and reflection for business undergraduates, *Journal of European Business Education*, **8** (2), pp 104–13

Flash, P, Tzenis, C and Waller, A (1995) *Using Student Evaluations to Increase Classroom Effectiveness*, University of Minnesota Office of Human Resources, Minneapolis

Forsyth, I, Jolliffe, A and Stevens, D (1999) *Evaluating a Course: Practical strategies for teachers, lecturers and trainers*, 2nd edn, Kogan Page, London

Honey, P and Mumford, A (1986) *Manual of Learning Styles*, 2nd edn, Ardingly House, Maidenhead

Honey, P and Mumford, A (1989) *The Manual of Learning Opportunities*, 2nd edn, Ardingly House, Maidenhead

King, M *et al* (1999) Student feedback systems in the business school: a departmental model, *Quality Assurance in Education*, **7** (2), pp 90–100

Kneale, P (1997) The rise of the 'strategic student': how can we adapt to cope?, in *Facing Up to Radical Changes in Universities and Colleges*, ed S Armstrong, G Thompson and S Brown, pp 110–30, Staff and Educational Development Association/Kogan Page, London

Kolb, D (1984) *Experiential Learning: Experience as a source of learning and development*, Prentice Hall, Englewood Cliffs, NJ

National Committee of Inquiry into Higher Education (1997) *Higher Education in the Learning Society: The report of the national committee (The Dearing Report)*, HMSO, London

November, P (1997) Learning to teach experientially: a pilgrim's progress, *Studies in Higher Education*, **22** (2), pp 289–99

Orpen, C (2000) Reconsidering the case-study method of teaching management, *Journal of European Business Education*, **9** (2), pp 56–64

Pedler, M (1992) *Action Learning in Practice*, 2nd edn, Gower, Aldershot

Reid, I and Parker, F (1995) Whatever happened to the sociology of education in teacher education?, *Educational Studies*, **21** (3), pp 395–413

Rickards, T (1999) *Creativity and the Management of Change*, Blackwell, Oxford

Schon, D (1983) *The Reflective Practitioner*, Basic Books, New York

Schon, D (1987) *Educating the Reflective Practitioner*, Jossey-Bass, San Francisco

Scott, S V (1999) The academic as service provider: is the customer 'always right'?, *Journal of Higher Education Policy and Management*, **21** (2), pp 193–202

Stephens, J *et al* (1998) Exploring business skills: an innovative approach to promoting lifelong learning, *Journal of Further and Higher Education*, **22** (3), pp 329–41

United Kingdom Central Council (1986) *Project 2000: A new preparation for practice*, UKCC, London

Velayutham, S and Perera, H (1993) The reflective accountant: towards a new model for professional development, *Accounting Education*, **2** (4), pp 287–301

Part C

Applying the principles

Having outlined the principles it is now necessary to put them into practice. As has been indicated, this is the main function of the chapters that comprise Part C of the book. They provide specific guidance, in respect of each of the aspects of curriculum design, development, delivery and appraisal outlined in the preceding chapters, for a selection of the core subject areas within business and management. The areas are listed in Table C.1, together with an indication of their scope in terms of curriculum content.

Table C.1 Selected core subject areas in the business and management curriculum

Subject Area	Chapter	Scope
Business Environment	8	economic, political, legal, socio-cultural, demographic and technological aspects
Business Organisation	9	organisational types, structures, cultures, groups, organisational theory and behaviour
Business Ethics	10	values, ethical theory, stakeholders, corporate responsibility
International Business	11	globalization, knowledge-based economy, cross-cultural capability, multicultural teamwork
Strategic Management	12	business policy, corporate strategy, competitiveness, managerial decision-making, business environment
Marketing	13	marketing decision-making, quantitative techniques, marketing research, strategic marketing, consumer buyer behaviour, retail marketing
Innovation and Entrepreneurship	14	new business 'start-ups', industry analysis, new business opportunities, business plans

Although often writing from very different educational perspectives, the chapter authors identify a number of themes of common concern. These include the domination of the curriculum by US texts (Chapters 10, 13) and case study material invariably based on large, private sector organisations (Chapters 9, 10, 12, 13); the importance of fostering a teamwork ethos and cross-cultural under-standing (Chapters 11, 13, 14); tackling the misinformed preconceptions of learners (Chapters 10, 13); the need to promote interdisciplinary understanding (Chapters 8, 9, 13, 14); and developing learning, teaching and assessment activities that reflect 'real world' practices by linking theory and practice (Chapters 13, 14).

The chapters also serve to illustrate the varied approaches to pedagogy within business and management education. These include problem-based learning (Chapter 8), cross-cultural learning (Chapter 11) and resource-based learning (Chapter 12). In addition, specific techniques are recommended, such as role plays and learning logs (Chapter 10), case studies (Chapters 9, 10, 12), simulations and field trips (Chapter 13) and business projects (Chapter 14).

The guidance contained in these chapters is intended for anyone and everyone who contributes to the learning experience of students in the area concerned. Whatever the scale and nature of the contribution it is important to be aware of the broader picture to ensure that as far as possible the 'joins do not show'. Ideally, as far as the learners are concerned, what they experience should be a 'seamless web'.

However, readers are encouraged to compare the more general picture with the situations that they encounter in supporting the learning of others. Whichever of the core subject areas outlined above one regards as being an area of specialism, there is much to be gained from analysing one's own experiences in the light of the comments and observations of others. This should serve both to stimulate new ideas and to challenge the legitimacy of existing educational practice. Arguably the greatest danger in teaching is losing the 'cutting edge' that emanates from a deep desire to innovate and experiment with the intention of enriching the learning experience of others. This is not a call for change for the sake of change but simply a recognition that good practice in learning, teaching and assessment demands an openness and a willingness to do things differently should circum-stances require it.

8

Business environment

Ranald Macdonald

Introduction

The business environment can be particularly demanding for many learners and educators since it is not a neat subject area or discipline in the way that its component parts may be viewed. It comprises all those elements forming the external context in which organisations find themselves undertaking their activities and, in a sense, this environment is unique to every organisation. As a result of the location in which an organisation operates, the types of activities it undertakes, the level of competition it faces, the different products or services that it offers and other factors, it will have to analyse, understand and respond to the environment in a way that it considers appropriate when managing and planning for the future.

The business environment therefore encompasses a wide range of issues, including political, economic, socio-cultural, technological, legal and ecological. Further, these need to be examined for their effects upon the strategy, behaviour and management of organisations at local, regional, national and international levels (Quality Assurance Agency, 2000).

Educational challenges

The emergence of the business environment as a subject area in its own right has largely come about as a result of the development of more generic business and management programmes within business schools. In these the emphasis is less on learners grappling with the intricacies of econometrics or the finer points of law, and more with the ability to see the 'big picture' of the world in which organisations operate before getting down to greater detail through the more functional studies, such as marketing, finance and operations. While these developments have predominated at undergraduate level, they are also mirrored at postgraduate level, not least with the widespread growth of MBA programmes and the consequent debate about 'breadth versus depth'.

An analysis of the business environment enables learners to place the activities and fortunes of individual organisations, which they may hear or read about, or for which they may work, within a wider context. As will be shown later, a most valuable source of stimulus material in this area is the mass media and, in particular, specialist papers such as the *Financial Times* or *Wall Street Journal*, and television programmes that deal with the world of business and finance. The ability of learners to understand what drives the price of coffee from Colombia or oil from Saudi Arabia, or to recognize the legal and social, as well as economic, issues in controlling the potential monopoly power of large enterprises, such as Microsoft, will also help them to see that the local baker's shop and neighbourhood supermarket have a wide range of external forces acting upon them.

As a result, the business environment provides an initial opportunity for learners to see a more integrated picture of the world in which organisations carry out their activities. It provides a setting for the study of the more specialist functional areas as well as preparing learners for further integrated approaches in capstone courses such as strategic management (see Chapters 6 and 12 and the section, 'Integration', in this chapter). Business environment can also draw on contemporary issues such as e-commerce, knowledge management, globalization and business ethics as they unfold. This makes it essential that both learners and educators move beyond textbooks as their main source of information to a wider range of resources such as newspapers and journals, television and radio, the Internet, business organisations and official sources of data of the kind highlighted in Chapter 5. Thus, in preparing and delivering business environment courses, educators face a variety of specific challenges.

Demonstrating environmental complexity

The educational background of many learners may not have prepared them for the more integrated approach of the business environment. They may well have studied some of the constituent elements of the subject – economics, law, politics or sociology – and therefore see them as discrete, stand-alone disciplines. Further, the subjects may have been studied in a fairly theoretical and 'academic' way, which may be far removed from the 'real' world in which learners have their own experience of working in, or relating to, organisations. The challenge for those responsible for business environment courses is to introduce learners to examples drawn from their everyday experience to show that, while it is possible to understand the economic or legal aspects alone, in reality they interact in a complex and often contestable way. A brief introduction to the privatization of previously state-owned public utilities, such as water or telecommunications in the UK, and the subsequent actions to ensure that a monopoly situation is not exploited, should help learners to see that the interaction of economics, politics, law and technology, at the very least, presents a very different picture of a highly complex world. However, this presupposes that educators have the necessary cross-disciplinary capability and enabling skills to help learners achieve such a goal.

Overcoming disciplinary constraints

Many of those responsible for business environment course development and learner support come from single-discipline, specialist backgrounds. Since the emphasis in a large proportion of HE institutions is to research, publish and teach in increasingly narrow fields, it is sometimes the case that business environment courses are given to new, less experienced staff or those who have not been able to succeed in a specialist area. Alternatively, such a course may have been given to someone to make up his or her required teaching hours. Whatever the circumstances, however, this subject area provides the opportunity for educators to draw together their knowledge and experience of the business world in a way that enthuses learners to find out more about its intricacies and construct their learning and understanding for themselves. The lack of a specialist background in all the component disciplines presents a stimulating challenge for educators and enables them to adopt a 'partnership in learning' approach with their students. Rather than being seen as the 'expert', they structure the learning environment and activities in a way that draws on their expertise as a 'teacher', in the truest sense, rather than as an economist, lawyer or sociologist.

There may also be the worry for some learners and institutions that courses such as business environment encourage breadth rather than depth. Here it is strongly contended that it is equally valid for learners to have developed the ability to make connections between different elements of their learning and thereby obtain a broad overview as it is for them to study single disciplines in great depth. The world of business is, by its very nature, integrated and broad, and learners need to be able to see the 'big picture' as well as the fine detail.

Navigating the wealth of material

As previously indicated, since business environment draws on so many discrete disciplines, learners have at their disposal a vast amount of material. Initially, this may well overwhelm them and it is important that they be helped to acquire the appropriate learning and study skills to navigate a route through the material. It is no good assuming that because students have successfully passed examinations to get on to a particular course that they have the necessary information literacy and associated time management skills needed for the business environment. Some writers (eg Needle, 1994; Brooks and Weatherspoon, 1997; Worthington and Britton, 2000; Capon, 2000) have produced textbooks that are designed to bring together the array of disparate materials from the various disciplines and also to present a series of integrated case studies and examples that enable learners to deal with the subject area in a more managed way. They do, however, acknowledge the need for students to do their own updating by reading newspapers and journals and monitoring other media. Here the contribution of information specialists to learner support should not be overlooked.

The vast array of materials at the disposal of learners makes plagiarism a particularly acute problem for business environment educators. Such a challenge can be met by both ensuring that students are aware that it is a serious academic offence to use other people's work without appropriate acknowledgement and designing assessment tasks that cannot be met simply by copying materials. Requiring plans, drafts and final reports over a period of time and perhaps using oral tests to check on learner understanding of what they have written are ways of minimizing the risk of plagiarism.

Avoiding a bias towards large enterprises

A final challenge arises from the need to counteract the tendency for there to be an overemphasis on multinational and other large enterprises at the expense of small and medium-sized organisations, which might be a form more familiar to learners as both employees and customers. Some writers have tried to address this explicitly (eg Stokes, 1998) but it is important for educators to direct students towards the activities of small businesses and to realize that they are just as affected by their external environment. Much has been written about small businesses, not least because of their importance to the economy, despite their poor survival rates. They probably experience the effects of the environment more identifiably than do large multinationals and, as such, provide good case material for students. Small business owners, while normally very busy, may be encouraged to talk to groups of students about their experiences. This can convey to students the impact of the environment on such organisations in a more immediate and vivid way than reading an article in a newspaper or case study in a book.

Aims, objectives and learning outcomes

As indicated in the previous section, the underlying aim of a business environment course is to introduce learners, in an integrated way, to the wide range of forces that impact upon organisations. This is achieved by bringing together a number of disciplinary perspectives. In this sense, business environment is essentially a foundation study 'about' business (see Chapter 1). This is a challenging aim and it is not always clear that it is reflected in the objectives pursued by writers in this field. For example, a cursory glance at a number of business environment texts reveals chapters on the economic, legal, technological, social, cultural and ecological environments, amongst others. While there may be an introductory chapter on the need to integrate the various aspects, most books then immediately go on to disaggregate them! However, in stressing the dynamism, complexity and turbulence within the business environment (Brooks and Weatherspoon, 1997) or its complexity, volatility and interaction (Worthington and Britton, 2000), some authors introduce techniques for examining and forecasting changes in the environment and the ways that businesses might respond.

Although the subject matter of business environment makes it essentially a study 'about' business, in its delivery there is plenty of scope for pursuing aims and objectives associated with a study 'for' business. This is because business environment is a valuable area for developing a range of skills. The very nature of the learning activities used in many business environment courses means that learners have to use information skills extensively and become competent in establishing the need for information; identifying sources; evaluating, analysing and interpreting information; and then communicating their findings to others. Further, given the multidisciplinary nature of the subject, information is unlikely to come from a single source. Similarly, the knowledge and techniques necessary to access and use the information are likely to require increasingly sophisticated self-management skills on the part of students. Depending on the particular learning approaches adopted, students are also likely to need good problem-solving and communication skills. Thus, in specifying objectives, it is important to be quite explicit about the skills, as well as the knowledge being acquired, thereby ensuring that they are appropriately developed and assessed.

Learners also need to acquire a certain intellectual flexibility or adaptability to be able to recognize and analyse complex issues and scenarios. This objective can be pursued by getting students to track an event, such as a take-over, serious environmental disaster, global market trend or public relations campaign. In this way, they can be made more aware of, and gain insights into, the complex and uncertain nature of the business environment. Encouraging learners to reflect on their own experiences of work, or as consumers, can be used to reinforce this awareness. However, care needs to be taken to ensure that students do not just adopt a formulaic approach to analysing the business environment but can examine each case on its individual evidence and circumstances.

An important objective of any business environment course should be that learners are introduced to an increasingly globalized world in which access to appropriate international sources of information is critical. The growth of the Internet and networked databases, including official statistics and daily newspapers, means that students are far more able to examine the international environment than was possible even a few years ago. At the same time, however, students should not lose sight of the local and national context in which organisations operate. As mentioned earlier, some of them will be employed in, or have contact with, small and medium-sized businesses, where the local economy is often of more direct importance than it is to the multinational. In this respect, the local knowledge that learners possess is a valuable resource (see Chapter 2). The information processing and analytical skills developed in this way can then be transferred to more international examples.

How these broader considerations can be translated into learning outcomes for business environment are illustrated in Table 8.1.

Table 8.1 Examples of learning outcomes for business environment

Area	Examples
Cognitive	Explain how the economic and political components of the business environment interact.
	Map the impact of the external environment on the activities of a small to medium-sized enterprise.
Affective	Demonstrate an open mindset with respect to the forces affecting business organisations.
	Demonstrate a willingness to work collaboratively in analysing issues associated with the business environment.
Adaptive	Locate and utilize a wide variety of sources of information about the external environment of different types of organisation.
	Communicate findings about the business environment in writing to others.

Creating and exploiting opportunities for learners to achieve these outcomes is the principal task of business environment educators.

Learning, teaching and assessment activities

Effective learning on business environment courses is characterized by students having the need to know something and engaging with tasks that enable them to focus on the underlying meaning of what is being learnt. They build on, and develop, a sound knowledge-base as a way of understanding what is happening in the 'real' world and generate lots of questions about both the content and the process of their learning. In so doing, they have at their disposal a number of dedicated resources of the kind illustrated in the box below.

Ideally, these resources should be used in conjunction with the more general media discussed earlier. They might also be supplemented by specialist sources focusing on one particular component of the environment. However, with specialist sources there is always the danger of resource overload and of learners failing to make connections across the disciplines so as to examine the complexity in which organisations find themselves operating.

In directing learners to the resources identified in the box on page 85, it is important to remember that the role of the educator is less the imparter of

Key resources for business environment

Leading journals

Interestingly to date there are no journals dedicated solely to the business environment, although a number do contain articles of relevance including:

- *Business Strategy Review*;
- *Harvard Business Review*;
- *Long Range Planning*;
- *Management Today*.

Popular textbooks

- Brooks, I and Weatherspoon, J (1997) *The Business Environment: Challenges and changes*;
- Capon, C (2000) *Understanding Organisational Context*;
- Needle, D (1994) *Business in Context: An introduction to business and its environment*;
- Worthington, I and Britton, C (2000) *The Business Environment*.

Organisations and useful Web sites

- The Industrial Society (www.indsoc.co.uk);
- The Institute of Management (www.inst-mgt.org.uk);
- The Trades Union Congress (www.tuc.org.uk);
- Business Education on the Internet (www.bized.ac.uk);
- Business Information Sources on the Internet (www.dis.strath.ac.uk/business/);
- Michigan State University Center for International Business Education and Research (http://ciber.bus.msu.edu);
- Thomson Learning: Business and Management (www.businesspress.co.uk);
- Prentice Hall: International Business Resources (www.prenhall.com/griffin/ib2/resources/links);
- The BBC Business News (www.bbc.co.uk/business).

knowledge and more the facilitator of learning who creates the appropriate learning environment and tasks. This means, in effect, providing opportunities for learners to develop and change their conceptions of the environment through what *they* do rather than what they are taught.

Thus, learning, teaching and assessment strategies and consequent activities should focus on what educators do to enable learners to develop and change their conceptions of the business environment and demonstrate achievement in this respect.

Table 8.2 Strategies for fostering a deep approach with examples from the business environment (based on Gibbs, 1992: 12–17)

	Strategy	Examples
Strategy 1	*independent learning*	Students are asked to choose their own organisation, story or issue as the basis for acquiring or demonstrating knowledge and understanding about the different responsibilities of national and local government.
Strategy 2	*personal development*	Learners on a group-based project involving a diversity of investigative tasks relating to the impact of the external environment on a medium-sized enterprise over a five-year period are required to review how working in a group helped or hindered their learning.
Strategy 3	*problem-based learning*	A current story, such as oil price increases or a change in government policy, provides the stimulus for examining the interaction of elements of the business environment prior to educator input on them. (This strategy is developed more fully in the section, 'Integration', in this chapter.)
Strategy 4	*reflection*	Students are asked to write a short commentary on how they would need to change their approach to investigating the impact of the socio-cultural environment on a business or public service to achieve a higher mark.
Strategy 5	*independent groupwork*	A group-based activity is subdivided into various aspects, such as legal, economic, political and technological, and allocated to individual students who then peer-tutor their colleagues before making a final presentation in which they emphasize the linkages between the different aspects.
Strategy 6	*learning by doing*	Teams of students take part in computer simulations and role plays on the response of a business organisation to the government's tax and spending policies.
Strategy 7	*developing learning skills*	Information gathering, analysis, interpretation and presentation are assessed as part of an activity to examine the impact on businesses of globalization.
Strategy 8	*project work*	Student groups are allocated different industries as the basis for examining European Union competition policy.
Strategy 9	*fine-tuning*	Lectures include an input from students relating the topic to the organisations they have been studying.

Examples of these strategies for business environment are provided in Table 8.2, which applies a framework developed by Gibbs (1992). This incorporates nine strategies, each of which has considerable potential for utilizing methods that encourage learners to adopt a deep approach to their learning (see Chapter 2).

In promoting these strategies, Gibbs emphasizes the need to align assessment with the method adopted and the intention of the educator, thereby minimizing the possibility that the assessment will allow, and even reward, learners for adopting a surface approach. One way of doing this is to apply the Structure of Observed Learning Outcomes (SOLO) taxonomy, developed by Biggs (1999) and others and increasingly adopted in Australia and elsewhere. The taxonomy can be used as a way of structuring curriculum objectives, whether the aim is to increase knowledge or deepen understanding, and can be used as the basis for developing grading schemes for assessment purposes (Macdonald, 1999). Tasks can be designed that target a particular level of the taxonomy or, alternatively, the categories can be used to assess the level of learning achieved. Table 8.3 illustrates how this could be used in the business environment, where an article from the *Financial Times* forms the basis of a data response question requiring students to explain the importance of the balance of payments and alludes to currency devaluations.

Table 8.3   The Structure of Observed Learning Outcomes (SOLO) model

Level	Features of Students' Answers to the Data Response Question
Prestructural	misses the point; shows little evidence of relevant learning (eg suggests that the balance of payments is to do with a company's finances)
Unistructural	meets only one part of the task and is unable to make connections between ideas or facts (eg identifies only one major component of the balance of payments)
Multistructural	several major relevant points or arguments introduced but not interrelated (eg lists the key components of the balance of payments, but cannot explain how they interconnect)
Relational	integration of concepts or ideas to form a coherent structure and meaning (eg from the figures given, calculates the visible and invisible balances and explains how any missing figures have been handled)
Extended abstract	more than answers the question and generalizes to a higher level of abstraction (eg explains the effect of a devaluation of the domestic currency on the current and capital accounts of the balance of payments)

A grading system could be constructed where a prestructural answer is awarded a fail grade; a unistructural, a D grade; a multistructural, a C grade; a relational, a B grade; and an answer that goes beyond what is expected an A grade. Further, within each category there may be levels indicating, for example, whether the student has achieved the level minimally, adequately or very well (Biggs, 1992).

Thus, in designing learning tasks and assessment in the business environment, as for other subject areas, it should first be clear what the outcomes are, then how the students will achieve them and finally how they will be assessed. All this should be done with a mind to what it is that is being learnt and assessed. Is it that students are able to list a series of statutes or policies, or is it that they are able to make connections between different variables? It may be necessary to start with a unistructural approach and then support learners in developing the appropriate use of relational, or even extended abstract, analysis.

In ensuring that assessment methods are aligned with learning outcomes and learning and teaching strategies, business environment educators face the additional challenge of ensuring that integration is not overlooked. Unlike some of the other subject areas covered in this book, business environment has a dual role of demonstrating the potential of an interdisciplinary approach as well as facilitating and underpinning linkages elsewhere in the curriculum.

Integration

In view of the multidisciplinary character of the business environment, it is not surprising that there are significant links between its content and that of other subject areas (see box below). Indeed, such links have the potential to serve as the primary means for securing a degree of horizontal, or even vertical, integration within the business and management curriculum.

Links between business environment and other subject areas

- *economics*, eg economic growth, financial institutions, inflation, unemployment, balance of payments;
- *law*, eg system of justice, consumer legislation, employment law, contract and agency law, codes of practice;
- *politics*, eg institutions of government, urban policy, European Union;
- *sociology*, eg demographic trends, culture and society, gender and the workplace.

Moreover, these links can be reinforced by adopting one of the most compelling educational approaches to integration, namely problem-based learning (see Chapter 6). As indicated earlier, this approach is one of the nine strategies suggested by Gibbs (1992) for fostering a deep approach to learning. Because of its potential for integration with respect to business environment, it is now going to be examined in more detail.

Problem-based learning has its roots in medical education at McMaster University in Canada (though others might claim to have been first) and has since attracted much interest in medical schools and other areas of professional education throughout the world. So, from architecture to engineering and from nursing to business studies, problem-based learning has been taken up with almost missionary zeal by many.

'The "McMaster approach", or the "McMaster Model" is founded on the belief that the study of health encompasses not only the problems of illness but the impact of biological processes, environment and lifestyle on the community and society. To keep pace with the continually expanding knowledge base, students must become lifelong self-motivated learners' (McMaster University, www-fhs.mcmaster.ca/).

This quotation could just as easily be written with 'business environment' substituted for 'health', and the impact of its constituent elements on business activity for the impact of biological processes, etc.

The essence of the approach is small-group, student-centred learning, with learners encountering 'real world' problems or issues as the basis for acquiring knowledge, understanding and skills. Here a distinction needs to be drawn between problem-solving education, where tackling the problems comes after the teaching has taken place, and problem-based learning, where the problem is the starting point for learning. Working in small groups, students address the problem or task in a fairly systematic way. This has been systematized as a series of seven steps or jumps. These steps are identified in the box below and illustrated with a business environment example.

Problem-based learning: the 'seven steps' applied to business environment

An example of a *problem* might be: 'It was reported yesterday that the Government was considering introducing legislation to control the profits of privatized public utilities. There has been public outcry over announced price rises and the recent bid by a French multinational for one of the main combined utility companies. The UK prime minister has consulted with the French premier and asked for the issue to be raised with the European Commission.' From this the seven steps might appear as:

1. *Clarify difficult terms or concepts.* What is meant by 'public utility' and 'privatization'?
2. *Define the problems to be tackled.* Why might the Government want to control profits and what is the link between this and privatization? What would a bid by a French multinational mean and why would the UK prime minister talk to the French premier? What role might the European Commission have in this?

3. *Establish what is already known.* The relationship between price, costs and profit is known. Is this relevant?
4. *Analyse the problem and clarify issues.* The problem seems to relate to many aspects of the business environment, at the very least political, economic, legal and possibly social. For example, it is necessary to know why the UK prime minister is taking an interest.
5. *Formulate learning objectives.* These could be derived from the following questions: What is the history of privatization? What are the various impacts of privatization and why would the government want to control these? Is there a problem with companies making excess profits? What is the relationship between consumers, companies, government, the European Union and other countries in economic, legal and social policy-making as it relates to the behaviour of companies?
6. *Carry out a self-study of the identified learning objectives.* This involves use of the World Wide Web, official publications and other sources to identify answers to the questions in Step 5, allocated among group members.
7. *Report back on findings to the group and synthesize.* Distil the findings of group members and agree on various answers to the problem. Prepare a report or presentation.

One of the key aspects of problem-based learning, and one where many users get it wrong, is that it is the students, perhaps prompted by the use of appropriate questions by the facilitator, who arrive at the learning objectives. This is what makes it different from the type of question at the end of a chapter in a textbook where what the students must do is quite clearly set out.

There is an increasingly varied literature on problem-based learning, and putting this phrase in one of the popular search engines on the Internet will yield thousands of entries! Some useful Web sites to complement the paper-based sources identified in Chapter 5 are shown in the box on page 91.

However, despite the wealth of materials to support problem-based learning, it is worth remembering that it is just one of the strategies proposed by Gibbs (1992) and that there are many other ways of achieving the same aim, to improve the quality of learning through the design of a curriculum that encourages a deep approach.

Through the application of integrated approaches, such as problem-based learning, and by providing learners with a genuinely interdisciplinary learning experience, business environment can serve as an exemplar for the business and management curriculum as a whole. Significantly, as the following two examples illustrate, where academic institutions have moved away from delivering business and management as a series of discrete subjects to a far more integrated approach, reflecting more closely the 'real' world of business, business environment is often a central feature of the curriculum design.

Useful Internet sources for problem-based learning

- Kenley, R (1995) *Problem-Based Learning: Within a traditional teaching environment* (www.arbld.unimelb.edu.au/ kenley/conf/papers/rk_a_p1.htm)
- *PBL Insight*, a newsletter for undergraduate problem-based learning from Samford University (www.samford.edu/pbl/)
- Woods, D (1996) *Problem-Based Learning: Helping your students gain the most from PBL* (http://chemeng.mcmaster.ca/pbl/pbl.htm)
- *Deliberations*, an electronic journal on teaching and learning; follow instructions to PBL (www.lgu.ac.uk/deliberations/home.html)
- PBL at the University of Delaware, lots of links to other Web sites and 'Dan tries problem-based learning: a case study' (www.udel.edu/pbl/)
- Problem-based learning in business education: curriculum design and implementation issues (http://mbawb.cob.ohiou.edu/papers.html)
- University of Maastricht, Educational Innovation in Economics and Business, plus links to other sites (http://www2.unimaas.nl/edineb/) and (www.unimaas.nl/um/onderwijs/index_uk.htm)

The first example relates to the integration of the business curriculum that has been undertaken at Auckland University of Technology in New Zealand. Here the Bachelor of Business degree has two main phases: the first comprising integrated studies and the second allowing for specialization and a semester of 'cooperative education' (a work placement). The integrated studies phase comprises a semester each of 'The New Zealand business environment', 'Managing information' and 'Managing the organisation'. The programme's brochure states:

> The business environment is complex and dynamic and no one discipline functions in isolation. For this reason we take an integrated approach to business for the first three semesters of the Bachelor of Business. This approach enables you to learn fundamental concepts and see the inter-relationships between law, economics, accounting, marketing, information technology, communication and management in the business environment. At the same time you will become a confident learner, developing the professional capabilities business requires: communication, teamwork, critical thinking, problem solving, research and use of technology. This understanding of business, together with your ability to see the interconnectedness in business, will give you a sound base for your study in your chosen majors or minors. (www.aut.ac.nz/corp/courseinfo/business/bus_integrated.shtml)

This quotation sums up what the business environment, and perhaps business and management in general, should be all about, helping learners to see the 'big picture' before expecting them to be able to make choices about specialist areas to study. While at Auckland, students cover a more comprehensive range of subjects during their integrated studies than might be feasible elsewhere, as well as integrating skill development into the learning, it does give an indication of what is possible.

Many programmes elsewhere follow the first-year business environment course with specialisms in the next year(s) before returning with a further integrated course in the final year in the form of strategic management or something similar. The skills and approach acquired from studying the business environment can therefore be further demonstrated later in a programme. Thus, a second example is provided by many Dutch *hogescholen* (the equivalent of the pre-1992 UK polytechnics) where the final semester of a four-year business programme is taken up with what is known as the 'graduation assignment'. To quote from one institution: 'The aim of the graduation assignment is putting into practice the knowledge, understanding and skills acquired in the study programme, with students themselves being responsible for the planning and execution of the assignment. This is to result in a concrete final product: a study, recommendation and/or solution to a business problem' (International Business School Breda, The Netherlands, 1999–2000).

Many other institutions will have, as part of their business studies programme, final-year projects or dissertations that give learners a high level of choice in terms of the study area and method of presentation. However, few make quite as explicit the links between all aspects of what has gone before and the demonstration of professional competence. This is what the business environment should be preparing learners for.

Reflection and evaluation

Given that educators are unlikely to be subject experts in all the various disciplines making up the business environment, there is a particular need for continual reflection on the processes of learner support. It may no longer be appropriate to be seen as 'the sage on the stage' but rather as 'the guide by the side'. This requires a significant move away from transmission models of teaching to a facilitation model of learning where students are being helped to change their conceptions of the world they are studying.

Initially many learners will find this approach confusing, disorientating and possibly demotivating. They may well turn to the facilitator with the accusation, 'You are paid to teach us.' In this situation, however, the goal of educators should be to help students learn! It requires continual reflection and the use of a range of methods to ensure that one does not lose one's nerve when students feel that their expectations have not been met (see Chapter 7).

Some of the more specific questions that can be used to guide reflection on business environment courses are provided in the box on page 93.

Examples of reflective questions for business environment educators

- What evidence is there to confirm that learners have appreciated the breadth and diversity of the business environment?
- Were learners able to make connections between different components of the business environment?
- Did the academic backgrounds of learners help or hinder their ability to see the 'big picture'?
- To what extent did learners have the opportunity of analysing the business environment of small to medium-sized enterprises as well as large multi-nationals?
- Have certain elements of the business environment (eg economic) been overemphasized and others (eg legal) been underemphasized?
- In researching aspects of the business environment did learners fully exploit all available sources?
- Was the support provided for students with respect to the development of their information-gathering skills adequate and were the services of information specialists sufficiently utilized?
- In using a problem-based learning approach did learners set relevant, rigorous and practicable objectives for their exploration of aspects of the business environment?
- Was an appropriate balance struck between, on the one hand, providing students with appropriate and timely guidance and, on the other, allowing them to learn directly from their experiences, including mistakes?

Whatever specific questions are used to guide the process, educators should constantly reflect on their practice so as to answer the underlying question, 'How might my students learn better?' For the business environment this relates, in particular, to the aims and objectives, where the integrated and holistic nature of the subject area can easily be diluted by reverting to an ill-thought-out conglomeration of different topics related to single disciplines. As indicated earlier, arguably the key question is, 'Have they got the big picture?'

Conclusion

In considering the business environment, this chapter has placed particular emphasis on some of the suggested strategies for encouraging a deep approach, in particular problem-based learning. Implicit in these strategies is the belief that educational practice should be guided by research into effective learning. This is not to suggest that the business environment is so different from other components of the business and management curriculum, except perhaps to the extent that it integrates such a diverse range of long-established discrete disciplines. Consequently, those providing learner support in other subject areas can apply much of the guidance, suitably modified, from this chapter.

Overall, the business environment provides an excellent means for presenting learners with the opportunity of seeing business and other organisations in their wider context. As such, it serves as a robust framework within which to foster the development of appropriate learning skills and should therefore receive due weight and attention in any business and management programme.

References

Biggs, J (1992) A qualitative approach to grading students, *HERDSA News*, **14** (3), pp 3–6

Biggs, J (1999) *Teaching for Quality Learning at University*, Society for Research into Higher Education/Open University Press, Buckingham

Brooks, I and Weatherspoon, J (1997) *The Business Environment: Challenges and changes*, Prentice Hall, Hemel Hempstead

Capon, C (2000) *Understanding Organisational Context*, Pearson Education, Harlow

Gibbs, G (1992) *Improving the Quality of Student Learning*, Technical and Educational Services Ltd, Bristol

Macdonald, R (1999) *Specifying Aims and Learning Outcomes*, The Open University, Milton Keynes

Needle, D (1994) *Business in Context: An introduction to business and its environment*, 2nd edn, Chapman and Hall, London

Quality Assurance Agency (2000) *Benchmark Statement for General Business and Management*, [online] http://www.qaa.ac.uk/crntwork/benchmark/business.pdf

Stokes, D (1998) *Small Business Management: A case study approach*, 3rd edn, Letts Educational, London

Worthington, I and Britton, C (2000) *The Business Environment*, 3rd edn, Pearson Education, Harlow

9

Business organisation

Ardha Danieli and Alan B Thomas

Introduction

The study of business organisation is one of the most enduring features of business and management education, and appears under a range of titles, including organisational analysis, organisational studies, organisational theory and organisational behaviour. As an early definition by Pugh suggests, it is primarily concerned with 'the structure, functioning and performance of organisations, and the behaviour of groups and individuals within them' (1971: 9). For convenience, a distinction can be drawn between the structural systems and elements (types of structure and culture) and the behavioural elements (group and individual actions). This has been institutionalized in the United States in the form of two sub-areas within business organisation: the macro, organisation theory, and the micro, organisational behaviour. In the UK, by contrast, organisational behaviour embraces both elements.

In this chapter use of the term 'business organisation' is intended to convey both the unit of analysis, the organisation, and the process of organising. However, the notion of the organisation as the unit of analysis is problematic because the field can be categorized in terms of four substantive levels:

- *individuals* – their personalities, identities, attitudes, perceptions, motivations and behaviours;
- *groups* – their nature and behaviour including decision-making, leadership, power, control and conflict;
- *the organisation* – the structures and cultures of organisations and how they change over time;
- *society* – the environment and the national cultures in which organisations are located.

With the increasing globalization of business activity, the international context in which organisations operate can be added to these levels (Adler, 1997; Hofstede, 1991). Thus, amongst those with an interest in business organisation considerable attention is given to the interrelationships between the various levels as they manifest themselves in the behaviour of organisations and their members. At the same time, globalizing trends coupled with the impact of information technologies have generated considerable interest in the virtual organisation, sometimes referred to as network or modular, and boundaryless organisations.

The origins of business organisation as a subject of study can be found in the works of the classical sociologist, Max Weber (1947), on bureaucracy; of Henri Fayol (1930), on principles of organisation; and of Frederick Taylor (1911), on 'scientific management', as well as the Hawthorne studies (Roethlisberger and Dickson, 1939), on group and individual behaviour. With the exception of Weber, these studies were closely concerned with exploring and improving managerial practice.

The earliest business organisation courses in the United States drew substantially on the body of 'classical administrative theory' developed by Fayol and his successors (Hugstad, 1983). Harvard Business School recognized organisational behaviour as a discrete area of study in 1962 with Fritz Jules Roethlisberger as the Head, and in 1970 London Business School appointed Derek Pugh as the first Professor of Organisational Behaviour in the UK (Buchanan and Huczynski, 1997). Subsequent research and challenges to these foundations have produced a rich body of materials to which both mainstream academics (eg Child, 1984; Mintzberg, 1983; Daft, 1998) and business consultants (Peters and Waterman, 1982; Hammer, 1995) have contributed.

Educational challenges

Those responsible for teaching business organisation face various challenges. These emanate from a number of related sources and include contention between differing approaches to delivering the curriculum; the complex, diverse and multidisciplinary nature of the subject matter; and the tension between theory and practice. They are compounded by the varied backgrounds of learners.

Choosing between orthodox and critical approaches

Traditionally, this subject area has been dominated by orthodox assumptions about the aims of teaching business and management. In the United States it is largely taken for granted that the aim of business teaching is to equip students with the knowledge and skills to improve business practice and contribute to 'the bottom line'. Here the emphasis is on developing the skills of students with respect to the identification of managerial problems and application of the 'correct' solutions. In other words, there is a bias towards teaching 'for' business as opposed to teaching 'about' business and a heavy emphasis on what has been described as the managerialist perspective (see Chapter 1).

Outside the United States, however, a wider range of approaches is in evidence. Many educators in this subject area are sceptical of the values of business and tend to see the teaching of business organisation within a 'liberal critical' or 'radical critical' tradition (Macfarlane, 1997; Thomas, 1997; Danieli and Thomas, 1999). As a result, the subject area has been exposed to a variety of alternative approaches, including those that treat it as a form of liberal study akin to political or religious studies (Grey and French, 1996) and those that see it as a 'critical' endeavour concerned with the 'emancipation' of individuals in the context of oppressive capitalist regimes (Alvesson and Willmott, 1994). Currently, business organisation is experiencing considerable ferment so that even the notion of what it means to offer a 'critical' analysis of organisational behaviour is contested, with some writers arguing that being critical does not entail 'emancipation' (Warwick Organisational Behaviour Staff, 2000). In the United States, interest in these approaches is beginning to grow with a workshop on 'critical' management included for the first time at the American Academy of Management Conference in 1999.

The 'liberal critical' tradition encourages students to adopt a questioning approach to all knowledge claims with a view to assessing their logical and empirical validity, thereby developing their resistance to dogma, propaganda and authority-based pronouncements (Brookfield, 1987). The development of 'radical critical' theories of business organisation includes debates about the usefulness of postmodernist organisational analyses (Hassard and Parker, 1993) and the exposure of the gendered nature of organisations and management (Savage and Witz, 1992; Collinson and Hearn, 1994; Marshall, 1984; Ferguson, 1984; Pringle, 1989). Faced with these significantly different approaches, learning facilitators have to decide not only which is most in keeping with their own 'world-view' but also the extent to which their learners should be made aware of the alternatives.

Handling multidisciplinary demands

The disciplinary roots of business organisation are numerous. Mullins (1999), for example, claims that the study of business organisation draws on sociology, psychology and anthropology. Others argue that the range of disciplines is wider and embraces 'psychology, social psychology, sociology, economics and political science, and to a lesser extent… history, geography and anthropology' (Buchanan and Huczynski, 1997: 3). The multidisciplinary character of business organisation has meant that the aspirations of some of the founding writers for an integrated science of organisation and management have proved difficult or impossible to fulfil (Pugh, 1971; Lupton, 1983).

Given the heterogeneity of business organisation, learners need to be made aware of this, rather than be encouraged to expect high degrees of uniformity and coherence. They also need to develop an understanding of the classical writings in not just one discipline but in a variety of disciplines, clearly a daunting and time-consuming task.

Another problem is that business organisation courses are often allocated insufficient time to enable educators to cover their subject area in the depth required to avoid oversimplification. Consequently, they are open to accusations from students of merely offering 'common sense'. This, coupled with the multidisciplinary nature of business organisation, can present educators whose own academic history is located within single disciplines with a significant challenge in making the study of business organisation both intellectually demanding and relevant to their students.

Coping with learner expectations concerning theory and practice

Implicit in the foregoing challenges is the tension between theory and practice. Here the impact on various categories of learner is greatest and the importance of the points made in Chapter 2 about being sensitive to the differences between them is most clearly in evidence.

While practising managers generally have little difficulty engaging with the more practical aspects of business organisation, they are often unable to devote a sufficient amount of reading time to the literature, especially that which is not directly concerned with improving managerial performance. They may therefore experience more difficulty when it comes to relating to abstract theoretical ideas and to demonstrating the academic rigour and critical reflection often expected on many courses. Managers may find it difficult to see the relevance of some theories to their own experiential knowledge or to see how they might use the theories to inform their practice. This is more likely when a 'liberal' and/or 'radical' critical approach has been adopted since these do not generally offer recipes for 'adding shareholder value'. Moreover, those who have substantial experience of managing business organisations are likely to be resistant to radical critiques of business practice. Such resistance arises from the investment that managers have made in their chosen career. To question business practice may be perceived as a personal criticism, so potentially devaluing their contributions to organisational performance. Resistance also emanates from the effort and resources that need to be invested by students in being open to alternative interpretations of business organisation; in becoming reflective practitioners (Schon, 1983); and in acknowledging the constraints within which managers and organisations operate.

Unless educators themselves have substantial business experience, and sometimes not even then, their credibility in seeking to inform practice with theory may be permanently in question, especially from senior managers looking for best practice solutions to their organisational problems.

Paradoxically, learners with little or no managerial experience present the opposite challenge. They may too readily identify with the more abstract aspects of the field without being able to translate these into practice or seeing the necessity of doing so.

For both types of learner, but particularly for practising managers, business organisation may be seen to lack 'face validity'. Unlike subject areas such as marketing (Chapter 13), accounting, strategic management (Chapter 12) and human resource management, it is not a business function with an identifiable location within an organisation.

Each of the challenges considered here underlines the importance of clarifying the aims and objectives of business organisation, together with the learning outcomes, at the beginning of any course so that the expectations of students can be effectively managed.

Aims, objectives and learning outcomes

The aims of business organisation curricula vary according to the orientations of those responsible for their planning and delivery. In the case of educators who see business and management education as being primarily 'for' business, the aim is likely to be essentially instrumental, namely to improve students' capacity to manage organisations. As one US textbook puts it: '[Our text] presents theories, research results, and applications that focus on managing organizational behavior in small, as well as large and multinational organizations... we illustrate how organizational behavior theory leads to research and how both theory and research provide the basic foundation for practical applications in firms, hospitals, educational institutions, and government agencies' (Gibson, Ivancevich and Donnelly, 2000: vii).

For educators committed to a more critical approach, however, the aim is rather different:

Instead of assuming the neutrality of management theory and the impartiality of management practice, each contribution challenges the myth of objectivity and argues for a very different, critical conception of management in which research is self-consciously motivated by an effort to discredit, and ideally eliminate, forms of management and organisation that have institutionalized the opposition between the purposefulness of individuals and the seeming givenness and narrow instrumentality of work-process relationships.
(Alvesson and Willmott, 1996: 4)

The broad objective of the former approach is enhanced competence in pursuing the established goals of business, such as profit or effectiveness, or of other types of organisation. For the latter it is resistance to, or emancipation from, dominant 'regimes of truth' (Foucault, 1979) and their associated practices. While both approaches may encourage critical reflection on the part of students, the former is likely to be located at the level of 'single loop' learning, while the latter will facilitate 'double loop' learning. The most basic assumptions about 'knowledge', 'control', 'organisational goals' and so on are not radically questioned under the former approach but are confronted head on under the latter. Examples of texts that exemplify this second orientation may be found in Jackson and Carter (2000) and Warwick Organisational Behaviour Staff (2000).

Specific learning outcomes for business organisation are extremely diverse and are likely to vary significantly according to the perspective adopted, and in particular the balance between developing managerial skills, on the one hand, and developing critical understandings, on the other. Table 9.1 provides illustrative examples of learning outcomes with each level of analysis serving as the context (see Chapter 4).

Table 9.1 Examples of learning outcomes for business organisation

Level of Analysis	Type of Outcome	Example(s)
Individuals	cognitive	Explain personality theories.
	affective	Accept individual differences in needs and goals.
	adaptive	Display ability to motivate others.
Groups	cognitive	Describe group development stages.
	affective	Manage emotions in groups.
	adaptive	Lead and participate in groups.
Organisation	cognitive	Recognize different types of organisational structure and culture, and analyse the implications of these for performance.
	affective	Display sensitivity to cultural differences within organisations.
	adaptive	Apply organisation and work design skills.
Society	cognitive	Demonstrate knowledge of different ethnic groups.
	affective	Display positive attitudes to cultural diversity.
	adaptive	Apply multicultural management skills.

These demonstrate the richness of business organisation as a sphere of learning. However, getting the balance right requires considerable ingenuity.

Learning, teaching and assessment activities

To the extent that the managing aspect of business organisation is essentially a practical and political skill, informed by management theories, and applied in a variety of workplace settings (Stewart, 1984), expertise can be developed using a range of methods, often in combination with each other. These will vary in the extent to which they engage the learner directly in practice. So, for example, the development of student understanding of motivation at work may combine private study of key theoretical texts, perhaps encouraging learners' imaginative engagement, with various techniques for motivating others. In addition, learners may be given the task of actually motivating a group to achieve a difficult objective under demanding conditions, so engaging them more directly with practice and encouraging them to apply, and so test out for themselves, the adequacy of the management theories elucidated in journals and textbooks (see box below).

Key resources for business organisation

Leading journals

- *Academy of Management Journal*;
- *Academy of Management Review*;
- *Administrative Science Quarterly*;
- *British Journal of Management*;
- *Gender, Work and Organization*;
- *Human Relations*;
- *Journal of Management Studies*;
- *Journal of Occupational and Organisational Psychology*;
- *Organization*;
- *Organizational Dynamics*;
- *Organization Science*;
- *Organization Studies*.

Popular textbooks

- Alvesson, M and Willmott, H (1996) *Making Sense of Management: A critical introduction*;
- Buchanan, D and Huczynski, A (1997) *Organizational Behaviour: An introductory text*;
- Daft, R (1998) *Organization Theory and Design*;
- Fincham, R and Rhodes, P (1999) *Principles of Organizational Behaviour*;
- Gibson, J, Ivancevich, J and Donnelly, J (2000) *Organizations: Behavior, structure, processes*;
- Hatch, M (1997) *Organization Theory*;
- Jackson, N and Carter, P (2000) *Rethinking Organisational Behaviour*;
- Marcic, D and Seltzer, J (1997) *Organizational Behavior*;
- Morgan, G (1997) *Images of Organisation*;
- Mullins, L (1999) *Management and Organisational Behaviour*;
- Thompson, P and McHugh, D (1995) *Work Organisations*;
- Weightman, J (1999) *Introducing Organisational Behaviour*.

Useful Web sites

- Critical Management Discussion List (http://www.mailbase.ac.uk/lists-a-e/critical-management);
- The Organisation and Management Theory Web Site (http://www.aom.pace.edu/omt/omt.html).

An introductory understanding of the principles of organisation can be conveyed by traditional lecture and seminar methods backed by one or more of the many excellent textbooks currently available listed in the box above. More usually, however, these are supplemented by case materials that offer opportunities for learners to apply the theories and frameworks conveyed by texts and lectures to examples drawn from the world of management practice.

Case studies

The use of case studies is widespread in the teaching of business organisation as in other areas of business and management (see Chapters 4, 5, 10, 11 and 12). When used as a focus for group discussion, they can help to enhance student skills of communication, argumentation, analytical reasoning and critical thinking (Thomas, 1996). They can prove fruitful for learners who have no work experience, by providing them with opportunities for considering real situations in which the issues they have examined have been either successfully or unsuccessfully managed. Case studies are also valuable for experienced managers who, without them, might struggle to see the relevance of more abstract ideas for organisational management.

As with the different aims of business organisation courses, the uses made of cases differ. Some facilitators employ them to develop students' skills of identifying and solving organisational problems. This approach, as Corbett (1994) argues, tends to position the student in a senior *management* position and so the solution to be prescribed is one that reflects management's concerns rather than those of other groups in the organisation. Here, case studies can be used either deductively, to test some organisational theories that have already been taught on the course, or inductively, to enable students to generate their own understandings of the issues and problems presented in the case and to engender debate amongst participants (see Clegg, Kemp and Legge, 1985; Gowler, Legge and Clegg, 1993). Alternatively, case studies can be utilized as vehicles for helping learners 'develop critical thinking and analytical skills in order to get beneath the surface reality of organisational life' (Corbett, 1994: 1). Further approaches include those of Griffith (1999) and Romm and Mahler (1991) (see also Chapter 5). For those business organisation educators who are keen to make use of case studies, several collections are available (see box at top of page 103).

While these collections are an extremely valuable resource, there is also much to be gained from educators looking for opportunities to develop their own case studies and encouraging learners to do the same.

Although widely adopted in business schools around the world, the case study method has not been without its critics (Argyris, 1980; Berger, 1983). It has been argued, for example, that some approaches are unduly hierarchical, even authoritarian, especially where there is a heavy emphasis on educators leading learners through a case to a conclusion. This can induce learner dependency on a dominant authority figure and is the very antithesis of student-centred learning. Consequently, case studies need to be handled with care.

Case collections for business organisation

- Adam-Smith, D and Peacock, A (1994) *Case Studies in Organisational Behaviour;*
- Cohen, A, Fink, S and Gadon, H (1994) *Effective Behavior in Organizations: Cases, concepts and student experiences;*
- Corbett, J (1994) *Critical Cases in Organisational Behaviour;*
- Daft, R and Sharfman, M (1995) *Organization Theory: Cases and applications;*
- Gowler, D, Legge, K and Clegg, C (eds) (1993) *Case Studies in Organizational Behaviour and Human Resource Management;*
- Oddou, G and Mendenhall, M (eds) (1998) *Cases in International Organizational Behavior;*
- Thomas, A (1996) *The Organizational Behaviour Casebook: Cases and concepts in organizational behaviour;*
- Tompkins, T (2000) *Cases in Management and Organizational Behaviour.*

Experiential methods

The expression 'experiential method' refers to those facilitation strategies and techniques that directly involve the learners in the examination of their own and others' behaviour. Possibilities range from asking learners to keep an experiential learning log in which behavioural observations are recorded and participation in games and role plays, to the mounting of large-scale organisational simulations. An example is provided in the box below.

Example of an experiential learning activity

The underlying purpose of this activity is to enable learners to compare theory and practice with respect to equality of opportunity in organisational life for different social groups. Having been introduced to the theoretical and legal underpinning of equal opportunity initiatives and anti-discrimination measures in the workplace, using a combination of directed reading and presentations, students are paired with someone from either a different ethnic and/or cultural background and/or gender to their own.

Their brief is to find out as much as possible in the time permitted (eg 15 minutes) about the biography (family, education, interests, beliefs, etc) and consequent experiences in organisational settings of their partner. In so doing, learners need to be sensitive to not only different biographical and related experiences but also the boundaries defining what it is acceptable to reveal about each other's lives.

Following a plenary session in which what has been learnt is shared more widely, but with due regard to the sensibilities of partners, learners note their observations in a personal development logbook, which might also be used for assessment purposes. These might make reference to the similarities and differences between theory and practice, as well as some critical reflection on the value of theoretical insights, and the implications of what has been learnt for working practices and organisational relationships.

Experiential methods are especially suitable as vehicles for connecting learners with various organisational processes, such as communication, decision-making, stress and conflict management, and to group processes including leadership and team-building. However, in these situations specific skills of group facilitation and the management of ambiguity are typically required of educators, who need to be able to work effectively in the absence of the usual protections of dominance and centrality afforded by the traditional teaching role.

Integration

Integration issues loom large in the field of business organisation. This is because business functions, such as marketing (see Chapter 13), accountancy and finance, research and development, and production, are all affected by structural consider- ations and manifest behaviour in specific organisational and cultural contexts. Thus, in principle, business organisation is linked directly to all these areas, as well as a variety of disciplines. Some of these linkages are listed in the box below.

Links between business organisation and other subject areas

- *marketing*, eg psychology of markets, consumer behaviour;
- *accountancy and finance*, eg participative budgets, reward structures and performance;
- *production*, eg team dynamics, employee participation and job design;
- *sociology*, eg organisational culture, managing diversity, organisational goals;
- *psychology*, eg motivation, personality and learning, group processes;
- *political science*, eg power structures, micropolitics, ideological orientations.

However, business organisation is perhaps most closely related to strategic management (Chapter 12), which has a strong organisational and behavioural component, and to human resource management. The latter is more policy- and practice-orientated than business organisation, but shares with it an interest in such matters as motivation theory, in relation to reward policies; organisation structure and group processes, in relation to job and work design; and personality and learning, in relation to selection, development and training.

Although learners should experience little difficulty in linking business organi- sation and human resource management, integration with strategic management may prove more challenging. In part, this arises from its location, for many learning facilitators, within the managerialist 'for' business camp. As a result any critical issues raised by business organisation may well be treated as irrelevant and dealt with accordingly. In addition, approaches in strategic management have tended to emphasize context and structure as opposed to the 'softer' aspects of behaviour.

Reflection and evaluation

The scope of business organisation, the uncertain character of much of the knowledge-base of the field and the wide variety of methods that can be adopted for learning and teaching purposes provide plenty of opportunity for reflection and evaluation on the part of educators. Indeed, to the extent that business organisation deals with the social, moral and political issues associated with the design and control of work in society, rather than purely technical problems, critical reflection can hardly be avoided (Thomas, 1993). Thus, educators might find it helpful to consider some of the questions set out in the box below to guide their reflection in what is essentially a controversial subject area.

Examples of reflective questions for business organisation educators

- Has the teaching of business organisation been set in its social and historical context?
- Were learners made aware of the nature and limitations of insights derived from the social sciences for the study of business organisation?
- Was the relationship between 'theory' and 'practice' discussed?
- Were learners provided with opportunities to compare and apply theories of business organisation with practical examples?
- Have learners been asked to evaluate theory in the light of their own experiences?
- Have learning assessments sought to measure the ability of students to think critically about business organisation?

Clearly, the box above does not contain a definitive list of questions. There are many others that could be asked and educators are encouraged to see the development of their own questions as a part of this process of reflection. This is essential to ensure that learners understand the value and validity of business organisation as a key area of study.

Conclusion

The study of business organisation is likely to continue to hold a key place in the business and management curriculum for the foreseeable future. The field has been given particular impetus recently by the onset of widespread changes in business practices associated with intensified national and international competition, the spread of new information technologies and the wholesale restructuring of leading businesses. In an era of 'permanent revolution', an understanding of the processes driving organisational developments, and of their effects, has become increasingly significant to learners. At the same time, the range of learning resources, methods and perspectives available to business organisation educators has never been greater. As the world of business itself becomes more challenging, so too do the tasks facing those who seek to learn and teach in this field.

References

Adam-Smith, D and Peacock, A (1994) *Case Studies in Organisational Behaviour*, Pitman, London

Adler, N (1997) *International Dimensions of Organizational Behavior*, 3rd edn, South Western College Publishing, Cincinnati

Alvesson, M and Willmott, H (1994) *Critical Management Studies*, Sage, London

Alvesson, M and Willmott, H (1996) *Making Sense of Management: A critical introduction*, Sage, London

Argyris, C (1980) Some limitations of the case method: experiences in a management development program, *Academy of Management Review*, **5**, pp 291–98

Berger, M (1983) In defense of the case method: a reply to Argyris, *Academy of Management Review*, **8**, pp 329–33

Brookfield, S (1987) *Developing Critical Thinkers*, Open University Press, Milton Keynes

Buchanan, D and Huczynski, A (1997) *Organizational Behaviour: An introductory text*, Prentice Hall, Hemel Hempstead

Child, J (1984) *Organization: A guide to problems and practice*, Harper & Row, London

Clegg, W, Kemp, N and Legge, K (eds) (1985) *Case Studies in Organizational Behaviour*, Harper & Row, Cambridge

Cohen, A, Fink, S and Gadon, H (1994) *Effective Behavior in Organizations: Cases, concepts and student experiences*, Irwin, Chicago

Collinson, D and Hearn, J (1994) Naming men as men: implications for work, organization and management, *Gender, Work and Organization*, **1** (1), pp 2–22

Corbett, J (1994) *Critical Cases in Organisational Behaviour*, Macmillan, London

Daft, R (1998) *Organization Theory and Design*, South Western College Publishing, Cincinnati

Daft, R and Sharfman, M (1995) *Organization Theory: Cases and applications*, West, St Paul

Danieli, A and Thomas, A (1999) What about the workers? Studying the work of management educators and their orientations to management education, *Management Learning*, **30** (4), pp 449–71

Fayol, H (1930) *Industrial and General Administration*, Geneva International Management Institute

Ferguson, K (1984) *The Feminist Case Against Bureaucracy*, Temple University Press, Philadelphia

Fincham, R and Rhodes, P (1999) *Principles of Organizational Behaviour*, Oxford University Press, Oxford

Foucault, M (1979) Governmentality, *Ideology and Consciousness*, **6**, pp 5–21

Gibson, J, Ivancevich, J and Donnelly, J (2000) *Organizations: Behavior, structure, processes*, 10th edn, Irwin, Burr Ridge

Gowler, D, Legge, K and Clegg, C (eds) (1993) *Case Studies in Organizational Behaviour and Human Resource Management*, Sage, London

Grey, C and French, R (1996) Rethinking management education: an introduction, in *Rethinking Management Education*, ed R French and C Grey, pp 1–16, Sage, London

Griffith, W (1999) The reflecting team as an alternative case teaching model: a narrative, conversational approach, *Management Learning*, **30** (3), pp 343–62

Hammer, M (1995) *Re-engineering the Corporation: A manifesto for business revolution*, Brealey, London

Hassard, J and Parker, M (eds) (1993) *Postmodernism and Organizations*, Sage, London

Hatch, M (1997) *Organization Theory*, Oxford University Press, Oxford

Hofstede, G (1991) *Cultures and Organizations*, McGraw-Hill, Maidenhead

Hugstad, P (1983) *The Business School in the 1980s*, Praeger, New York

Jackson, N and Carter, P (2000) *Rethinking Organisational Behaviour*, Financial Times/Prentice Hall, Harlow

Lupton, T (1983) *Management and the Social Sciences*, Penguin, Harmondsworth

Macfarlane, B (1997) In search of an identity: lecturer perceptions of the business studies first degree, *Journal of Vocational Education and Training*, **49**, pp 5–20

Marcic, D and Seltzer, J (1997) *Organizational Behavior*, South Western College Publishing, Cincinnati

Marshall, J (1984) *Women Managers: Travellers in a male world*, John Wiley, Chichester

Mintzberg, H (1983) *Structure in Fives: Designing effective organizations*, Prentice Hall, Englewood Cliffs, NJ

Morgan, G (1997) *Images of Organisation*, Sage, London

Mullins, L (1999) *Management and Organisational Behaviour*, 5th edn, Financial Times Management, London

Oddou, G and Mendenhall, M (eds) (1998) *Cases in International Organizational Behavior*, Blackwell, Oxford

Peters, T and Waterman, R (1982) *In Search of Excellence: Lessons from America's best run companies*, Harper & Row, New York

Pringle, R (1989) *Secretaries Talk: Sexuality, power and work*, Verso, London

Pugh, D (ed) (1971) *Organization Theory: Selected readings*, Penguin, Harmondsworth

Roethlisberger, F and Dickson, W (1939) *Management and the Worker*, Harvard University Press, Cambridge, MA

Romm, T and Mahler, S (1991) The case study challenge – a new approach to an old method, *Management Learning*, **22** (4), pp 292–301

Savage, M and Witz, A (eds) (1992) *Gender and Bureaucracy*, Blackwell Publishers/The Sociological Review, Oxford

Schon, D (1983) *The Reflective Practitioner*, Temple Smith, London

Stewart, R (1984) The nature of management: a problem for management education?, *Journal of Management Studies*, **21** (3), pp 323–30

Taylor, F (1911) *Principles of Scientific Management*, Harper & Row, New York

Thomas, A (1993) *Controversies in Management*, Routledge, London

Thomas, A (1996) *The Organizational Behaviour Casebook: Cases and concepts in organizational behaviour*, International Thomson Business Press, London

Thomas, A (1997) The coming crisis in western management education, *Systems Practice*, **10** (4), pp 681–702

Thompson, P and McHugh, D (1995) *Work Organisations*, Macmillan, Basingstoke

Tompkins, T (2000) *Cases in Management and Organizational Behavior*, Prentice Hall, New York

Warwick Organisational Behaviour Staff (Antonacopoulou, E *et al*) (eds) (2000) *Organisational Studies: Critical perspectives (vol 1: Modes of Management; vol 2: Objectivity and its Other; vol 3: Selves and Subjects; vol 4: Evil Empires?)*, Routledge, London

Weber, M (1947) *The Theory of Social and Economic Organization*, Oxford University Press, London

Weightman, J (1999) *Introducing Organisational Behaviour*, Addison Wesley, Longman, Harlow

10

Business ethics

Bruce Macfarlane and Roger Ottewill

Introduction

Business ethics is often linked with social or corporate responsibility for learning and teaching purposes. This is because both are essentially normative in their orientation and concerned with the issue of values in business and management. Thus, they serve as an antidote to the technical and value-neutral character of much of the business and management curriculum. Business ethics draws substantially on the application of ethical theory as a means of analysing business behaviour. Corporate social responsibility is a constituent component of business ethics that acknowledges that organisations have obligations, extending beyond their formal legal duties, to a range of stakeholders.

Although business ethics has been taught at Harvard Business School since 1908, it did not become well established in the United States until the 1970s, where it now forms part of the curriculum in 90 per cent of business schools (Stark, 1993). Elsewhere growth in this subject area has been slower, with much of the provision in the UK dating from the late 1990s (Cummins, 1999).

Current interest in business ethics and corporate social responsibility can be explained by reference to a number of key drivers. High-profile financial scandals, environmental disasters and growing criticism of the power of multinationals operating in the developing world are among the contributing factors. The Guinness/Distillers takeover battle in the UK, the fatal gas leak from the Union Carbide plant in India and the silicone breast implant controversy in the United States are just a few examples of widely reported incidents. Governments have reacted to corporate misdemeanours by increasing the regulation of business activity. In the United States, for example, the Lockheed bribery scandal prompted legislation during the post–Watergate era in the form of the Foreign Corrupt Practices Act (1977) while, in the UK, whistleblowers are now afforded legislative protection in the wake of the *Herald of Free Enterprise* and Piper Alpha disasters. Moreover, corporate governance is no longer a matter left to the discretion of the boardroom. Enlightened entrepreneurs have come to recognize that they are living in a climate of heightened public scrutiny in which they are accountable to a wide range of stakeholders and have responsibilities that extend well beyond profit maximization.

Educational challenges

It is against the backdrop of scandal and controversy that the teaching of ethics to business and management students has evolved both as an integral part of the curriculum and as a discrete subject area. As implied earlier, business ethics provides a counterbalance to the operational-based subject areas such as strategic management (Chapter 12) and marketing (Chapter 13) that have tended to dominate the traditional business and management curriculum. It provides an opportunity for learners to think critically about some of the central tenets and cherished assumptions of business behaviour while producing more sensitized and sophisticated decision-makers. In pursuing this objective, however, educators are faced with some significant challenges.

Getting beyond scepticism

Challenging the scepticism of learners is perhaps the key task facing anyone who provides learner support in the spheres of business ethics and corporate social responsibility. This is because business ethics often appears in the curriculum at a relatively late stage after many of the attitudes of learners towards, and assumptions about, business behaviour have become firmly established. Given the emphasis on the operational aspects of business and management, mentioned earlier, learners can gain the false impression that the study of business is a value-free zone.

Learners often begin a business ethics course having already internalized a set of assumptions and market-based orthodoxies. Many assume that the only goal of business is profit maximization and have never questioned this (Gowen *et al*, 1996). The mindset of many learners is also underpinned by an entrenched belief in business life as a legitimately separate sphere of human behaviour. Business life, according to this view, is a game with different rules, a 'dog-eat-dog' culture removed from the niceties of private life. 'Business ethics' is a contradiction in terms.

Thus, it is essential to get learners to confront their own presuppositions, often based on ethical relativism, at an early stage of a business ethics course. One way of doing this is by tackling the 'sceptical' literature about business ethics and asking learners to identify the contradictions and assumptions contained in classic articles by, for example, Milton Friedman (1970) or Albert Carr (1968). An alternative approach is to use a negotiation role play (Asherman and Asherman, 1995) to demonstrate the importance of trust and mutual benefit to both parties in any bargain or to ask students to identify the adjectives they would associate with the words 'business' and 'professional'. This latter technique can provide starkly contrasting word lists but reveal in the process a false dualism. Many of those 'in business' are professional people such as accountants, bankers and lawyers. These techniques begin to unravel the notion that business life is purely amoral and highlights the fact that many managers are committed to ethical standards within a professional context.

An analogy with war may also be used as a means of tackling scepticism. A state of war is frequently invoked as a metaphor for business activity but is usually represented in Machiavellian terms as taking place without regard to any moral rules. The work of Walzer (1977) has demonstrated the shortcomings of this 'realist' depiction of war and the considerable evidence of moral rules throughout the history of warfare. Learners might be asked to identify 'rules' of war, such as treating prisoners of war with respect, not bombing innocent civilians, or limitations on the actions of soldiers (Macfarlane, 1999). If we recognize the legitimacy of the phrase 'war crimes', in this most conflictual form of human activity, then how can we deny that there is a place for ethics in business life? Students can be asked to build on this analogy by identifying the moral 'rules' of war in business.

While learners may recognize that ethical considerations ought to play a role in business this view may be shaped entirely by the notion of enlightened self-interest. 'Good ethics is good business' is a well-worn slogan. However, it can represent a cynical 'stance' that do-gooding is just about public relations. While it is self-evident that a poor ethical reputation can adversely affect a company's long-term profitability this argument is based on a purely strategic imperative. In confronting this view, a distinction might be drawn between the internal, or 'private', world of the business organisation (eg dealing with employees) and the external, or more 'public', world of business relationships (eg communicating with customers). In other words, not all business activity tends to be exposed to the same level of public scrutiny and, therefore, acting ethically only as a means of avoiding adverse publicity fails to provide a rationale for action on all occasions. It is, moreover, a morally bankrupt position offering no imperative to act ethically apart from prudential self-interest.

Teaching rather than preaching

For those dealing with ethical issues in learning and teaching a significant challenge concerns the extent to which they should come 'off the fence'. Usually this involves striking a difficult balance between making explicit their own values and creating a climate in which participation is maximized and mutual respect for different positions is maintained.

Many educators in this field have commitments to particular religious or ethical positions. There is always a danger, however, in being perceived by learners as too 'preachy'. Ethics teaching naturally involves discussion and argument about differing interpretations of right and wrong. In this respect, learning facilitators play a crucial role as class arbitrators giving everyone a fair opportunity to contribute and encouraging all shades of opinion. Taking an overtly partisan stance might stifle contributions from less assertive learners. At the same time, students have to be encouraged to re-evaluate their own assumptions by making clear one's own. This is all part of the process of tackling scepticism about the legitimacy of business ethics and demonstrating a commitment to the subject!

Most writers on business ethics agree that it should be about raising ethical awareness rather than 'moral conversion' (eg Cooke and Ryan, 1988; Trezise, 1994; Gowen *et al*, 1996). Above all, business ethics should enable learners to make informed and reasoned ethical choices and help them in the process of developing their own personal ethical code.

Meeting the needs of inexperienced learners

Learners with little or no direct experience of ethical issues in a business and management context need to be 'broken in' gently. One way of doing this is to focus initially on intracorporate issues. Topics such as workplace bullying, discrimination, surveillance and personality testing will connect more closely with any experience they might have had, which is likely to be as a front-line employee in a service industry setting. Approaching the study of business ethics via familiar territory means that ethical theory can be applied on the basis of the actual (or potential) experience of learners (see Chapter 2). Such learners can then move on to apply theory in less familiar contexts, such as the ethics of international business. Nonetheless, it is inevitable that the influence of organisational culture and leadership on the ethical 'climate' of an organisation is likely to be better understood by more mature learners.

While students can be led from the familiar to the unfamiliar in terms of their own experiences, learners at all levels may still find it daunting to get to grips with ethical theory. Business and management students are not accustomed to a curriculum geared towards philosophy, such as that of Kant or Rawls. Building an understanding of different ethical positions tends to be a slow process that, if rushed, can result in oversimplistic interpretations. Linking the learning of separate ethical theories to an appropriate case study illustrative of this mode of reasoning is one possible approach to this challenge. However, the traditional emphasis on seeking to solve moral quandaries, via the rule-based theories of Kantianism, utilitarianism, rights and contractarianism, is subject to criticism from advocates of a virtue ethics approach who argue that this results in context-free, character-free decision-making (eg McCracken, Martin and Shaw, 1998). Adopting a virtue-based approach has important implications in terms of the choice of case study material. The focus on the development of good habits and character within virtue ethics also implies a greater emphasis on the fostering of affective learning outcomes rather than rule-based templates for decision-making.

Aims, objectives and learning outcomes

What then is the purpose of including a study of business ethics in the business and management curriculum? Stiles, Jameson and Lord (1993) contend that there are five aims for a business ethics course: stimulating the moral imagination; identifying ethical issues; bringing out a sense of moral obligation in accordance with the learner's value set; developing analytical competence; and tolerating disagreement. Other commentators (eg de Rond, 1996) stress that the aim of teaching business ethics should be to improve the decision-making skills of learners, ensuring that this incorporates a consideration of the ethical dimension. Typically, with this aim in mind, learners on a business ethics course will initially be exposed to a range of principle-based ethical positions such as utilitarianism, Kantianism or rights theory. These theories are then applied to case study material to facilitate 'ethical' decision-making. There are even simplified decision-making models available that cherry-pick aspects of ethical theory in a step-by-step approach, such as Blanchard and Peale's (1988) 'ethics check'. An emphasis is placed on the importance of avoiding decisions that may have costly implications for the ethical reputation of the business. Issues for discussion might include the ethics of new product development, bribery or whistleblowing.

An alternative, or possibly complementary, aim for a business ethics course is to provide learners with opportunities for developing a broader, critical perspective with regard to the purposes and effects of the business system. This approach to business ethics might focus more on issues that lie outside the practical decision-making control of individual managers. It also involves a more fundamental questioning of the business system, drawing on an array of economic and political theorists, such as Marx, Galbraith and Schumacher, rather than moral theorists like Kant and Bentham, and thereby connects more readily with the notion of social responsibility. Issues for discussion might include the effects of globalization, property rights and pollution, and 'fair' wages.

The two contrasting approaches to business ethics sketched out above, and summarized in Table 10.1, are a manifestation of the wider debate regarding the purpose of a business and management education, to which attention was drawn in Chapters 1 and 4. Thus, leading texts on business ethics tend to reflect either the 'managerialist' or 'critical' conceptions of the curriculum. Most emphasize the application of moral theory as a basis for managerial decision-making. Chryssides and Kaler (1993), for example, argue that business ethics is essentially a practical study 'for' business while hinting that moral theory is vital in providing a rationale. 'It [ie business ethics] has, then, an essentially practical purpose. We inquire not simply to be informed, but to inform our actions; to provide those actions with a

Table 10.1   Alternative curriculum models applied to business ethics

	Managerial Model	**Critical Model**
Theoretical foundations	ethical theory	economic, political and social theory
Practical applications	whistleblowing; bribery; advertising	globalization; 'fair' wages; meaningful work

better and sounder basis than they might otherwise have' (Chryssides and Kaler, 1993: 12).

However, other texts take a more eclectic view of business ethics as a general study about the business system and its relationship with society. In this respect, Hoffman and Frederick's (1995) anthology includes readings on the concepts of economic justice and meaningful work. They also state that an evaluation of the business system is part of their purpose. One of the four tasks of the anthology is: 'An ethical investigation of the context in which American business is conducted – that is, capitalism or the free market. Does the system truly contribute to a good society and reflect our most important social values? In particular, is it a just system, one that reflects our beliefs about the fair distribution of goods and services?' (Hoffman and Frederick, 1995: 2).

By contrast, Lippke (1995) espouses an avowedly radical view that business ethics should be about confronting the structure of capitalism from an egalitarian perspective.

There is no reason, in principle, why both the 'managerialist' and 'critical' approaches cannot be embodied in the objectives and the learning outcomes of a business ethics course. Outcomes can also be mapped against the general framework outlined in Chapter 4, with the cognitive most closely equating to the 'critical' and the affective and adaptive occupational skills to the 'managerialist'. Ethical theory serves as the knowledge-base upon which attitudes and values are re-examined and employment-related skills, such as decision-making and persuasion, are developed. Some examples are provided in Table 10.2.

Table 10.2   Examples of learning outcomes for business ethics

Area	**Examples**
Cognitive	Evaluate the value of ethical theory in determining the propriety of a course of action.
	Explain the regulatory environment with respect to a particular profession.
Affective	Manifest a tolerance of disagreement in discussing an ethical dilemma facing a business organisation.
	Demonstrate sensitivity to ethical issues arising within the 'public' world of business.
Adaptive	Apply decision-making skills in resolving moral issues in the workplace.
	Use persuasion skills to convince others of the efficacy of a moral stance.

Cutting across these outcomes is a range of ethical issues that can be conceptualized as a series of overlapping areas starting from the organisation and moving outward, as illustrated in the box below. This is closely linked to the mapping of stakeholder interests and incorporates aspects of social responsibility.

Mapping ethical issues

- *intracorporate issues*, eg privacy and employee surveillance, discrimination, bullying, whistleblowing;
- *customer issues*, eg marketing and advertising techniques, pricing, product safety and development;
- *intercorporate issues*, eg 'spying' on competitors, price wars, treatment of suppliers, use of marketing power, hostile take-overs;
- *societal issues*, eg multinationals and the developing world, bribery and culture, pollution and environmental standards.

Such issues provide the focus for much of the learning, teaching and assessment within business ethics.

Learning, teaching and assessment activities

In designing learning, teaching and assessment activities for business ethics and social responsibility, it is important to recognize that most of the leading textbooks and case study material still tend to be authored by US writers and researchers. Thus, educators must adjust their strategy to take account of the cultural context in which learning is taking place. The first major British textbook, *Key Issues in Business Ethics* (Donaldson, 1989), only appeared at the end of the 1980s, while UK and European case study material is still rated as inadequate (Cummins, 1999). However, popular new UK and European-based texts and an evolving European research community are beginning to redress this imbalance, albeit slowly, as illustrated by the resources listed in the box below.

Key resources for business ethics

Leading journals

- *Business and Society Review;*
- *Business Ethics: A European review;*
- *Business Ethics Quarterly;*
- *Ethical Perspective;*

- *Journal of Business Ethics*;
- *Teaching Business Ethics.*

Popular textbooks

- Chryssides, G and Kaler, J (1993) *An Introduction to Business Ethics*;
- Trevino, L and Nelson, K (1999) *Managing Business Ethics: Straight talk about how to do it right.*

Organisations and useful Web sites

- Australian Business Ethics Network (www.bf.rmit.edu.au/Aben);
- European Business Ethics Network (www.eben.org);
- Institute of Business Ethics (www.ibe.org.uk);
- Institute of Global Ethics (www.globalethics.org);
- International Society of Business, Economics and Ethics (www.synethos. org/isbee);
- New Academy of Business (www.new-academy.ac.uk);
- Transparency International (www.transparency.de).

Moreover, there is also scope for students with considerable work experience to generate their own learning resources. If provided with adequate guidance, they should be able to produce mini case studies that can serve to enrich their own learning experience and that of their peers, thereby contributing to the ongoing development of one of the traditional methods of learning, teaching and assessment in business ethics.

Case studies

Most of the best-known and widely used business ethics case studies share a number of characteristics. First, they tend to represent well-publicized examples of unethical behaviour. The Ford Pinto, Dow Corning and silicone breast implants, Union Carbide and the Bhopal disaster in India, the *Herald of Free Enterprise* and Nestlé Infant formula milk scandal are examples of this phenomenon. There is a danger, though, that by focusing on a large number of such cases, often involving a combination of corporate negligence and significant loss of life, this will encourage the view among learners that business practice is almost exclusively 'unethical'. While salutary lessons can be drawn from such cases, a balance needs to be struck between high-profile wrongdoing and more positive examples of business practice often demonstrating the associated importance of leadership and culture in influencing behaviour. Organisational role models, such as The Co-operative Bank in the UK, or other case study material offering positive examples of business practice, like *Stories of Virtue in Business* (Weber, 1995), can act as a counterweight in this respect, especially for facilitators committed to a virtue-based approach. Case studies focusing on character failure, rather than a corporate fiasco, can introduce further variety while providing an insight into why collective decision-making can falter under competitive pressure (McCracken, Martin and Shaw, 1998).

Second, the overwhelming majority of organisations featured in case studies tend to be large multinational corporations. Since sole traders and business partnerships, along with public and voluntary sector bodies, play a significant role in the economy and society generally, case studies should also focus on the ethical challenges facing these types of organisation. The unity of ownership and control in unincorporated bodies means that owners often find it easier to 'walk the talk' of their own ethical code. Inviting visiting speakers from these types of organisations locally is one way of redressing the imbalance in available case study material.

Last, like most case studies those in business ethics conventionally place learners in the position of a senior executive or, sometimes, a middle manager (Badaracco and Webb, 1995). This conveys the false impression that business ethics is only about managerial decision-making when it equally involves front-line workers facing ethical dilemmas while interacting with colleagues and customers.

Although care needs to be taken to create the right balance with respect to the use of case studies, they can act as a valuable tool for evaluating the link between ethical theory and the justification for decisions in business practice. As in other subject areas, such as business organisation (Chapter 9) and strategic management (Chapter 12), case studies are extremely helpful as a means of both stimulating general class-based discussion and assessing the ability of individual learners, or groups of students, to apply ethical theory correctly and creatively.

Role plays

By confronting learners with moral dilemmas in a business setting, role plays can be an effective learning tool. Used creatively, they also make it easier for learners to appreciate many of the extraneous factors that contribute to decision-making, such as personality clashes, organisational culture, prejudices and leadership style. A simple whistleblowing role play (see box on page 117) can reveal some of these complexities.

Role plays can also be used to focus on critical decision-making dilemmas facing an organisation's employees in relation to a variety of stakeholders, such as co-workers, customers, suppliers and environmental pressure groups. Even with a large group of students in a formal lecture setting, they can be deployed, with learners working in pairs for short periods and using a selection of responses to demonstrate the complexity of ethical issues.

Reflective learning logs

Reflective learning logs provide a means of combining learning and assessment in a business ethics context. Maintaining a log enables learners to record their experiences and reflections. It also provides educators with a means of assessing student

A whistleblowing role play

Role card 1: The whistleblower

You are about to enter the office of your line manager. You work as a sales executive and have become increasingly concerned about the activities of Bill who heads up your sales team. Although Bill is a great motivator and you admire his sales record, you have noticed that he routinely overclaims on expenses by as much as 20 or 30 per cent. You know this because Bill has asked you to pass on his claims to the Finance Department on several occasions when you have worked jointly together and incurred the same real level of expenses. When you confronted Bill about the matter he just shrugged his shoulders and retorted, 'So what? What's the big deal? Everyone does it?' You feel his actions amount to theft and show little respect for the company's stakeholders. After much agonizing on the right course of action you have decided to tell your line manager.

Role card 2: The line manager

You are just about to have a formal meeting with Karen, a sales executive, who has requested to see you. Rumours have been circulating that she is about to make some kind of complaint about Bill. You know Bill well and understand his value to the company. He is the company's most successful sales executive, currently leading a team that includes Karen. Bill's very much his own man and a bit of a lovable rogue in his own way. Although he is unorthodox, he gets results and your department is currently being squeezed to meet a target to increase sales by 30 per cent this quarter. You have heard on the grapevine that Karen is not a 'team player' and tends to be a bit of a 'whinger'.

development, as illustrated on page 118. By connecting ethical theories to their own experiences, learners can begin to reflect on the forces that shape decisions and draw lessons for future action. Although some learners may have limited experience on which to reflect, most will be able to draw on something of relevance, such as part-time employment or voluntary work. Clearly, learning logs are particularly well suited to postgraduate and mature learners, who are in a stronger position to connect ethical theory with their own working environment. An example is given in the box on page 118.

A learning log, which should normally be written in the first person, may be used in a more open-ended way as a kind of personal diary in which students make their own decisions about log entries, perhaps producing a summary reflection or commentary. It might also be adapted for a virtue-based approach to business ethics by using it exclusively as a means by which learners can self-track their own character development.

The ethics learning log

First entry: Where do you stand?

Summarize your *opinions* and *attitudes* concerning the role of ethics in business and society. Distinguish between what you think *happens* and what you think is *right*. Do you think the business world has its own rules? Are moral rules even relevant to business practice? Is business like a 'game' with 'winners' and 'losers'? Are ethics only relevant to 'private life'? What is the role of business in society? Is profit maximization its only obligation? Above all, be as frank as possible in expressing your point of view.

Second entry: Evaluate the theories

Reflect on the ethical theories and associated cases that have been studied so far and comment on how these have influenced your thinking. Which theory/theories have you found has influenced your thinking the most? Drawing on ethical theories, which is the most practical and fairest to apply in resolving decision-making dilemmas? You might want to connect your argument with your own working experiences.

Third entry: The critical incident

Describe a 'critical incident' you have experienced or witnessed in a work-based setting, involving an aspect of ethics, either as an employee or as a customer. Reflect on whether you, or other persons, made the right ethical decision(s). Were there factors that explain the decision reached, regardless of whether you now consider this the right one? You should change the names of real organisations and individuals involved in order to protect their identity.

Fourth entry: The reflection

Reflect back on your first log entry. Do you still hold the same attitudes and opinions? How has your thinking about business ethics developed since the beginning of the course? If your thinking has changed, try to explain why. What have you learnt from this course? How useful will it be to you in future, particularly with respect to your career?

Other methods

Other ways of approaching learning and teaching in business ethics include the discussion of key readings either in class or via Web-boards; linking work experience to the needs of the wider community via 'service-learning' (Friedman, 1996); computer simulations (Schumann, Anderson and Scott, 1997); video case studies (Hosmer, 1997); and using wider literature (Shephard, Goldsby and Gerde, 1997) or even controversial movies (see box at the top of page 119) as a basis for stimulating debate about a range of ethical issues (Berger and Pratt, 1998; MacAdams and Duclos, 1999).

Business ethics at the movies

- *Bonfire of the Vanities* (1988);
- *Business as Usual* (1987);
- *Glengarry Glen Ross* (1992);
- *Rising Sun* (1986);
- *The Insider* (1999);
- *Tin Men* (1987);
- *Wall Street* (1987).

Integration

Despite the value-neutral approach to many parts of the business and management curriculum, ethical considerations do apply. Indeed, there are established research communities focusing on the ethical dimension of accountancy and marketing education, for example. Potential links between business ethics and a selection of business-related subject areas are illustrated in the box below.

Links between business ethics and other subject areas

- *strategic management*, eg stakeholder theory, corporate governance, social responsibility, global business operations;
- *human resource management*, eg personality and drugs testing, employee surveillance, discrimination, bullying;
- *leadership and organisational culture*, eg leadership styles and values, codes of conduct;
- *business economics*, eg sustainable development, 'free' goods and the environment;
- *business law*, eg advertising regulations, anti-trust laws;
- *marketing*, eg deceptive advertising and pricing, advertising to children, pyramid selling.

Thus, rather than teaching ethics as a discrete subject, many institutions of HE have sought to integrate it as a core theme throughout their business and management curriculum. Alternatively, strategic management (Chapter 12), the traditional capstone of the curriculum both in the UK (Gammie, 1995) and North America (Bart, 1988), has been used as a vehicle for considering ethical issues. This makes sense given the increased regulation of the company boardroom, the need for large corporations to address the concerns of multiple stakeholders, the effects of monopolistic market power and the impact of strategic decisions on regional employment, national economies and developing nations.

However, one of the difficulties in teaching ethics as part of strategic management is that there is often limited time and space in which to challenge the sceptical attitudes of learners and/or to create an understanding of ethics as more than a strategic constraint. There is also the danger that learners will simply equate ethics with the legal/regulatory framework if study is confined to topics such as corporate governance. One way of creating a better understanding is by focusing on the impact of strategic decisions from a range of stakeholder perspectives. This might include the implications of change for employees, the limits of 'fair' competition, the relationship between market power and the public interest, and the effects of global competition on national cultures. Broadly, an ethical dimension within a strategic management course should enable learners to appreciate the values inherent in strategic decision-making.

Reflection and evaluation

Teaching business ethics involves encouraging students to think reflectively and critically about the rights and wrongs of business activity. This is a demanding process to support and requires a reciprocal level of reflection and evaluation from educators. Reflecting on whether the right learning environment was achieved requires thought to be given to a range of questions relating to the challenges mentioned earlier and the extent to which aims have been achieved. Some examples of the kinds of question that might be asked to facilitate reflection and evaluation are provided in the box below.

Examples of reflective questions for business ethics educators

- How much initial scepticism did learners display at the commencement of their study of business ethics?
- How effective was the approach used to reduce any initial scepticism?
- Was the balance right between 'teaching' and 'preaching'?
- Did the class tolerate different ethical perspectives during discussion?
- Were learners given the opportunity of evaluating ethical theory?
- Were learners able to develop and express their own individual ethical position?
- Did learners share their own working experiences as part of the learning process?
- To what extent were learners able to draw on personal experience as a basis for engaging with ethical principles and theory?
- Were learners provided with a sufficient variety of case studies and examples to illustrate the range of ethical dilemmas in different types of organisation?

Given the importance of reflection and evaluation in dealing with values, it might also be appropriate to incorporate questions of this kind into the learning and assessment strategy. For example, learners could be asked to appraise the values espoused by the institution responsible for their learning environment as a means of enhancing the rigour of the evaluation process.

Conclusion

Business ethics remains something of a 'Cinderella' subject area on many business and management programmes with no adequate career structure, at least for UK academics in this field (Cummins, 1999). However, courses in business ethics are beginning to play an increasingly important role in business and management education. They provide learners with a rare, and often belated, opportunity to reflect on their assumptions about business life and the relationship between organisations and wider society. Teaching this subject offers a range of interesting and important educational challenges not least of which is demonstrating that ethical considerations should be fundamental, rather than tangential, to the conduct of business life.

References

Asherman, I and Asherman, S (1995) *25 Negotiation Role Plays*, HRD Press, Amherst

Badaracco, J and Webb, A (1995) Business ethics: a view from the trenches, *California Management Review*, **37** (2), pp 8–28

Bart, C (1988) The undergraduate business policy course in Canada: academics' approaches and practitioners' prescriptions, *Management Education and Development*, **19** (4), pp 311–17

Berger, J and Pratt, C (1998) Teaching business-communication ethics with controversial films, *Journal of Business Ethics*, **17**, pp 1817–23

Blanchard, K and Peale, N (1988) *The Power of Ethical Management*, William Morrow and Company, New York

Carr, A (1968) Is business bluffing ethical?, *Harvard Business Review*, **46**, pp 143–53

Chryssides, G and Kaler, J (1993) *An Introduction to Business Ethics*, International Thomson, London

Cooke, R and Ryan, L (1988) The relevance of ethics to management education, *Journal of Management Development*, **7** (2), pp 28–38

Cummins, J (1999) *The Teaching of Business Ethics at Undergraduate, Postgraduate and Professional Levels in the UK*, Institute of Business Ethics, London

de Rond, M (1996) Business ethics, where do we stand? Towards a new enquiry, *Management Decision*, **34** (3), pp 54–61

Donaldson, J (1989) *Key Issues in Business Ethics*, Academic Press, London

Friedman, M (1970) The social responsibility of business is to increase profits, *The New York Times Magazine*, September 13, pp 32–33, 122, 124, 126

Friedman, S (1996) Community involvement projects in Wharton's MBA curriculum, *Journal of Business Ethics*, **15**, pp 95–101

Gammie, B (1995) Undergraduate management education: an analysis of rationale and methodology, *International Journal of Educational Management*, **9** (4), pp 34–40

Gowen, C *et al* (1996) Integrating business ethics into a graduate program, *Journal of Business Ethics*, **15**, pp 671–79

Hoffman, W and Frederick, R (1995) *Business Ethics: Readings and cases in corporate morality*, McGraw-Hill, New York

Hosmer, L (1997) A question of power: Hydro-Quebec and the great whale controversy – a 35 minute video for in-class use, *Teaching Business Ethics*, **1** (1), pp 97–106

Lippke, R (1995) *Radical Business Ethics*, Rowman and Littlefield, Lanham

MacAdams, T and Duclos, L (1999) Teaching business ethics with computer-based multimedia? A cautionary analysis, *Teaching Business Ethics*, **3** (1), pp 57–67

Macfarlane, B (1999) Re-evaluating the realist conception of war as a business metaphor, *Teaching Business Ethics*, **3** (1), pp 27–35

McCracken, J, Martin, W and Shaw, B (1998) Virtue ethics and the parable of the Sadhu, *Journal of Business Ethics*, **17**, pp 25–38

Schumann, P, Anderson, P and Scott, T (1997) Using computer-based simulation exercises to teach business ethics, *Teaching Business Ethics*, **1** (3), pp 163–81

Shephard, J, Goldsby, M and Gerde, V (1997) Teaching business ethics through literature, *Teaching Business Ethics*, **1** (1), pp 33–51

Stark, A (1993) What's the matter with business ethics?, *Harvard Business Review*, **71** (3), pp 38–47

Stiles, P, Jameson, A and Lord, A (1993) Teaching business ethics: an open learning approach, *Management Education and Development*, **24** (3), pp 246–61

Trevino, L and Nelson, K (1999) *Managing Business Ethics: Straight talk about how to do it right*, Wiley, Chichester

Trezise, E (1994) Practical reflections on teaching business ethics to undergraduates, *Business Ethics: A European review*, **3** (3), pp 180–85

Walzer, M (1977) *Just and Unjust Wars: A moral argument with historical illustrations*, Basic Books, New York

Weber, C (1995) *Stories of Virtue in Business*, University Press of America, Lanham

11

International business

Karina Jensen

Introduction

With the increasing globalization of business activity and the advent of the knowledge-based economy, the importance of international business for business and management students cannot be overstated. Success in the global market-place depends increasingly upon developing new approaches to leadership education and economic literacy that are truly cross-cultural in their orientation. New leadership skills embrace a commitment to a global mission, coupled with the ability to understand and lead multicultural teams and to harness and transfer organisational practices into innovative solutions worldwide. The new economy demands an understanding of the similarities and differences of international business environments, including political, social and technological settings, as well as the development of intercultural managerial effectiveness.

Since international business has become a priority for today's business organi-sations, it is important to address the question of how best to facilitate learning in this field. Best practice, as evidenced by some of the leading international business schools in Europe and the United States, indicates that the development of global or cross-cultural competency skills is becoming of increasing importance in the learning environment for students in this subject area. Moreover, as organisations continue to face a changing global economy, so educators must be alert to the implications of these developments for the form and content of the learning experiences of their students.

Educational challenges

Arguably the overriding challenge facing those engaged in the design and delivery of courses in international business is to develop a curriculum that will enable learners to operate successfully in the global economy. Thus, there needs to be a shift from an 'about' business focus to one in which far higher priority is given to a study 'for' business (see Chapter 1). The vocational importance of international business has been strengthened by the expanding global economy, as has the need for those who can fill positions of global leadership. In a 1997 study, where US Fortune 500 firms were surveyed, 85 per cent did not believe that they had an adequate number of global leaders. Another study of 40 global leaders in 50 firms across Europe, North America and Asia showed that the top strategies for developing the mindsets of global leaders were identified as multi-cultural teams, international travel, global training programmes and transfer assignments overseas (Gregersen, Morrison and Black, 1998). Moreover, Jonathan Winter, Managing Director of Whiteway Research International, has argued that a successful business graduate needs to be able to manage a lifelong relationship between work and learning. In preparation for a 21st-century career, he has recommended that graduates obtain attributes and skills, such as self-awareness, reflective learning, cross-cultural sensitivity, teamwork, foreign languages and international experience (Winter, 1997). On the one hand, the international business professional needs to recognize the local and global strengths of structures, operations and resources and, on the other hand, the global manager must possess the cultural knowledge and communication skills to motivate people within a multicultural business environment.

The demand for these attributes is creating a new recruitment model for business professionals. As indicated earlier, the critical new human resource requirement is cross-cultural competence, where the global manager requires a broader knowledge base with openness and adaptability to different cultural approaches (RAND Institute on Education and Training, 1994).

Preparing learners 'for' international business

Although institutions of HE recognize the need for international business skills, corporate criticism of internationally educated individuals continues to grow. Companies emphasize the global nature of business and the need to manage an increasingly diverse work force, which make it essential for managers to integrate business and cross-cultural knowledge. However, a study on global preparedness and human resources found incongruity between university preparation and corporate needs and expectations in Europe and the United States (RAND Institute on Education and Training, 1994). With cognitive, interpersonal, social and communication skills receiving greater attention from employers, the ability to apply knowledge successfully appears to rely on the concurrent and effective use of these skills in a genuinely cross-cultural learning environment. Thus, the challenge for universities and educators is to embrace a new learning process based on the cross-cultural learning model (see Table 11.1).

Table 11.1 The cross-cultural learning model (Jensen, 2000)

From a Parochial View	To a Global View
sciences	humanities and sciences
teaching	learning partnership
learning content	cultural learning process
goal-directed, structured and learning	conscious, reflective and collaborative learning
personal development	cultural self-awareness
teamwork	cross-cultural team learning
monocultural approach	multicultural approach
country-specific education and training	lifelong learning of cultural contexts

However, successful implementation of such a model depends on securing attitudinal change. Hence, the commitment of educators is of particular importance, as is their willingness and ability to foster in their learners personal traits of flexibility, adaptability, openness, cultural empathy, commitment, innovation and entrepreneurialism. All of these are viewed as key success factors in the emerging global, knowledge-based economy. Yet, the corporations in the RAND (1994) study did not believe that institutions of HE could fulfil these requirements. A worldwide survey of international business education in the 1990s further corroborates the view that most universities seek to provide only an awareness of the international dimension of business, rather than to develop cross-cultural competence or expertise (Arpan, Folks and Kwok, 1993). In other words, the emphasis is still very much 'about' rather than 'for' international business. Thus, although there may be a formal commitment to internationalization in mission statements and strategic plans, institutions of HE still face considerable challenges in this respect.

Internationalizing curriculum content

As Akhter and Ahmed (1996) point out, there has been insufficient internationalization of the curriculum. In response, the challenge is to put into practice the three levels of international knowledge that most effectively describe the learning process: global awareness, global understanding and global competence (Kedia and Cornwall, 1994), through the development of appropriate models. While traditional management models clearly paved the way for strategic thinking and structural frameworks in business, they rarely addressed the dynamics of human interaction in the global market-place. Multinational companies have realized that they need to look beyond their traditional management models and organisational structures to develop global competitiveness, multinational flexibility and world-wide learning capability simultaneously (Moore, 1996). The intersection of global strategy and culture has also demanded increased attention to international organisational behaviour and global human resource systems. Aside from the global integration of functions, operations and facilities, the emerging organisational structure requires an international perspective for managing knowledge. Taken together, these considerations can be conceptualized as an emerging international business learning model (see Figure 11.1).

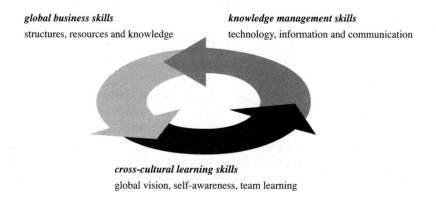

global business skills
structures, resources and knowledge

knowledge management skills
technology, information and communication

cross-cultural learning skills
global vision, self-awareness, team learning

Figure 11.1   Emerging international business learning model (Jensen, 2000)

Underlying this model is the need for a global vision and for learners to question their preconceptions with respect to other cultures.

Fostering a global vision

The ability to exchange ideas and pursue activities across international borders and to create intercultural learning communities is crucial to the fostering of a global vision. Clearly, this presents a challenge in terms of the cross-cultural development of educators, which depends, to a significant extent, on the establishment and maintenance of international linkages between universities (May and May, 1996) and securing access to international learning resources. Indeed, a network of shared information between education partners and multinational companies offers a valuable knowledge bank for learning facilitators. Technology further facilitates network outreach programmes through the use of the Internet, electronic databases and communication systems. These initiatives considerably increase the availability and quality of international resources for staff development, research, course content and case studies. In short, educators must take the lead in exploiting opportunities for giving practical expression to the imperatives of a global vision. In so doing, they can lay the foundations for facilitating the process of cross-cultural learning.

Facilitating cross-cultural learning

From the perspective of cross-cultural learning, perceptions of students concerning the complexities of international business often need to be challenged. The ability to explain how economic, government, political and financial issues affect international business is inherently tied to the ability to recognize and understand culturally different operating environments. This requires the acceptance and integration of different cultural beliefs and values. It also involves the basic recognition and understanding of the learners' own philosophical beliefs and value system. Group exercises and simulations using artificial cultures can assist in opening mindsets and perspectives for learners. Such exercises might make use of an international trade scenario where members of groups represent significantly different cultures, which require behaviour modification. The next step is to expose learners to real, as opposed to artificial, cultural differences.

Here, a key challenge for educators is to leverage cultural diversity for in-depth practice of intercultural communication and teamwork. The learning environment therefore needs to incorporate international students and culturally diverse groups in order to develop the cross-cultural capability required within international business settings. This requires a simulated or 'real world' project, based upon teamwork with culturally diverse members. Field-based projects in international business provide very effective learning situations. A good example is the selection of culturally diverse and cross-disciplinary teams to perform feasibility studies and market entry analyses for companies in foreign markets. Aside from gaining practice in international business strategy, the projects address capability needs for cross-cultural management issues through the teamwork process (Ottewill and Laughton, 2000). Such projects are, of course, an example of valuing students as a resource rather than viewing them simply as empty vessels to be filled with knowledge and expertise (see Chapter 2).

International business represents an intense and diverse learning environment that can no longer be sustained with traditional methods of monocultural learning, such as business models, cultural profiles or country research. Although helpful, they serve only as a supplement for learning the real interactions that take place in changing and culturally diverse business environments. Genuine cross-cultural learning involves knowledge of oneself in relation to other cultural contexts (Vaill, 1996). Moreover, the open and adaptive mindset required for cross-cultural learning is essential for performing effectively in work situations that straddle the globe and for adjusting to the distinctive mentalities and styles associated with different cultures. Cross-cultural learning is characterized by conscious, reflective and collaborative practices that involve actual business scenarios, simulations and projects as well as a commitment to learning that is lifelong.

Aims, objectives and learning outcomes

In responding to the growing demand for global management skills and cross-cultural competence, the aims and objectives of international business courses need to incorporate the features identified in the previous section, within the context of a commitment to lifelong learning. The key components are a global focus, cross-cultural consciousness-raising and the development of communication and teamwork skills. In articulating such aims and objectives the distinction between educators, business professionals and students is gradually disappearing with the emergence of the concept of a broadly defined global learning community. This is based on collaborative partnerships and team-building, which serve to facilitate communication and develop better understanding for mutual learning and knowledge creation. Such a perspective is clearly reflected in the European Union's Policy on Education. The goal of creating a 'Europe of Knowledge' is based upon the concept of lifelong learning processes concerning pan-European integrated education. The development plan includes mental mobility (open-mindedness), virtual mobility (technology use), partnerships, pilot projects, linguistic development and a European resource network (European Commission, 1999).

Turning specifically to learning outcomes, these can be mapped against the framework of cognitive, affective and adaptable occupational skills outlined in Chapter 4 (see Table 11.2). International business and cross-cultural management theory supplies a knowledge-base for cognitive application, whereas cross-cultural sensitivity, self-awareness and teamwork provide the affective attributes and adaptable occupational skills.

Table 11.2 Examples of learning outcomes for international business

Area	Examples
Cognitive	Evaluate business and cross-cultural models and theories in relation to a particular aspect of globalization Compare and contrast the economic environments of a range of countries
Affective	Maintain an open mindset and tolerance for different cultural perspectives on business problems Demonstrate sensitivity to cross-cultural issues in employee relations
Adaptive	Apply teamwork and process facilitation skills in conducting feasibility studies Utilize reflective, entrepreneurial and action learning skills when experiencing different cultures for the first time

Learning, teaching and assessment activities

Effective learning, teaching and assessment activities in international business need to be set within a multicultural learning environment supported by appropriate social, technology and knowledge architectures. Individual and group learning can be explored through the development of social processes involving teams, self-management, empowerment and collaboration. Technology is applied as a tool that assists further learning through networks and software for access to information. A strong knowledge network is created through action-reflective learning processes that promote shared knowledge and collective business intelligence and through leveraging the resources available within the business and academic communities. There are numerous organisations, materials and sources of expertise that can provide assistance in designing and delivering courses in international business (see box below).

Key resources for international business

Leading journals

- *International Business Education Development*;
- *International Business Review*;
- *International Journal of Training and Development*;
- *Journal of Higher Education*;
- *Journal of International Business Studies*;
- *Journal of Management Development*;
- *Journal of Teaching in International Business.*

Popular textbooks

- Adler, N J (2000) *International Dimensions of Organizational Behavior*;
- Czinkota, M R *et al* (2001) *Global Business*;
- Doz, Y L and Prahalad, C K (1999) *The Multinational Mission*;
- Marquardt, M (1998) *The Global Advantage*;
- O'Hara-Deveraux, M and Johansen, R (1994) *Global Work*;
- Sarathy, R and Terpstra, V (2000) *International Marketing*;
- Trompenaars, F and Hampden-Turner, C (1998) *Riding the Waves of Culture*;
- Vaill, P B (1996) *Learning as a Way of Being.*

Organisations and useful Web sites

- Academic Libraries of the 21st Century (http://www.library.tamu.edu/21stcentury/orgbooks.html);
- Cultural Studies Center (http://www.popcultures.com/internat.htm);
- European Commission on Higher Education (www.europa.eu.int/comm/education/socrates/erasmus/links.html);
- International Business and Technology (www.brint.com/international.htm);
- International Business Resources on the WWW (http://ciber.bus.msu.edu/busres.htm);
- International Business Simulations Inc (www.ibsim.com);
- International Business Web Sites (http://rigel.pepperdine.edu/resources/guides/bibintl.htm);
- Internationalist Guide to Business (www.internationalist.com/business);
- International Society for Organizational Learning (SoL) (www.solonline.org).

Case studies

There are a number of case studies that address various issues and problems in international business. The European Institute of Business Administration (INSEAD) and the Harvard Business School have produced most of the classic case studies that incorporate international and cross-cultural elements of business management. These include Procter and Gamble Europe: the Vizir Launch, Saatchi and Saatchi, DuPont in Titanium Dioxide, Renault–Volvo, and BMW–Rover. There are several other leading institutions that also provide international case studies through the European Case Clearing House (see Table 5.1). In order to provide an effective overview for students of international business, case studies normally incorporate a market or organisational situation that demands analysis within cross-cultural and cross-disciplinary contexts. In the case of Saatchi and Saatchi, the case demands an evaluation of the company's core competence, its competitive environment and its organisational structure within a multicultural setting. In evaluating the case, learners are required to examine the strategic issues in developing a global service organisation. This analytical approach offers a comprehensive look at the complex issues facing multinational organisations.

In order to provide learners with a realistic and current picture of international business, it is important to select case studies that address issues associated with the new knowledge-based economy. Case studies can also be developed using 'live' material from business leaders and companies within the alumni and corporate network (see Table 5.2). A case study could be based on a group project involving a company analysis focused on either a sponsor organisation or a course member's organisation. A business analysis is then conducted on a company's current international opportunities or an emerging opportunity overseas. This can be founded on either the local learning community or a global learning network. For example, in creating learning partnerships with other business schools, students on the MBA programme of the International Graduate School of Management at the University of Navarra in Spain (IESE) have the opportunity to participate in a Global Roll Out Workshop (GROW). Linked with students from other business schools around the world, learners form multinational teams in order to develop a global marketing strategy for a real company.

When addressing the challenge of globalization and new technologies, students on the International Management School of the Ecole Nationale des Ponts et Chaussées MBA programme in Paris are asked to assume the role of managers trying to develop a new business or to increase the international market value of an existing business. This approach has been used in the Innovation and Technology Management course, which draws upon business leaders from participating companies who serve as guest speakers in order to present the challenges and the opportunities of managing international businesses and new technologies. Through the sponsoring company, learners are expected to rely upon various research vehicles including company contacts, industry publications and the Internet. In following the problem-solving process, students need to examine different fields of management in order to:

- identify key organisational and market issues or questions;
- target the international business issue and specify the research methodology;
- review and present the limits, applications and implementation of the technology;
- propose market solutions and recommendations.

In order to emphasize the international business focus, teamwork incorporates a multicultural element where group projects focus on one or more foreign countries.

Case studies can be transformed into a more effective learning tool through the active participation of students and companies. A case study analysis incorporating teamwork and a group project can serve as a powerful experiential learning environment and means of assessment.

Simulations and role plays

In providing learners with realistic global market scenarios, computer-based business simulations offer a multimedia environment for practising analytical, communication and decision-making skills. Within the simulation, an action learning approach, or 'learning by doing', is applied through engagement with a series of events and outcomes. There are different levels of learning that address the varying needs of practising managers and of students with limited or no direct experience of business. For example, MARKSTRAT-INTERNATIONAL is designed for use by executives in general management in order to provide an environment for a broad integration of tools in global corporate strategy. For those with limited experience, there is the INTERCOMP simulation that takes learners through the international business process of direct exports, contractual entry and foreign production.

A further impressive example of an international business simulation is a virtual course at the University of Washington, in the United States. This incorporates the international business simulation (IBSIM) developed at the University of California, San Diego by Professor Alex Kane. This is designed to give students a first-hand opportunity to experience the competitive environment of international business through a dynamic, complex, Internet-based simulation of a global economy. Students are members of corporate, government or media teams and need to organise effectively to develop strategies and make decisions under time pressure in a competitive context. As members of a team, students have managerial responsibilities and their performance is evaluated by the organisation. As individuals, students negotiate their salaries, manage their personal financial portfolios and rate the performance of their governments.

IBSIM simulation is a non-traditional, experiential learning simulation that tests and extends student abilities to work in the international arena. It gives learners the opportunity to apply and integrate diverse tools and knowledge derived from other courses. It provides an intense experience through its competitive nature, unforgiving deadlines and performance-based grade evaluation. There is no textbook since all information and preparation is taken from the simulation.

Cross-cultural team exercises

Cross-cultural teamwork can make a valuable contribution to the development of the affective and adaptive occupational skills of learners. In order to do so it is necessary to focus on teamwork, structure and process models. In this way, learning needs are clearly centred on three key phases of teamwork: entry, process and action. During the entry or initial phase, learners need time for socialization in order to share, build trust and strengthen interpersonal relationships. Having established a sense of trust and commitment, they can proceed to the second phase concerning the work process. This demands the discussion and exchange of team ideas and approaches. Formal instruction concerning team processes, tools and methodologies provides teams with a stronger framework for communication and cultural resource assessment. The final phase results in action and implementation of the team project. This requires additional support and guidance concerning interpersonal and time management issues.

There are several exercises that can be applied inside or outside the classroom setting for creating openness and trust and for developing awareness of individual expectations and cultural values amongst learners during the team-forming stage. One simple exercise that addresses team expectations requires learners to record their thoughts on two pieces of paper. On one sheet, they write the expectations for themselves in the team and, on a second sheet, they write their expectations of the other team members. These reflections should be recorded and discussed amongst the team members to encourage awareness and understanding of different work styles.

To further the process of team-building, educators need to equip learners with facilitation models. A simple model that works well in the context of cross-cultural team-building has been developed by an organisation called IDEO. It is based on the following principles:

- defer judgement;
- build upon the ideas of others;
- have one conversation at a time;
- stay focused on the topic;
- encourage different ideas.

In addition, there are a number of learning models available for cross-cultural teamwork, most notably those developed by Nancy Adler (1997) (see box on page 133).

To highlight cultural differences, teams can be allocated a culture and given a list of attributes and behaviours that need to be demonstrated during their interactions

---

Adler's models for cross-cultural teamwork

Team structure model

- Set a common goal and framework.
- Discuss and agree upon common work rules.
- Assess group resources.
- Define group roles.
- Assign tasks and timeline.
- Evaluate results.

Intercultural learning model

- Recognize differences.
- Encounter shocks.
- Consider possibilities (understand your own cultural assumptions).
- Be open to the culture (take responsibility for cultural learning).
- Pursue learning (how different cultural approaches may benefit groupwork).
- Transcend boundaries (view cultural differences as opportunities not barriers).
- Appreciate diversity.

---

with other teams. The objective for each is to negotiate a contract for the exchange of goods or service with another team. After the first exchange between the teams has taken place, a discussion should ensue on the observations of cultural differences and any necessary behavioural modifications.

Integration

Today, many institutions and organisations apply international business as a cross-disciplinary integrative theme drawing together key subject areas, including strategic management (Chapter 12), marketing (Chapter 13) and finance. Indeed, many business and management programmes are designed to ensure the incorporation of international business courses and material in the curriculum. However, integrative initiatives of this kind need to be underpinned by securing a global direction in the scope of the activities of business schools and the orientation of learning facilitators. For those who work in international business education there are a number of institutions that sponsor research and instructional programmes, such as the Center for International Business Education and Research, Duke University; the University of South Carolina; Thunderbird – the American Graduate School of International Management; the Centre for European Studies;

and London Business School. These all promote and support initiatives for global case studies, teaching and research, and share a global focus, integrated course content, innovative methods and a culturally diverse and collaborative learning environment. Educational innovations are applied through action learning or field-based projects involving academic and corporate settings. They offer educators and learners alike an experiential and interactive focus together with coursework, which is often cross-disciplinary, modular and theme-based.

The cross-disciplinarity of international business is illustrated in the box below. This indicates just some of the links with other components of the business and management curriculum.

Links between international business and other subject areas

- *strategic management*, eg globalization, global alliances, global missions;
- *human resource management*, eg cross-cultural competency, leadership education, global human resource systems;
- *organizational development*, eg organizational configurations of multi-nationals, cross-cultural teamwork processes;
- *technology and innovation*, eg research and development product design, e-business, e-banking;
- *marketing*, eg transnational marketing, global brands;
- *finance*, eg international monetary arrangements, International Bank for Reconstruction and Development ('World Bank'), investment planning;
- *economics and trade*, eg direct exports, foreign production, General Agreement on Tariffs and Trade, European Union;
- *business law*, eg mergers and acquisitions, international codes of practice for multinationals, US Foreign Corrupt Practices Act (1977).

Reflection and evaluation

In reflecting upon the changing nature of international business education, two important and related considerations are the extent to which advantage has been taken of the student mix, in terms of its cultural diversity, and how far learners have been exposed to a genuinely cross-cultural learning experience. In the United States, the educational value of international students in business schools has often been ignored (RAND Institute on Education and Training, 1994). By contrast, European business schools are more advanced in attracting and developing a multi-cultural student body. As the importance of a culturally diverse work force continues to be underscored by executives in leading companies, business schools are increasing their recruitment efforts to attract more foreign students. Leveraging cultural diversity for team learning processes is therefore an important focus for the development of international managers. However, while cross–cultural team learning may be applied through course projects, there is frequently little opportunity for the evaluation of individual and group learning processes. Aside from recognizing and understanding cultural differences, it is also important for students to learn from cultural diversity in the interests of providing them with an insightful cross–cultural learning experience.

The box below provides some examples of reflective and evaluative questions for educators to use in considering the extent to which they have created a truly cross–cultural learning environment as well as demonstrating their commitment to reflective practice.

Examples of reflective questions for international business educators

- To what extent has the cultural mix of students been exploited for learning and teaching purposes?
- What steps have been taken to contribute to the emergent global learning community?
- Have case studies provided students with the means of securing an effective overview of one aspect of the global economy?
- How far is the vision of students still limited geographically/culturally?
- In undertaking assignments, have students been able to access and evaluate resources from around the world?
- What evidence is there to indicate that students have become more cross-culturally aware?
- Were learners provided with opportunities for reflecting upon cross-cultural teamwork processes?
- In what ways has the principle of an open mindset been applied?
- Have new technologies that help to develop a global knowledge network been effectively incorporated into the student learning experience?

Designing and posing similar questions should facilitate the creation of a learning experience with a 'for' international business focus and one in which pride of place is given to the development of cross–cultural competency.

Conclusion

The future role of international business education in the knowledge-based economy is dependent upon the ability to create global learning networks. In seeking to equip learners with the reflective, conscious and collaborative learning skills that they need to manage effectively in the culturally diverse global economy, universities must utilize every opportunity for establishing and maintaining rich links with similar institutions throughout the world.

Moreover, cross-cultural learning practices to achieve interpersonal and intercultural awareness need to be applied within experiential contexts. The ability to apply cross-cultural learning is becoming more important in international business than traditional practices, such as language training and overseas study, with openness and adaptability to different cultural perspectives being viewed as a higher priority by a growing number of universities and companies.

At the same time, new modes of pedagogic thinking are required if the needs of learners, faced with an increasingly dynamic international business environment, are to be met. This is hampered where there is an overemphasis on goal-directedness and on requiring learners to value goals set by others rather than themselves (Vaill, 1996). Managerial leadership is no longer just a set of technical skills; rather it is one of learning skills, with cross-cultural, cross-functional and multi-lingual knowledge being among the most highly valued assets in the global management arena (O'Hara-Deveraux and Johansen, 1994).

Finally, as the growing importance of learning cannot be shouldered by universities and business schools alone, a partnership between academic institutions and the business community has to be forged. While this is needed for business and management education in general, it has a particular resonance for international business as the globalization of business activity is paralleled by the globalization of educational endeavour.

References

Adler, N J (1997) *International Dimensions of Organizational Behavior*, 3rd edn, South Western College Publishing, Cincinnati

Adler, N J (2000) *International Dimensions of Organizational Behavior*, 4th edn, South Western College Publishing, Cincinnati

Akhter, S H and Ahmed, Z U (1996) Internationalizing business curriculum, in *International Business Education Development*, ed Z U Ahmed, pp 1–4, International Business Press, New York

Arpan, J S, Folks Jr, W S and Kwok, C C Y (1993) *International Business Education in the 1990s: A global survey*, Academy of International Business, USA

Czinkota, M R *et al* (2001) *Global Business*, 3rd edn, Harcourt College Publishers, Texas

Doz, Y L and Prahalad, C K (1999) *The Multinational Mission*, Simon and Schuster, New York

European Commission (1999) [online] http://europa.eu.int/comm/education/leonardo/leonardo2_en.html

Gregersen, H B, Morrison, A J and Black, J S (1998) Developing leaders for the global frontier, *MIT Sloan Management Review*, Fall, pp 21–31

Jensen, K (2000) Cross-cultural learning practices for business education, in *Educational Innovation in Economics and Business V: Business education in the changing workplace*, ed L Borghans *et al*, pp 321–43, Kluwer Academic Publishers, Dordrecht

Kedia, B L and Cornwall, B T (1994) Mission based strategies for internationalizing US business schools, *Journal of Teaching in International Business*, **5** (3), pp 11–25

Marquardt, M (1998) *The Global Advantage*, Gulf Publishing, Texas

May, B H and May, D R (1996) Implementing internationalization, in *International Business Education Development*, ed Z U Ahmed, pp 35–40, International Business Press, New York

Moore, J F (1996) *The Death of Competition*, Harper Business Publishing, New York

O'Hara-Deveraux, M and Johansen, R (1994) *Global Work*, Jossey-Bass Publishers, California

Ottewill, R and Laughton, D (2000) East meets west: using multi-cultural groupwork to develop competences required by tomorrow's international managers, *Journal of Teaching in International Business*, **12** (1), pp 1–22

RAND Institute on Education and Training (1994) *Global Preparedness and Human Resources*, RAND, California

Sarathy, R and Terpstra, V (2000) *International Marketing*, 8th edn, Harcourt College Publishers, Texas

Trompenaars, F and Hampden-Turner, C (1998) *Riding the Waves of Culture*, McGraw-Hill, New York

Vaill, P B (1996) *Learning as a Way of Being*, Jossey-Bass Publishers, California

Winter, J (1997) Skills for graduates in the 21st century, *EMDS International Careers*, **26**

12

Strategic management

Peter L Jennings and June Fletcher

Introduction

A variety of terms is used to describe the subject area covered in this chapter. These include corporate strategy, business policy and management strategy. For the purposes of the chapter, however, strategic management has been chosen as the preferred descriptor.

Although such descriptors are often used interchangeably, they do represent differences of emphasis and focus. The debate and argument over their precise definition and application to specific managerial activities in organisational settings typify the ambiguity that surrounds the subject area. Its multifaceted nature reflects roots that span a number of academic disciplines, such as economics, organisational behaviour, finance, accountancy and sociology. While none dominates, each contributes a specific ethos that translates into a preferred style of learning and teaching, presenting particular challenges for learners and educators alike.

The subject area first became established in mainstream management education in the United States in the late 1940s and early 1950s, as corporate, strategic or long-range planning. Strategic management courses have now developed well beyond these initial foundations and can be found in virtually all business and management programmes in HE. Traditionally occupying a final-stage, capstone position, they serve to integrate other business and management subject areas and provide an organisation–wide view of business development. It is also the case that an increasing number of vocational award programmes, such as National Vocational Qualifications for managers in the UK, now include elements of strategic management.

Recent changes have seen the strategic management curriculum segmented in order to be offered at a variety of levels and in different contexts, including non-business-related programmes. In responding to changing programme structures, in many instances the principal focus is now upon a narrower, specific element of the subject area. At the same time, the curriculum has been extended to take into consideration the increasingly international nature of the business environment and the orientation and aspirations of business leaders (see Chapter 11).

Educational challenges

The expansion of learning and teaching in the field of strategic management has been driven principally by the desire for learners to understand and explain why certain organisations consistently outperform their competitors and remain leaders within their field (Macmillan and Tampoe, 2000). However, effective managers not only have to be capable of grasping these explanations, but also have to be able to put strategic management ideas into practice. Thus, the learning experience, especially for those approaching the subject for the first time or without relevant managerial experience, needs to balance the quest for theoretical, conceptual and academic knowledge with an appreciation of the practicalities of applying such understandings in real situations, where the performance of organisations is influenced significantly by managerial decisions.

The burgeoning literature covering strategic management is testimony to its growing inclusivity, with an increasing number of issues considered to be of a strategic nature, including strategic human resource management and strategic marketing. If programmes are to reflect all these areas, an understanding of the interrelationship between the founding disciplines is required from learners. However, this would necessitate a huge curriculum with learning activities extending well beyond the time and resources normally available within conventional programmes. Hence, educators are faced with making some difficult and challenging choices in meeting the needs of learners with varying degrees of managerial experience.

Emphasizing theory or practice

While acknowledging the symbiotic relationship between theory and practice, a common dilemma is whether to concentrate upon academic principles or upon managerial practice. An academic orientation is more suited to full-time learners with limited managerial experience and a practical orientation to experienced managers.

The former concentrates upon learning 'about' strategic management. Emphasis is placed upon critical evaluation of contemporary theory with learners developing specific conceptual understandings and related cognitive skills. These are then located within a broader framework incorporating other, related subjects, which build collectively toward achieving a degree of vertical integration (see Chapter 6). The relevance of theory to practice and the relationship between the two is covered in an illustrative manner by the provision of examples from real organisations.

The practical orientation for experienced managers focuses upon learning 'for' strategic management. Emphasis is placed upon those practical skills that learners need to become more proficient strategists. Here academic and personal transferable skills are developed to the extent that they have direct impact upon a manager's strategic capability. Theory and concepts are explored only in order to explain the rationale underpinning managerial action and 'real world' examples. Practical activities and illustrations are central to this approach, which may include elements of experiential learning. Courses adopting such an approach are often designed specifically for the needs of business organisations.

Determining the focus

Alternatively, or interwoven within the selected position on the theory–practice continuum, educators are faced with the challenge of deciding on which of the specific dimensions of strategic activity to focus, namely content, context or process. Courses labelled 'business policy' tend to focus upon content and context at the level of direct competition between the enterprise and its immediate rivals. Emphasis is placed upon those aspects of business activity that enhance competitiveness and that have a positive influence upon potential and existing customers. 'Corporate strategy' courses, while also tending to emphasize content and context issues, often have a broader focus and encompass larger enterprises. Strategy is examined from a senior management perspective including an appreciation of the balance and relationship between a variety of corporate activities at the business level. Courses covering 'management strategy' tend to place their emphasis upon process issues and examine the specific actions taken by senior managers to lead and direct strategic activity and change. Naturally both content and context figure, but to a much lesser extent. The common element in all instances is the inseparability of the enterprise and its environment, irrespective of whether strategic activity is viewed as a proactive or reactive managerial activity. Hence there is a close relationship with the business environment (Chapter 8) and ideally there should be close co-operation between facilitators in these two subject areas.

Resolving the role of competing paradigms

A growing literature also illustrates the development of differing conceptual representations of strategic management processes and styles. Each has its own distinctive characteristics and strengths, strongly related to the context within which it is applied (Chaffee, 1985). The challenge is to decide whether one particular style should dominate or whether no specific conceptual representation should be favoured, with learners being required to evaluate and appraise the merits of all the available options.

The traditional linear sequential representation is strongly process-driven and remains extremely popular for courses that target experienced managers and practitioners. The broad principles are often recognizable within the long-term or strategic planning routines found in many medium- to large-sized organisations. It provides a focus for exploring the relationship between the various stages in the process, as well as the content and techniques that might be applied in each step. Many of the earliest versions of linear sequential models can be criticized for an overemphasis on strategy formulation, at the expense of explicit consideration of strategic implementation. The challenge for anyone choosing to adopt a linear sequential approach is to ensure that both of these important processes are given adequate attention.

Adaptive representations are much less process-driven, requiring a stronger conceptual understanding. Advocates argue that this group of theoretical models is the closest to reality for the majority of practising strategic managers, since they focus attention upon the relationship between the organisation and its environment and the need for constant, simultaneous attention to a wide variety of different issues. The absence of strong process means that courses that emphasize an adaptive orientation tend to give priority to the application of specific tools and techniques in particular contexts. The dichotomy between strategy formulation and strategy implementation becomes subsumed within the wider debate and tends not to feature so prominently.

Interpretive/cultural representations may be regarded as purely theoretical or academic representations, since they generally lack specific process advice for practitioners. Neither do they give explicit attention to particular tools and techniques. Supporters argue that the strong human orientation most accurately reflects the psychological and sociological dimensions of strategic management, being founded upon the concept of organisations as subsets of society. Courses centred upon the interpretive paradigm tend to emphasize critical evaluation and conceptual understanding, with limited reference to practical application. Consequently, learners may be disparaging of the limited extent to which useful, practical advice is provided.

A further option is to design a curriculum that deliberately seeks to compare and contrast the various representations. Here learners are challenged to link each representation to situations and circumstances affecting various enterprises.

Responding to differences in managerial experience

As has been implied, an underlying challenge facing educators arises from the widely differing backgrounds and work experience of learners studying strategic management. Since professional and vocational courses often specify tight entry requirements, they provide facilitators with a defined foundation upon which to build. Mainstream, full-time courses in HE are aimed at learners with broadly similar levels of managerial experience, which is often limited.

However, postgraduate programmes are often composed of learners from a wider range of backgrounds in terms of managerial practice. Here a balance needs to be struck between the comparative strengths and weaknesses of students in order to equalize the understanding and capabilities of all, over the duration of the programme.

Learners tackling a strategy course for the first time are often overwhelmed by the sheer volume of material available. Strategic management can be perceived as both difficult and demanding but, at the same time, highly relevant to career prospects. A defensive reaction to personal fear and anxiety might well be hostility towards the subject matter and the facilitator (see Chapter 2). It is important to defuse any hostility quickly and to take steps to reduce the anxiety. This task is not helped by the frequently unfamiliar and often ambiguous use of terminology that litters strategic management learning resources.

A related challenge is to reflect the reality of a broadly based, all-pervasive managerial activity that has significant implications that need constant attention. Dividing the student learning experience into digestible chunks allows learners to make progress in coming to terms with unfamiliar ground. However, learners with direct managerial experience realize that dividing the subject matter in this way is purely an academic construct, with no basis in practice. They may feel that as this does not correspond to their experience, its value is questionable. In this situation learners should be encouraged to reflect upon alternative forms of practice that may challenge some of the taken-for-granted, underlying assumptions that, without analysis and questioning, become ingrained in routine practice. As a result of dividing the curriculum, learners without direct managerial experience may not fully appreciate the holistic nature of the subject matter. Introductory learning activities should reinforce the interdependence of the topics that follow, perhaps by relating issues to the learners' experience as customers of enterprises that are themselves practising strategic management.

Of course, the choices highlighted in this section are not necessarily mutually exclusive and a survey of current courses with a strategic orientation would reveal a wide range of alternative focuses and emphases. The choice of focus defines the boundaries for the course, which are reflected in the aims, objectives and learning outcomes and in the content of learning activities, facilitator-directed readings and class contact sessions. It also provides an important reference point against which to judge the extent to which course content meets learner expectations.

Aims, objectives and learning outcomes

Clearly, there is a very close relationship between the choices that may be made in defining the boundaries and the content of strategic management courses and their aims, objectives and anticipated learning outcomes. Non-accredited and bespoke programmes often provide sufficient flexibility for educators to work directly with the learners in jointly defining required learning outcomes that fully reflect student expectations. Formal accredited programmes are normally much more restricted, since strategic management must integrate with other subject areas in achieving overall learning objectives. Here, aims, objectives and learning outcomes would normally be specified well in advance of actually meeting learners, and some modifications may be necessary as the course unfolds, to reflect learner experience, backgrounds and expectations.

In broad terms, the underlying purpose of studying strategic management is to examine its contribution to the performance of the organisation (Johnson and Scholes, 1999). This extends to developing an appreciation of how and why organisations act strategically at the corporate and business levels (Finlay, 2000), and may encompass the development of skills in the formulation and implementation of strategic plans (Macmillan and Tampoe, 2000).

Learners are often already aware, from their general life experience if not from other subject areas, that for business, commercial and even voluntary organisations the central strategic question concerns the development of an effective competitive position. The aims and objectives of a strategy curriculum must reflect the fact that competitive positioning requires the assessment and balancing of influences arising in the external environment with the internal operations of the organisation. Management must be able to identify changes in the environment, determine their significance and facilitate appropriate, innovative change within the organisation to maintain a basic match between environmental opportunities and organisational strengths, whilst addressing environmental threats and organisational weaknesses.

Curriculum aims should also demonstrate that the culture of the organisation, and the cultures of the markets in which the enterprise operates, are a very significant influence upon the decisions made, the style of management, internal structuring and the climate of change that prevails. Nevertheless, the fundamental capability to create and sustain a viable competitive position can only be found in the people who make up the organisation. When comparing the effectiveness of many organisations, learners need to appreciate that the quality of leadership and competent management are the keys to explaining superior performance.

Strategy courses typically aim to provide an understanding of the principal functions and processes of strategic management and the corporate environment within which strategic managers and leaders operate. Often it is *not* a prime objective that learners become proficient, specialized strategists (Eden and Ackerman, 1998). Inevitably some of the creative and analytical skills so necessary for effective strategic management will be developed, but this is regarded very much as an additional benefit. It is essential, however, that students develop an in-depth appreciation of the range of strategic choices that an organisation may pursue in response to the modern, dynamic, corporate environment. Thus, upon completion of their studies the place and the contribution of strategic management to the wider organisational perspective and performance should be apparent to learners.

Learning outcomes can be usefully mapped in terms of the general framework presented in Chapter 4. Some examples are provided in Table 12.1.

Table 12.1 Examples of learning outcomes for strategic management

Area	Examples
Cognitive	Explain alternative approaches to strategic management. Understand and use theoretical concepts, models, frameworks, tools and techniques that support the processes of strategic management. Evaluate the appropriateness of alternative styles of strategic management in differing operating circumstances.
Affective	Demonstrate an openness to new ideas and an awareness that in many situations there is a range of alternatives that should be evaluated. Manifest a tolerance of others through working together effectively, efficiently and co-operatively as a team member and, when appropriate, organising, guiding and motivating other team members.
Adaptive	Draft a strategic plan for an organisation. Apply decision-making skills in selecting appropriate strategies for different types of organisation. Persuade others of the efficacy of a recommendation with respect to the future strategic direction of an organisation.

Learning, teaching and assessment activities

Clearly the final design of learning, teaching and assessment activities needs to be closely aligned to the principal focuses for the course and the anticipated learning outcomes. While a number of common elements may be found in most strategy courses the degree of emphasis may shift to reflect overall aims and objectives. Whatever the emphasis, the key is to apply a strategic approach to curriculum content and pedagogy.

Courses seeking to develop strategic planning skills may concentrate upon activities that enable learners to gain experience in using tools and techniques for environmental analysis, strategic capability and the identification and evaluation of alternative development options. Exercises involving the application of alternative paradigms and models of strategic management, and exposure to the realities of managing strategic management in practice, may be favoured where process-driven aims and objectives have been adopted. Role plays and simulations highlighting values, attitudes, culture, organisational politics and the behaviour of stakeholders and coalitions may be utilized in a course founded upon the adaptive model of strategic management. In each case there is much to be gained from adopting a learner-centred approach to course delivery.

Resource-based learning

Given the wealth of material available, both paper-based and electronic (see box on page 145), one option is to adopt a form of resource-based learning (RBL) integrating elements of open learning with face-to-face facilitation (Jennings and Ottewill, 1996).

Key resources for strategic management

Leading journals

- *Academy of Management Journal;*
- *Academy of Management Review;*
- *California Management Review;*
- *Harvard Business Review;*
- *Journal of Business Strategy;*
- *Journal of Management Studies;*
- *Journal of Strategic Change;*
- *Long Range Planning;*
- *Organizational Dynamics;*
- *Sloan Management Review;*
- *Strategic Management Journal.*

Popular textbooks

- Eden, C and Ackerman, F (1998) *Making Strategy: The journey of strategic management;*
- Finlay, P (2000) *Strategic Management;*
- Johnson, G and Scholes, H K (1999) *Exploring Corporate Strategy;*
- Joyce, P and Woods, A (1996) *Essential Strategic Management;*
- Lynch, R (2000) *Corporate Strategy;*
- Macmillan, H and Tampoe, M (2000) *Strategic Management;*
- Mintzberg, H, Ahlstrand, B and Lampel, J (1998) *Strategy Safari;*
- Mintzberg, H, Quinn, J B and Ghoshal, S (1998) *The Strategy Process;*
- Segal-Horn, S (1998) *The Strategy Reader;*
- Stacey, R D (2000) *Strategic Management and Organisational Dynamics.*

Organisations and useful Web sites

- Cambridge Corporate Management, mini case studies (www.cambcorp. co.uk/);
- European Case Clearing House (www.ecch.cranfield.ac.uk);
- Financial Times (www.ft.com);
- Fortune Global 500 (www.fortune.com/fortune/global500);
- Strategic Management Club OnLine (www.strategyclub.com);
- Strategic Management Courseware (www.anbar.co.uk/courseware/);
- The Business Case Web Site (www.businesscases.org/interface/index. html);
- The Strategic Planning Society (www.sps.org.uk).

Using RBL is also extremely valuable in situations where there are reductions in formal learner–facilitator contact with a resultant shift of emphasis towards greater student responsibility and self-instruction (Rowntree, 1990). If managed effectively it can provide all the positive benefits of learner-centredness while maintaining a degree of control through the provision of facilitator-directed activities and learning (Race, 1989).

Underlying RBL is the belief that for learners to gain maximum advantage from encounters with educators, whether on a regular weekly basis or less frequently, in blocks of time or at summer schools, thorough preparation is essential. Thus, as much attention, if not more, needs to be given to the support and guidance that are provided for learners 'at a distance' as to the planning of face-to-face encounters.

To prioritize a student-centred approach during these encounters, learners need to be provided with a broad package of information to guide them through not only the subject matter but more importantly the abundance of learning resources at their disposal. Such a package might include a detailed course outline, incorporating a commentary on the aims, objectives and learning outcomes; open-learning-style material and self-assessment activities to complete in preparation for learner–facilitator encounters; and copies of PowerPoint presentations.

Guidance on relevant background reading, including textbooks, is also essential (see box, 'Key resources for strategic management'). Until the publication of *Exploring Corporate Strategy* by Johnson and Scholes in 1983, the vast majority of textbooks covering strategy issues emanated from the United States. The success of Johnson and Scholes prompted many UK and European academics to publish their own texts. Hence, educators now have at their disposal a wider range of academic material, of US, British or European origin, specializing in corporate strategy, business policy and management strategy. These cover linear sequential, adaptive or interpretive models, emphasizing content, context or process and are designed to develop academic and/or practical skills. Coverage is comprehensive and choice is largely personal. However, while nobody should feel obliged to 'reinvent the wheel', it is in keeping with the spirit of the RBL approach advocated here that they supplement published material with additional learning resources, customized to reflect individual preferences and to put their distinctive stamp on the student learning experience.

Moreover, the dynamic nature of strategic management demands the use of the most up-to-date and contemporary material available. Consequently, educators will need to rely heavily upon current journals, Web sites (see box, 'Key resources for strategic management') and research-based conference proceedings, and ensure that these are incorporated into learner support packages before the findings have made their way into textbooks. Those engaged in learner support might also take advantage of training and development seminars provided by a number of commercial organisations that are designed to illustrate the application of established tools and techniques, such as portfolio analysis, balanced scorecard and scenario planning, in practical situations. In this way, innovation in delivery and assessment methods can be stimulated.

If learners are adequately prepared through the provision of carefully planned guidance, there is no longer any need for learner–facilitator contact to concentrate on the delivery of straightforward factual or conceptual material or even the introduction of new topics. Rather, it can be used to reinforce, or add value to, prior learning through the application of a variety of interactive and assessed activities, including groupwork, video analysis, feedback on self-assessment exercises and tasks associated with learners' current workplace experiences. Time is also available for briefings and surgeries to support formative and summative assessment (Jennings and Ottewill, 1996). In practice, the boundary between the various types of learning and assessment experience becomes blurred.

In this context, group activity is particularly valuable in enabling learners to pool their collective knowledge and experience. This facilitates the critical evaluation of current theoretical perspectives. It also allows educators to draw upon those learners who have practical managerial experience as living examples of the concepts being discussed.

Given that strategic management is a live subject, whether introductory or more specialized, the need for flexibility is crucial. This demands the exploration of real-life, topical issues as they arise. Additionally, students need to be encouraged to draw upon and discuss some of the business problems and situations encountered in their general life or business experience. In this way the problems and situations may serve as a catalyst for assessed activities, such as research projects and presentations.

Case studies

Many of the principles inherent in RBL can be reinforced through the judicious use of case studies. For case studies to be effective, prior preparation and clear guidance are usually essential, as is the willingness of students to learn interactively.

In strategic management, like other areas of business and management (see Chapters 4, 5, 9, 10 and 11), case studies are seen as a valuable learning activity and one that can also be utilized for assessment purposes. Founded upon the traditional Harvard case study method (Barnes, Christensen and Hansen, 1994), case studies can contribute to the achievement of many learning objectives.

First, case studies can add to knowledge and understanding by providing 'real world' illustrations that demonstrate the practical application of theoretical concepts. In short, they serve to illustrate the integration of theory and practice. Asking students to locate the products, or strategic business units, of the case study organisation in terms of the Boston Consulting Group Matrix is a simple example.

Second, case studies can provide the platform for mini-simulations in which learners, either individually or collectively, are challenged to recommend managerial action that should be taken in response to a particular situation of strategic importance. Learners are asked to assume the role of a senior executive within, or act as a consultant to, the enterprise in question. When using case studies in this way and before any contact with learners, it is important to establish exactly what actions have been taken by management since the close of the case study. This will allow formative feedback to be given to students, who will be able to compare their recommendations with the actual decisions of the senior managers involved.

Third, case studies provide an ideal opportunity to develop critical faculties by engaging the learner in the evaluation of managerial action. Similarly, critical evaluation may extend to appraising the practical relevance and application of theory and conceptual frameworks with the objective of questioning whether current research is sufficiently robust to reflect fully the richness of strategy in practice.

Last, for many learners their personal experiences and backgrounds provide 'living' case studies (see Chapter 5). With appropriate support, experienced learners can develop their own case studies, which not only enhance their own learning but may also be shared within their peer group. This helps to overcome one of the serious weaknesses of text-only published case studies, their inability to reflect fully the cultural, behavioural, psychological and sociological dimensions of strategic management. Incorporating video material may help to alleviate some of this weakness, but immersion in the specific context of an important strategic issue is most beneficial, especially for active learners. The use of case studies, especially where these are self-generated and related to current practical experience, is a common form of summative assessment in all types and styles of strategy courses.

Published text-based case studies, sometimes with accompanying videos, are available from a variety of different sources (see box, 'Key resources for strategic management'), while current newspapers and periodicals provide a source of contemporary illustrations and examples. Formally published case studies covering strategy issues tend to focus almost exclusively upon medium-sized and large organisations, which often introduces elements of international, multinational and global strategic management. As in the case of business environment and business ethics, it is relatively difficult to find published case studies covering small firms (see Chapters 8 and 10) and dealing with new business venture creation (see Chapter 14). Thus, it is important to ensure that the course does not implicitly suggest that strategic issues are identical in all organisations, irrespective of their context. Where possible, involving students in the local business community through consultancy-style assignments, or inviting visiting speakers to contribute to learner–facilitator contact sessions, helps to redress this imbalance (see Chapter 5). In instances where assignments have been generated through contact with local businesses it is important to seek their involvement with the assessment and feedback process, via, for example, students presenting a short report and/or oral presentation.

Naturally, companies attract the attention of case study authors when there is a major issue to debate. Thus, most case studies either relate the background to a spectacular failure or provide a detailed exemplar of best practice. This tends to give the impression that good strategic management consists only of major managerial decisions in high-risk situations and ignores the, often long, periods of steady management and comparatively minor change that typify most of corporate life. Rarely are learners asked to advise management in situations where the most appropriate course of action is to maintain the status quo, making no major changes in strategic direction!

The realism of case studies can be enhanced through the incorporation of role plays and simulations. These also provide considerable benefits in terms of both formative and summative feedback and assessment. Learners are exposed to the realities of coping with the broad range of managerial issues needing attention and prioritization. Unfortunately, role plays do not adequately portray the pressures and risks to which strategic managers are routinely exposed. Real-time simulations are rarely practical in HE situations. Role plays may be used to simulate specific elements of the strategic management process, such as the decision to subcontract a particular production routine. These can be particularly useful as small-group activities interjected to break up large group lecture sessions into active learning segments. However, the best application is grounded in experiencing the total process, which invariably necessitates considerable time and learning resource. Strategic management courses may be structured around an extended role play as the core learning method with supporting activities interwoven to illustrate and explore specific concepts at appropriate points. Moreover, with a certain amount of creative and strategic thinking, elements of formative and summative assessment can be built into this learning experience.

Integration

Strategic management has consistently figured as a core, compulsory course in the final stages of both undergraduate and postgraduate programmes (Bart, 1988; Gammie, 1995). Typically, the subject is considered and debated both as an academic discipline in its own right and as a fundamental integrative mechanism for the business and management curriculum. Educationally, it serves to integrate material first introduced and presented elsewhere in the programme. Experientially, it enables learners to draw upon their current and recent experience to examine and analyse issues of immediate relevance and concern to their learning context. In particular, strategic management highlights the interaction between specialist, functional areas of business activity. Examples of links between strategic management and other subject areas are set out in the box on page 150.

However, its integrative potential can be undermined by the current vogue in the UK of responding to the pressure for dividing the curriculum into smaller self-contained components studied at various stages throughout the overall programme. This accelerating trend tends to militate against the integrative approach, as learning becomes increasingly segmented and learners are encouraged to build qualifications on a credit accumulation basis.

Moreover, a natural tension exists between, on the one hand, seeking to learn about strategy via a capstone course or, on the other, developing understanding

---

Links between strategic management and other subject areas

- *business environment*, eg environmental analysis, transactional interdependencies, dynamism and complexity, competitive rivalry, industry analysis, value system analysis;
- *business organisation*, eg structure, culture, strategic capability, value chain analysis, portfolio analysis, core competencies, stakeholder analysis, organisational politics;
- *business ethics*, eg values, regulatory environment, employer responsibilities, job design and motivation, reward systems, corporate governance;
- *international business*, eg business development, globalization, multinational and international organisations, technology transfer, licensing;
- *knowledge management*, eg information systems, strategic decision-making, facilitation mechanisms, intellectual property, patents and copyright;
- *innovation and entrepreneurship*, eg new technology, creativity, new business venture creation, spin-outs, intrapreneuring, corporate entrepreneurship;
- *business functions (eg finance, human resource management, marketing and operations)*, eg horizontal and vertical integration, organisational hierarchy, strategic contribution, evaluation of strategic options, strategic implementation.

---

through exposure to strategic concepts in related subject areas at an earlier stage of study. Inevitably the former might mean some overlap in the sense that learners will have previously encountered relevant ideas, techniques and materials from subject areas like marketing (Chapter 13). By retaining strategic management as a capstone course, it is not normally intended to repeat or directly cover material crucial to other subject areas, but rather to explore the interrelationships between different parts of the business and management curriculum.

Reflection and evaluation

Effective strategic management requires reflective observation and analysis, which make possible learning from previous experience. In designing their courses, educators should also seek to evaluate the decisions taken and choices made. Reflective evaluation enables them to assess whether an appropriate learning environment has been created and whether the course design adequately reflects the background, experience and expectations of learners. This may extend to considering the detailed subject content and its contribution to achieving the desired learning outcomes. Examples of reflective questions are to be found in the box on page 151.

Examples of reflective questions for strategic management educators

- To what extent did learners display and express fear and anxiety connected with the nature and demands of strategic management at the beginning of the course and how effective were the initial learning activities in overcoming these concerns?
- Did the curriculum content adequately reflect the baseline strategic experience of the majority of learners?
- Was an appropriate balance struck between the study of strategic management theory and practice?
- Did the learners' summative assessment results demonstrate an understanding of interrelationships between strategic management and learners' earlier studies?
- Did learners cope adequately with the ambiguity inherent in many aspects of strategic management?
- To what extent did learners with first-hand experience of strategic decision-making have opportunities for sharing their knowledge and understanding with those who were less experienced?
- Was there an appropriate range of learning activities to engage all students in actively learning how to manage strategically?
- Were learners provided with a suitable range of case studies, illustrations and examples covering both 'high-risk' and 'steady-state' scenarios?
- Were learners able to evaluate and reinforce or modify their own stance toward strategic management activity?

While reflective evaluation tends to be an activity reserved for post-course analysis, in strategic management it is particularly helpful to seek opportunities to assess learner attitudes and opinions of content, structure and design during the early stages of the course (see Chapter 7). This enables those responsible for learner support to make modifications, where appropriate, that have an immediate and positive impact on learning activities, thus enhancing the enjoyment and achievement of learners.

Conclusion

Strategic management can make a significant contribution to developing learners' awareness and understanding of the influences on the performance of contemporary organisations. Today, many strategic management courses are provided for learners who have little or no direct experience of the strategic issues that they study and discuss. Strategic management, therefore, tends to provide a glimpse into their possible future responsibilities and careers.

Leading a well-designed, appropriately resourced and challenging strategy course is a tremendously satisfying experience for those involved and provides many opportunities for personal development. The dynamic nature of the subject matter furnishes a ready outlet for personal research and demands that educators are active in keeping up with recent developments within the business world. There is a growing, some might argue overgrown, supply of readily prepared learning materials, both paper-based and electronic. However, educators will almost certainly seek to customize such materials to suit their own personal interests, as well as the backgrounds, practical experience and expectations of learners. Thus, learning and teaching in strategic management is an important and interesting challenge for both learner and educator alike. Both can draw satisfaction from the knowledge that the effective achievement of learning outcomes will make a significant contribution to the performance of their present or future organisations.

References

Barnes, L B, Christensen, C R and Hansen, A J (1994) *Teaching and the Case Method*, 3rd edn, Harvard Business School Press, Boston

Bart, C (1988) The undergraduate business policy course in Canada: academics' approaches and practitioners' prescriptions, *Management Education and Development*, **19** (4), pp 311–17

Chaffee, E (1985) Three models of strategy, *Academy of Management Review*, **10** (1), pp 89–98

Eden, C and Ackerman, F (1998) *Making Strategy: The journey of strategic management*, Sage Publications, London

Finlay, P (2000) *Strategic Management*, Pearson Education Ltd, Harlow

Gammie, B (1995) Undergraduate management education: an analysis of rationale and methodology, *International Journal of Management Education*, **9** (4), pp 34–40

Jennings, P L and Ottewill, R (1996) Integrating open learning with face-to-face tuition, *Open Learning*, **11** (2), pp 13–19

Johnson, G and Scholes, H K (1999) *Exploring Corporate Strategy*, 5th edn with case studies, Prentice Hall Europe, Hemel Hempstead

Joyce, P and Woods, A (1996) *Essential Strategic Management*, Butterworth Heinemann, London

Lynch, R (2000) *Corporate Strategy*, 2nd edn, Pearson Education Ltd, Harlow

Macmillan, H and Tampoe, M (2000) *Strategic Management*, Oxford University Press, Oxford

Mintzberg, H, Ahlstrand, B and Lampel, J (1998) *Strategy Safari*, Prentice Hall Europe, Hemel Hempstead

Mintzberg, H, Quinn, J B and Ghoshal, S (1998) *The Strategy Process*, Prentice Hall Europe, Hemel Hempstead

Race, P (1989) *The Open Learning Handbook*, Kogan Page, London

Rowntree, D (1990) *Teaching Through Self Instruction*, Kogan Page, London

Segal-Horn, S (1998) *The Strategy Reader*, Blackwell, Oxford

Stacey, R D (2000) *Strategic Management and Organisational Dynamics*, 3rd edn, Pearson Education Ltd, Harlow

13

Marketing

Andrew Perkins

Introduction

Marketing has been taught in US universities for much of this century and in Europe from the mid-1960s, where it has established itself as a subject area in its own right since the late 1970s (Evans and Piercy, 1980). It is therefore a relative newcomer to HE and its status as a proper academic discipline worthy of serious study was initially subject to much debate and criticism. However, globalization has led to increased levels of competition in the markets of many industrialized nations. This in turn has meant that the efficient production of goods and services is no longer a sufficient basis for guaranteeing the survival and prosperity of business enterprises. Today, an ability to understand consumers, identify attractive target markets and communicate effectively with them is an essential requirement for organisations that wish to survive and prosper. This has created an increased need for employees with marketing knowledge and skills, with the result that there has been a rapid rise in demand for marketing education.

Any attempt to define the scope of marketing must incorporate three views of the subject area. First, it is a philosophy of business where the customer is seen as being at the centre of an organisation's strategy. Second, it is a function dedicated to carrying out a set of specific activities in much the same way as human resource management, finance or production. Last, it is a social process by which individuals and organisations obtain the goods and services they need. Marketing education inevitably reflects all three perspectives. Moreover, in recent years, there has been a shift in emphasis within the marketing curriculum away from techniques and processes for maximizing sales to those designed to secure long-term profitable relationships with customers.

Throughout this chapter, marketing is seen as a complex and diverse multidisciplinary subject area closely related to professional practice. An indication of its diversity and breadth is the range of marketing specialisms that learners are now often able to study within the context of a business and management programme. These include international marketing, consumer buyer behaviour, marketing research, not-for-profit marketing, retail marketing, marketing management and planning, marketing communications, physical distribution management and strategic marketing.

Educational challenges

With the increasing popularity and diversification of marketing courses, educators in this subject area face many challenges. As they seek to respond to the growing demands of organisations for people with both generic and specialist marketing skills, there is a need to ensure that courses are relevant and up to date. Here, recognition of the increasingly competitive and turbulent nature of business is particularly important. Thus, the rapid pace of product innovation, the enhanced power of information technology to capture data on consumers, the success of Asian companies and the power of international brands can all be seen as drivers in stimulating and developing interest in marketing as a subject of study and in shaping curriculum content. More specific challenges faced by those involved in the design and delivery of marketing courses are discussed below.

Being sensitive to cultural context

Modern marketing education has been colonized by US academics, despite marketing originating in the UK in the period following the Industrial Revolution (Fullerton, 1988). Writers who have developed and dominated marketing thought since the 1950s, like Drucker, Levitt, Borden, Buzzell and Kotler, have been from the United States. Likewise many of the leading journals in the field are published in the United States.

While the teaching of marketing may have benefited from the straightforward and highly structured designs of the textbooks that US writers and their publishers have produced, these are by no means unproblematic for those supporting the learning of non-US students. The cultural provenance of most of the texts is clear. The illustrative material often relates to large US corporations and it includes scenarios from the American way of life with names, places and prices in dollars to match. This can create cultural resistance amongst learners from elsewhere. One response to this challenge is to choose European editions of US texts, such as Kotler *et al* (1999) and Solomon, Bamossy and Askegaard (1999). Another is to select books produced by authors based outside the United States (eg Antonides and van Raaij, 1998; Brassington and Pettitt, 2000; Lambin, 2000), since international editions of US texts seldom succeed in convincingly throwing off their cultural roots. It is also possible to integrate non-US cases into the student learning experience, from providers such as the European Case Clearing House (see Table 5.1).

It is only recently that European scholars have taken issue with this US hegemony of marketing education. As a result, many learners based outside the United States have been presented with a narrow and distorted view of marketing. This is shaped by the US marketing environment with its huge domestic market and distinctive and highly competitive mass-marketing infrastructure. Hence, approaches to learning facilitation focus on the mass marketing of packaged consumer goods produced by large corporations targeted at individuals and households. Services and industrial marketing tend to be treated as special cases. European scholars have criticized such approaches for their dependence on limited 'real world' data and for their concentration on one kind of marketing. Learners studying in the European Union, for example, are living in predominantly service economies. There is a strong probability that they are either current or potential employees of small and medium-sized enterprises, marketing services to organisational buyers rather than individual consumers. The possibility also exists that they will be involved in marketing in the not-for-profit or public sector. The challenge facing educators, then, is to expose learners to a range and variety of markets, products and customers that take account of different organisational settings. In so doing, they should be mindful that there are various models of marketing, not just the one that prevails in the United States. Examples of alternative models are the Germanic-Alpine, the Nordic, the Latin and the Asian. Thus, those responsible for the support of learning need to ensure that their teaching is relevant to the learners' cultural context.

Coping with multidisciplinary demands

Marketing is not a discrete, specialist subject area in the same way as economics, law, accountancy or psychology. It draws on a number of disciplines including economics, financial and management accounting, psychology, sociology, anthropology, semiotics and law to inform professional practice (Baker, 2000a). These disciplines contribute to an understanding of the workings of the market and to making sound marketing decisions. Thus, marketing is integrative in a similar way to other subject areas within business and management, such as business environment (Chapter 8) and business organisation (Chapter 9), as well as non-business subjects, such as architecture. Just as the purpose of architectural students studying physics is to build structures that do not fall down, so the purpose of marketing students studying economics is to build a pricing strategy on the basis of solid foundations.

The disciplinary eclecticism within marketing education presents facilitators with two related challenges. First, those using a variety of specialist, disciplinary material within the marketing curriculum often find themselves in the position of having to venture beyond their sphere of competence. Here the challenge is that, without a specialist background in the disciplines concerned, they may have limited critical awareness of relevant research in these areas. There is no simple solution to this challenge. One approach might be to take advantage of the expertise of colleagues from other disciplines. They can give advice or directly contribute on a collaborative basis. Another is that proposed in Chapter 8, namely to view the educator's role, not as an expert in every area covered in the curriculum, but as a partner engaged in a jointly owned process of learning with students. Nonetheless, wherever possible, educators do have a responsibility for enhancing their awareness of contributing disciplines by taking advantage of sources that are designed to assist them in this respect, such as Foxall and Goldsmith (1998). Such sources provide a means of understanding the linkages between particular disciplinary fields of relevance to marketing. They can be supplemented with texts covering specialist topics for marketers, such as finance and accountancy (Schmidt and Wright, 1996; Wilson, 1999).

A second and related challenge is the varied backgrounds of learners. Some may be unfamiliar with the principles of marketing, while others may have practical experience. The latter can serve as a resource through participation in group learning with inexperienced fellow students. Whatever the background of learners, in order to help them appreciate some of the more theoretical aspects of marketing, it may be necessary to move from the familiar to the unfamiliar (see Chapter 2). For example, a discussion of well-known sales promotion techniques can be used as a first step in helping students relate to more complex material concerning the psychology of consumer buyer behaviour. In this way, learners can be provided with the means of linking theory and practice.

Fostering quantitative awareness

Learners often come to the study of marketing with the perception that it is a 'soft' option. They regard it as a creative activity, more art than science, more within the realm of the imagination than reason and with little need for mathematical or financial skills. The fear of having to deal with quantitative information of a financial or statistical kind can be a significant barrier to learning. Notwithstanding the wider academic debate about whether marketing is an art or a science (Brown, 1996), it is necessary to produce marketers who understand the financial implications of the marketing decisions they take. They also need to be able to interpret the statistical information available to them on the markets they are targeting. Here, educators face two challenges. First, they need to confront the misapprehension that marketing is not about finance or statistics. Second, they need to help learners overcome the fear they often have in making sense of financial or statistical information.

How can these challenges be met? Ideally, from an early stage of their studies learners should be made aware that a knowledge of quantitative issues is essential to marketers. The performance of business organisations is measured in quantitative terms and marketers need to be able to communicate the financial implications and quantitative logic of the strategies they propose to others within the organisation and beyond. They need the ability to understand the key financial statements, such as the balance sheet, the profit and loss account and cash flow statements, as well as apply techniques like ratio analysis, budgetary control and quantitative survey methods.

There are a number of ways of enhancing quantitative awareness among marketing students. The use of simulations such as MARKSTRAT3 (which is discussed more fully later in the chapter) gives learners direct, if simulated, experience of the effect of marketing decisions on the financial performance of a business. This requires them to process, on a continuous basis, financial and statistical information as they take marketing decisions. Consequently, it gives learners the opportunity to understand for themselves the impact of marketing decisions on the financial performance of an organisation.

There are also textbooks designed specifically for this purpose like Schmidt and Wright (1996). Furthermore, facilitators can select case studies that give learners experience of practising techniques for the analysis of financial statements. These put learners in the position of consultants and force them to consider the financial implications of the strategies they propose as solutions to the problems presented in case studies. It is also a valuable exercise for learners to evaluate the quantitative data presented in authentic marketing plans. At the same time, it helps to get students to consider the implications of statistical and cost data for the proposals they make in seminar discussions. For example, they need to be able to justify the expenditure on a television advertising campaign in terms of the strategic benefits the organisation will reap. Likewise, for a full appreciation of topics, such as sales promotion, foreign market entry, advertising or new product development, financial awareness is essential. Finally, marketing strategies should be evaluated in terms of their impact on important measures of financial performance, such as shareholder value (Doyle, 2000).

In addition to finance, learners need enough of a grounding in statistics to be able to interpret and evaluate marketing research reports. This includes a knowledge of basic sampling issues, techniques of data analysis and the use of information technology applications like SPSS.

Aims, objectives and learning outcomes

In determining the aims, objectives and learning outcomes of a marketing course, particular attention needs to be given to its strongly vocational orientation. In the UK this is evidenced by the fact that marketing is formally recognized as a profession (Baker, 2000b; Bradley, 1995). It has its own professional body, namely the Chartered Institute of Marketing, which plays an important part in shaping and influencing the HE curricula. Thus, it is a subject area that is primarily 'for' business rather than 'about' business (see Chapter 1). In other words, the aim of a marketing education is generally seen as the preparation of professionals who are able to make sound marketing decisions and manage the marketing activities of the organisations that employ them. Nonetheless, this does not preclude the incorporation of 'about' business concerns within the marketing curriculum. For example, most introductory texts contain sections on issues relating to the social responsibility of marketers, such as the societal marketing concept (Kotler, 2000), green marketing, consumer ethics and the role of marketing in society (Baker, 2000a; Bradley, 1995). Marketing touches upon so many areas of human life and activity that it is important to produce marketers with compassion and a sense of social responsibility. Having said that, these dimensions need to be seen in the context of sound marketing decisions from a commercial point of view.

Marketing, then, is a complex area of study directly related to professional practice. Central to marketing education are skills of analysis and decision-making relevant to marketing management coupled with an awareness of the broader social implications of marketing activities. How these can be expressed as learning outcomes is illustrated in Table 13.1.

Table 13.1   Examples of learning outcomes for marketing

Area	Examples
Cognitive	Evaluate the utility of portfolio analysis as an aid to marketing planning. Conduct a detailed and comprehensive analysis of complex marketing situations.
Affective	Demonstrate an appreciation of the wide-reaching social implications of marketing activities.
Adaptive	Draw up a comprehensive marketing plan with associated costs and schedules. Apply teamwork skills in developing a marketing strategy.

Learning, teaching and assessment activities

Although leading marketing textbooks provide an accessible framework and associated materials, they need to be treated with caution. As indicated earlier, they may be too culturally specific in nature. They may also be limited in scope. Hence, there is a need to broaden the range of materials that learners use. In so doing, educators have at their disposal a wide variety of resources, a selection of which are listed in the box on page 159.

At the same time, given the vocational nature of marketing education, facilitators need to find ways of bringing the 'real' world into their teaching as much as possible. Beyond the standard use of case studies and guest speakers for this purpose, there is a variety of methods by which this can be achieved. Computer-based simulations, field trips and student research projects are three such examples.

Key resources for marketing

Leading journals

- *Asia–Australia Marketing Journal*;
- *European Journal of Marketing*;
- *Harvard Business Review*;
- *Industrial Marketing and Management*;
- *International Journal of Research in Marketing*;
- *International Marketing Review*;
- *Journal of Consumer Research*;
- *Journal of International Marketing*;
- *Journal of Marketing*;
- *Journal of Marketing Management*;
- *Journal of Marketing Research*;
- *Journal of the Academy of Marketing Sciences*;
- *Journal of the Market Research Society*.

Popular textbooks

- Brassington, F and Pettitt, S (2000) *Principles of Marketing*;
- Kotler, P (2000) *Marketing Management*;
- Kotler, P *et al* (1999) *Principles of Marketing*;
- Wilson, R and Gilligan, C (1997) *Strategic Marketing Management*.

Organisations and useful Web sites

- Academy of Marketing (www.stir.ac.uk/Departments/Management/ Marketing/academy/am-web.../index.ht);
- American Marketing Academy (www.ama.org);
- Chartered Institute of Marketing (www.cim.co.uk);
- Great Ideas for Teaching Marketing (www.swcollege.com/marketing/ gitm/gitm.html#1);
- Marketing Education Review (http://cbpa.louisville.edu/mer/e-marketing. htm).

Computer-based simulations

MARKSTRAT3 is an example of a marketing simulation that integrates learning, teaching and assessment activities very effectively. It can serve as a useful basis for learning facilitation, fulfilling the dual purpose of developing learners' marketing decision-making skills and fostering their collaborative teamwork aptitudes. While MARKSTRAT3 also provides a valuable theoretical element, where learners receive instruction in the theory behind marketing decision-making, it is principally concerned with bringing the reality of marketing decision-making to life.

Following a briefing about the simulation and the key elements of teamwork skills, learners are formed into teams of four or five with a class of approximately 20 learners constituting one industry. The teams work as 'companies', which compete against each other for a period of 7 to 10 weeks. Learners in each company make a wide range of key marketing decisions over this period involving product markets, new product development, advertising, distribution, sales force deployment, segmentation and targeting, pricing and finance. These decisions are informed by market research reports, which companies are able to 'purchase' each week during the simulation period.

Each company starts with the same share price. At the end of each session, learners communicate their decisions to the facilitator, who then activates the computer program for the simulation. At the beginning of the following session, each company is notified of the results of its decisions. This continues for a number of weeks and the company with the highest share price at the end of the simulation period is the winner. Learners thus have 'realistic' experience of marketing decision-making and a simulated opportunity for relating theory to practice.

The assessment of learners is based on both the success of the company in terms of its final share price and written evidence produced by students with respect to the analysis that informed the decision-making process. Learners are asked to keep a weekly diary that records the rationale for each decision. On completion of the simulation period, students write up full reports on their company's performance. This summarizes the decisions they took, the thinking behind each one and how decisions relate to marketing theory. In their reports they also evaluate the strengths and weaknesses of the company's performance. Hence, learners are assessed both on the performance of the company and on the quality of analysis in the final report. The use of this simulation thus integrates learning, teaching and assessment. It also assists with the development of teamwork skills and the bringing of the 'real' world into the marketing classroom.

Field trips

One of the great advantages of teaching a subject like marketing is that students are surrounded by marketing activities in daily life and can exploit these for learning purposes. Advertisements, sales promotions, retail stores, trade fairs and sales literature are all good resources for learning and teaching purposes. One useful way of using this abundance of material is via a field trip in which learners visit sites of commercial operations in order to learn how they are organised from a marketing perspective.

For example, as part of a retail marketing or consumer behaviour course, students can visit stores and carry out observations and interviews to learn the principles of store design and layout (see box on page 161).

Field trips of this kind provide a clear opportunity to involve managers of the retail outlets visited in the assessment and feedback process. For example, learners could be asked to make an oral presentation or write a report focusing on an

---

Field trip tasks

Example 1: Visit to a supermarket

1. Identify the specific physical features that are designed to move consumers in particular patterns around the store and encourage them to purchase particular products.
2. Interview one of the managers about how shelf space is allocated. What and who determines which products are placed on the shelves? How much space are they allocated? At what level are they displayed on the shelf and why?

Example 2: Visit to local clothing shops

1. Visit five small local clothing shops and assess their layout. What similarities and differences are there and what factors account for these differences? In the light of what you have observed, what layout changes, if any, should be recommended?
2. Consider the components that help create store atmosphere. Describe the atmosphere in each store. To what extent was it consciously created?
3. Conduct a store image analysis for each shop. Ask a group of customers to rate each store on a set of attributes and plot these on a graph. On the basis of the findings, are there any areas of competitive advantage or disadvantage that should be brought to the attention of store managers?

(Adapted from Solomon, Bamossy and Askegaard, 1999)

---

analysis of store image, including recommendations for improvement, thereby providing consultancy-style feedback for retail managers.

Mini research projects

Another useful way of bringing the 'real' world into the teaching of marketing is to set mini research projects. These typically involve learners in conducting small-scale surveys interviewing consumers in order to explore marketing concepts at first hand (see box on page 162).

Mini research projects provide an opportunity for learners to deploy and understand the limitations of using different research tools in relation to marketing, such as questionnaires, interviews and focus groups. They also help to remind students of the importance of quantitative rigour during the collection, analysis and interpretation of statistical data.

There are various other ways in which the 'real' world of marketing practice can be drawn into the student learning experience. Given that marketing campaigns, messages and symbols are part of the everyday life of the modern

---

Market research projects

Example 1: Brand image

Some marketers believe that a significant proportion of consumers develop images of brands based on advertising rather than on product experience. If this is true, one would expect beliefs about brands to reflect advertising themes. Select a product category in which different advertising themes can be associated with brands (eg pain relievers, airlines, paper towels). Construct a vocabulary of product attributes, including the advertising themes. Ask a sample of 50 consumers to rate the brands in the product category utilizing the vocabulary.

- Are brands rated higher on criteria used in the brand's advertising?
- Do both heavy and light users of the product category rate brands in accordance with the advertising themes?

(Adapted from Assael, 1998)

Example 2: Consumer decision-making

Select an electronics product that costs several hundred pounds (eg a DVD, stereo, personal computer). Conduct in-depth interviews with consumers who have purchased the item within the past year.

- Describe the decision-making process underlying the purchase of the product and the choice of brand.
- To which model does the decision-making process conform?
- What are the implications of the decision-making process for: (a) market segmentation; (b) product positioning; and (c) advertising strategy?

(Adapted from Solomon, 1995)

---

consumer this is not difficult to achieve. An analysis of television advertisements is an obvious example, which also serves to illustrate the importance of psychology in marketing. Ensuring that students are able to make such connections is vital if they are to come away with an integrated understanding of marketing.

Integration

Since marketing is both a synthetic discipline and a philosophy of business, there are numerous links with other subject areas that form part of the business and management curriculum. These are illustrated in the box on page 163.

Links between marketing and other subject areas

- *law and ethics*, eg advertising regulation, advertising to children, consumer protection legislation, predatory pricing;
- *economics*, eg utilities, exchange theory, economic man and rationality, theory of monopolistic competition, pricing, price elasticity;
- *psychology*, eg perception, learning and memory, needs and motivation, personality, management of rewards;
- *sociology*, eg roles, social class, groups, family life cycle, culture, subculture, power;
- *strategic management*, eg resources, competencies and strategic capability, stakeholder theory, resource allocation and control;
- *human resource management*, eg organisation design and structure, culture and organisational effectiveness, culture and innovation;
- *accounting and finance*, eg financial statement analysis, performance measurement, ratio analysis, variance analysis, marketing and distribution audits.

Making these links explicit to learners is important. Human resource management and accounting and finance are areas closely related to marketing where the links tend to receive limited attention within many programmes. Yet managing a team of fellow professionals, such as sales managers, market analysts and advertising managers, is central to marketing management. Further, competence in managing marketing budgets, interpreting quantitative data and justifying expenditure on marketing activities necessitates quantitative awareness. Ensuring that students incorporate the full organisational implications of their proposals when constructing a marketing plan is an effective way of achieving a degree of integration.

Reflection and evaluation

Marketing educators need to reflect on the extent to which they are achieving a variety of goals. Delivering a marketing course involves the complex task of crafting a set of learning, teaching and assessment strategies that enable learners to develop a base of knowledge and a set of skills in preparation for current or future organisational roles. This means that educators need to strike a balance between theory and practice through providing learners with experiential learning activities. Moreover, since the marketing environment is changing rapidly, learners need to understand not only the bases of traditional marketing practices but also the implications of new technologies like the Internet and interactive multimedia for contemporary marketing.

Some specific questions to guide the process of reflection and evaluation are provided in the box below. Of course, for individuals the nature and range of these questions will depend upon the particular orientation of the learning, teaching and assessment strategies adopted.

Examples of reflective questions for marketing educators

- Have students understood that marketing is a science as well as an art?
- Have students become proficient in the application of relevant financial and statistical techniques?
- Have students understood the social and ethical implications of marketing activities?
- Have sufficient experiential learning activities been created within the course?
- Are learners capable of working collaboratively as members of a marketing team?
- Do students appreciate the contribution of other disciplines to decision-making in marketing?
- Were learners exposed to a variety of business environments, case studies, examples and sectors so that they could appreciate the diversity of marketing activities?
- Was adequate use made of the local marketing environment?
- To what extent did the course draw on the personal marketing experiences of students?
- Were learners able to develop skills like leadership, teamwork, communication, problem solving and information technology that are valued by employers?
- Were learners made aware of the implications of new technologies for marketing?

Conclusion

Marketing is prone to misunderstanding from two main sources. It is often regarded as a 'soft' option by learners new to the subject. In addition, it is viewed with some suspicion by academics from other disciplines. In reality, however, it has reached maturity both as an academic subject in its own right and as a key business function and discipline. It is proving to be a popular choice for students entering HE, while other more traditional disciplines struggle to meet recruitment targets. Those involved in the provision of marketing education have the dual challenge, which is crucial for the survival and prosperity of business organisations, of mastering an emerging and complex body of knowledge and contributing to the preparation of future managers able to supervise marketing activities.

References

Antonides, G and van Raaij, F (1998) *Consumer Behaviour: A European perspective*, Wiley, Chichester

Assael, H (1998) *Consumer Behaviour and Marketing Action*, South Western College Publishing, Cincinnati

Baker, M (2000a) *Marketing Strategy and Management*, Macmillan Business, London

Baker, M (2000b) *Marketing Theory: A student text*, Thomson Learning, London

Bradley, F (1995) *Marketing Management*, Prentice Hall, Hemel Hempstead

Brassington, F and Pettitt, S (2000) *Principles of Marketing*, Financial Times/Prentice Hall, Harlow

Brown, S (1996) Art or science? Fifty years of marketing debate, *Journal of Marketing Management*, **12**, pp 243–67

Doyle, P (2000) *Value-Based Marketing*, John Wiley, Chichester

Evans, M and Piercy, N (1980) Undergraduate marketing degree curricula in the United Kingdom, *Business Education*, Autumn, pp 151–62

Foxall, G and Goldsmith, O (1998) Personality and consumer research: another look, in *European Perspectives on Consumer Behaviour*, ed M Lambkin *et al*, pp 130–37, Prentice Hall, Hemel Hempstead

Fullerton, R (1988) How modern is modern marketing? Marketing's evolution and the myth of the production era, *Journal of Marketing*, **52**, pp 108–25

Kotler, P (2000) *Marketing Management*, Prentice Hall International, New Jersey

Kotler, P *et al* (1999) *Principles of Marketing*, Prentice Hall Europe, Hemel Hempstead

Lambin, J-J (2000) *Market-Driven Management*, Macmillan Business, London

Schmidt, R and Wright, H (1996) *Financial Aspects of Marketing*, Macmillan Business, London

Solomon, M (1995) *Consumer Behaviour: Buying, having and being*, Prentice Hall, New Jersey

Solomon, M, Bamossy, G and Askegaard, S (1999) *Consumer Behaviour: A European perspective*, Prentice Hall, New Jersey

Wilson, R (1999) *Accounting for Marketing*, International Thomson Business Press, London

Wilson, R and Gilligan, C (1997) *Strategic Marketing Management*, Butterworth Heinemann, Oxford

14

Innovation and entrepreneurship

Philippa Gerbic and Andrew McConchie

Introduction

Innovation and entrepreneurship in the 'real' world is intensely creative and dynamic, characterized by individuals who are driven toward success and thrive on uncertainty, opportunity and challenge. It is therefore disappointing to observe that the richness of this subject area can often be lost in those learning and teaching environments that have traditionally been characterized by teacher-led curricula, knowledge transmission, examinations and a consequent lack of student interest and motivation. A 'real world' approach to innovation and entrepreneurship can provide a means for learners to become engaged in framing problems of interest to them and solving these through the application of self-generated knowledge. To energize, inspire and intellectually stimulate learners, educators need to adopt an approach that no longer treats knowledge as a transaction but acts, rather, as a catalyst for transformational learning. In short, there is much to be gained from being innovative and entrepreneurial when designing and delivering courses in this field.

While capabilities in innovation and entrepreneurship are often viewed as advanced outcomes for degree programmes, there is no reason why they cannot be developed at an earlier stage of study. Innovation and entrepreneurship courses provide opportunities for all business and management students to have a near 'real world' experience of new business development. In other words, they serve as a framework within which learners can begin the process of acquiring the attributes of entrepreneur as innovator, that is someone who thinks outside traditional boundaries and who, in order to remain in business, must entwine knowledge from marketing, management, finance and an array of other subject areas.

The guidance in this chapter has been informed by the experience of delivering a course entitled New Business Development (NBD). This forms part of a four-year Bachelor of Business degree programme at the Auckland University of Technology. In NBD, interdisciplinarity reinforces a 'real world' approach where learners grapple with complex problems in entrepreneurially driven individual and collective learning activities. In this respect, innovation and entrepreneurship very much reflects the 'for' business orientation discussed in Chapter 1.

Educational challenges

As a relatively new subject area in business and management, innovation and entrepreneurship presents learning facilitators with some exciting challenges. At the same time, given the nature of the subject matter, there is a particular need to be creative in responding to them.

Unlocking entrepreneurial potential

For educators in innovation and entrepreneurship, helping learners unlock their entrepreneurial potential is a critical challenge. While there is considerable accord in the entrepreneurship education literature about the importance of developing entrepreneurial propensity from secondary education level (eg Chamard, 1989; Filion, 1994), most learners have never had the opportunity of thinking of themselves as entrepreneurs or of developing a new business idea, prior to commencing a business and management programme in HE. Thus, HE has a particular responsibility for developing and sustaining an enterprise culture, on which the competitive advantage of many countries depends.

Arguably, learners with work experience are more likely to be receptive to the demands of an entrepreneurship education than those without such experience. In the case of the NBD course, learners are generally full-time workers with a minimum of five years' work experience. They enter degree-level study with credits (one-year full-time equivalent) in business fundamentals, such as marketing, accounting, management, economics, statistics and law, and often bring with them a wide variety of experience in business and the community. They know the business field in which they wish to specialize and see their degree as a key stage in their career. Thus, they display many of the characteristics of adult learners by taking responsibility for their own learning, appreciating autonomy and being motivated by significant amounts of choice in the programme (Merriam and Caffarella, 1991). At the same time, they are often aware of the importance of becoming more entrepreneurially adept for career development purposes, with the result that educators can work more effectively with what has been called in Chapter 2 'the grain of the students'. For learners without these characteristics, more attention may well have to be given to preparing the ground.

However, even where learners possess work experience, many have a view of business that is static and an understanding of it based on a series of unconnected disciplines and functions. As yet, they are not fully aware of the dynamism, complexity and interconnectedness inherent in business activity. They have good stores of knowledge but little experience in mobilizing this through problem solving or critical thinking. Some learners have not worked in groups. Many are unaware of the ways in which basic research skills can be employed to help business decision-making. They have yet to develop independent learning, and reflective and metacognitive skills. Thus, in some respects, they are not as different from learners without work experience as might initially be thought. For both types of learner, innovation and entrepreneurship can serve as an excellent vehicle for unlocking the potential and developing the skills of those committed to driving the economy forward. In so doing, however, a related challenge is the need to anticipate and respond positively to change.

Preparing learners for the changing environment

The environment for business is now one characterized by rapid change, uncertainty, supercomplexity, ambiguity, dilemmas, pressure of work, diversity and multiple and conflicting views about the way forward. To succeed, learners require problem-framing and decision-making skills, technical competence and a propensity to reflect and self-monitor (Schon, 1983; Eraut, 1994; Barnett, 1999). Globalization and increasing mobility have created new diversity and opportunity. E-business and the knowledge-based economy require new approaches to business processes, structures and relationships.

This means that there is a need for innovation and an entrepreneurial spirit. For the entrepreneur, rapid change is not something to be feared; rather it should be embraced, as it signals opportunities to be exploited. In such a world, there is a call not only for entrepreneurs who can inspire, energize, stimulate and motivate themselves, but also for transformational leaders who can implant similar qualities in their colleagues and employees (Bass, 1990). In a UK study (Harvey and Knight, 1996), employers indicated that they wanted graduates who have not only intellectual abilities but also personal attributes such as adaptability, flexibility, self-motivation, self-reliance and an ability to work independently and collectively. Graduates are expected to be transformative, that is creative and innovative in the face of change; committed to lifelong learning; and capable of contributing to the evolution of the organisation through inspirational interpersonal and leadership styles and teamwork.

Thus, learning facilitators in innovation and entrepreneurship are faced with designing curricula that will equip graduates with such capabilities. Moreover, they need to help learners develop their own explanatory frameworks and a deep understanding of central concepts. New approaches are needed to develop capable and confident graduates, and the learning and teaching of innovation and entrepreneurship provides many opportunities to respond to this formidable challenge.

Aims, objectives and learning outcomes

The most important educational aim of a course in innovation and entrepreneurship, according to an in-depth survey of 15 experts in this field, is a greater awareness of the processes involved in the creation of a new business (Hills, 1988). A related aim is the development of a learning experience that engages the students. Such an experience must be challenging and relevant to the 'real' world; specify ends and facilitate means; create opportunities for new learning; involve teamwork; and provide feedback and reflection on performance. Relevance to the 'real' world is crucial for the credibility of any course in innovation and entrepreneurship.

In the case of NBD, the overall aim is to develop a deep understanding of innovation and entrepreneurship from a number of disciplinary perspectives. It also provides opportunities for students to develop a better understanding of themselves as learners and members of groups. A key objective is the development of entrepreneurial propensity with the emphasis being on pre-'start-up' activities. It does not examine post-'start-up' activities, although there is provision for this in the final stage of the Bachelor of Business programme through co-operative education (see Chapter 6). Like other courses in entrepreneurship, NBD is characterized by the deployment of an interdisciplinary pedagogy. Using this approach enables greater depth to be achieved in both knowledge-bases (eg new product development, promotion strategy and business law) and skill-bases (eg research, problem solving and critical thinking).

Learning outcomes for innovation and entrepreneurship courses can be classified in terms of the framework outlined in Chapter 4 (see Table 14.1).

Tensions exist between the achievement of cognitive outcomes, which require development of discipline knowledge, and of adaptive and affective outcomes, which require attention being given to skills and dispositions. While adaptive and affective outcomes are often difficult to develop, particularly in the case of 'hard' skills like statistical analysis and technical competence in aspects of human resource management, an inclusive approach to skill building as well as knowledge acquisition is essential for innovation and entrepreneurship (Vesper and McMullan, 1988). This may be resisted in situations where educators see themselves solely as subject experts, with the result that they are reluctant or unwilling to give time to the development of critical thinking, problem solving, teamwork or self-monitoring skills. Hence it is essential that this issue be addressed as an integral part of curriculum and staff development.

Table 14.1   Examples of learning outcomes for innovation and entrepreneurship

Area	Examples
Cognitive	Analyse the nature and structure of a selected industry Identify and evaluate business 'start-up' opportunities Understand the nature of, and prospective customers for, a new product Develop a plan that tests the feasibility of a new business venture Demonstrate transformed understanding of the integrated and interconnected nature of business activity
Affective	Appreciate the importance of entrepreneurial activity for the economy Cope with uncertainty, risk, ambiguity and lack of information Be open-minded about the roles and values of different business disciplines Be prepared to experiment with new ideas for business ventures Develop a holistic perspective with respect to new business opportunities
Adaptive	Operate effectively as a member of a group in generating new ideas for a product or service Demonstrate problem-solving and research skills in determining the viability of new products or services Act autonomously in pursuing new lines of enquiry Monitor performance and progress of the group and group members in meeting targets Evaluate personal creative and innovative capabilities in a business setting

Learning, teaching and assessment activities

As in other subject areas, there are many resources that can be used by educators in designing learning, teaching and assessment activities for innovation and entrepreneurship. Examples are provided in the box on page 171.

How such resources are deployed and the types of teaching approaches adopted vary considerably across programmes (eg Zeithaml and Rice, 1987). However, empirical studies generally support the notion that 'applied' teaching approaches result in more successful entrepreneurship outcomes. McMullan and Boberg (1991) compared project and case study approaches to teaching entrepreneurship and found the former more effective in developing analysis and synthesis skills. Gartner and Vesper (1994) came to similar conclusions, adding that projects requiring product-based business plan development were more successful, though they had mixed results with group projects.

Research relating to curriculum content is limited. Knight (1991) proposes the following framework: opportunity identification, strategy development, resource acquisition and implementation. As NBD is focused on pre-'start-up' activities, it has expanded Knight's initial stages as follows: strategic environmental scanning,

Key resources for innovation and entrepreneurship

Leading journals

- *American Journal of Small Business;*
- *Entrepreneurship Theory and Practice;*
- *Frontiers of Entrepreneurship Research;*
- *International Small Business Journal;*
- *Journal of Business Venturing;*
- *Journal of Small Business and Entrepreneurship;*
- *Journal of Small Business Management.*

Popular textbooks

- Brandt, S C (1983) *Entrepreneuring: The ten commandments for building a growth company;*
- Drucker, P (1990) *Innovation and Entrepreneurship;*
- Handy, C (1999) *The New Alchemists;*
- Harvard Business School Press (2000) *Harvard Business Review on Entrepreneurship;*
- Osteryoung, J S, Newman, D L and Davies, L G (1997) *Small Firm Finance: An entrepreneurial perspective;*
- Peter, J P and Donnelly, J H (2000) *A Preface to Marketing Management;*
- Rule, R C and Dickinson, C C (2000) *Rule Book of Business Plans for Startups;*
- Timmons, J A (1999) *New Venture Creation: Entrepreneurship for the 21st century.*

Useful Web sites

- Business Owner's Toolkit (www.toolkit.cch.com/scripts/sohotoc.asp);
- Business Plans (www.bplans.com/);
- Canada/British Columbia Business Service Sector Online Small Business Workshop (www.sb.gov.bc.ca/smallbus/workshop/busplan.html);
- MIT Enterprise Forum's Business Plan Resource Guide (http://web.mit.edu/afs/athena/org/e/entforum/www/Business_Plans/bplans.html).

opportunity identification, opportunity testing, strategy development and planning. Bechard and Toulouse (1991) argue for an approach that moves beyond a content focus to one based on contemporary adult education and learning theories. These can be equated with Dana's (1987) contention that entrepreneurial learning style preferences fit with active classroom participation and the need for particular attention to be given to student learning skills.

Such considerations have been to the fore in the design of NBD, as has the recognition that, in a subject area like innovation and entrepreneurship, assessment activities can serve as the main drivers for learning. As well as being used to judge performance against learning outcomes, they can create purposeful and motivational learning opportunities (Boud, 1995). Assessments, therefore, comprise a series of learning activities that are sequentially arranged to provide a manageable learning progression through various new business development stages. These culminate in the capstone assessment item that is considered to be the central component of any course on innovation and entrepreneurship, namely the development of a business plan. Throughout the course, regular structured classes and associated independent learning run alongside assessment tasks and, at times, act as the forum for them.

The principal components are described below. Each serves as a valuable learning and assessment opportunity in its own right. While together, they provide a robust framework for helping learners enhance their entrepreneurial and creative capabilities.

Industry analysis

To be a successful innovator and entrepreneur, it is important for learners to have an understanding of the nature and structure of particular business sectors or industries. This requires significant skills in secondary research and application of a range of industry analysis tools.

For formative and/or summative assessment purposes, learners can be asked to write a report that requires them to undertake secondary research into a sector or industry. Allowing learners to choose a sector or industry, conduct research and undertake an analysis creates greater engagement. This is because the assessment is focused on the 'real' world and offers students opportunities to connect or engage with it by integrating their learning with their own experiences, aspirations and interests (Beane, 1997).

However, some sectors/industries are very complex and it is impossible for facilitators to be knowledgeable about all of them. Since there is no single comprehensive instrument for analysing a sector or industry, facilitators need to concentrate on presenting a range of analytical tools that students synthesize and apply. Here, it is more important for educators to demonstrate expertise with respect to the tools rather than comprehensive knowledge of any particular sector/industry. Such tools include Porter's competitor analysis, SWOT analysis, PEST analysis, value chains, market segmentation, ratio analysis and perceptual mapping.

In this way, conceptual tools, and associated theoretical perspectives, are used as frameworks for the examination of practice within the sector/industry where learners wish to locate their new business idea. At the same time, learning is situated in a particular context and revolves around authentic activities such as using conceptual tools that reflect the beliefs, practices and values of the community

(Brown *et al*, 1989). The learning is also student-centred, so the role of educators is to support the development of learners' internal frameworks.

The learning involved in the synthesis of various industry analysis tools can also be seen as an active process of constructing rather than acquiring knowledge. Moreover, industry analysis requires the application of sophisticated secondary research skills, which many learners lack, thereby providing an additional opportunity for learning. Tasks that require synthesis and application can be said to challenge learners to a greater extent than those involving just one of these capabilities.

Business opportunities and new venture evaluation

With respect to their chosen sector/industry, learners need to know how to perform a systematic search for new business opportunities as well as how to analyse and evaluate them. There are many different tools for identifying opportunities for new businesses and evaluating these opportunities to determine ideas that are worthy of further development (see box below).

Selected tools for identifying and evaluating new business opportunities

- Drucker's seven sources of innovative opportunity;
- Boston Consulting Group Matrix;
- GE planning grid;
- 7-S model;
- Competitive strength versus market attractiveness model;
- AD little business profile matrix.

In this context, a good assessment format is the oral presentation (see Chapter 5) in which learners promote and/or demonstrate their business idea, thereby providing an opportunity to develop persuasive communication skills. In addition to educators and learners, the audience for these presentations can include representatives from the small business sector, including bankers, venture capitalists, government enterprise agencies and accounting firms. For example, in the case of NBD a major international accountancy firm is used for this purpose. As well as hearing about new business opportunities, everyone present can contribute to the provision of formative feedback.

Learners can benefit a great deal, both individually and collectively, from being required to give each other detailed feedback on particular outcomes and suggestions for improvement (Brown and Knight, 1994). The process can also serve to enrich the dialogue between facilitators and learners, with the former assisting in the generation of ideas for dealing with possible shortcomings, suggesting new thought pathways and providing moral support and encouragement. For learners with limited experience, facilitator intervention is vital. However, where learners are expected to operate with high levels of autonomy, how to structure formative feedback, with respect to time, process and focus, and how to develop a climate in which student self-evaluation is the norm are significant issues that need to be addressed by the teaching team.

Primary market research

Having invested a great deal of energy in generating a business idea, learners might well fail to see some of its flaws and weaknesses. Consequently, they need to test out their assumptions regarding customer needs and find out whether, and to what extent, these would be satisfied by their product or service offering. This can be achieved by conducting primary market research (see box below).

Key elements in primary market research

- identify research questions;
- compare and contrast a variety of methods;
- choose an appropriate research methodology;
- explain and justify the methodology;
- apply the methodology (eg via a sample survey tool);
- draw conclusions in relation to research questions and the suitability of the method.

It has been argued that the skills needed for primary research are best developed within a discipline and professional knowledge framework, since this is more likely to increase understanding and secure transfer to other contexts (Blagg *et al*, 1993). Nonetheless, educators in the field of innovation and entrepreneurship still need to check that learners can apply skills developed elsewhere to business settings, such as those associated with assessing the viability of new products and services, and, if necessary, to offer support to enable them to do so.

Business plan project

Focusing on problems that have a 'real world' emphasis and promote a deep approach to learning (see Chapter 2) are the key curriculum design ideas behind projects involving the preparation of a business plan. In analysing 'real world' problems, learners are engaged in actively looking for meaning and understanding. If learners can find and relate knowledge to new situations, apply theory to 'real world' problems, organise content into a coherent whole and distinguish between evidence and argument, this will result in qualitatively superior outcomes and enhance their satisfaction (Ramsden, 1992).

Assessment can be more 'real world' if the project relates to an idea, plan or proposal with which learners identify personally (Beane, 1997), rather than one where they do not have a sense of ownership. The preparation of a business plan that tests the feasibility of a new business idea, identified by a group of learners, is a considerable challenge. It requires them to determine goals, adapt knowledge and processes, address problems and create strategies and, where possible, a competitive advantage to ensure that the idea will succeed. This kind of project is usually closely connected to learners' lives, interests and aspirations, particularly if the plan is based on fulfilling an unmet need identified within their own community.

In order to succeed in the business plan project, learners must demonstrate that the plan is technically competent in a variety of respects (see box below).

Basic requirements of a business plan

- executive summary;
- organisational overview;
- market analysis;
- legal environment and compliance issues;
- marketing and promotion objectives and strategy;
- operations objectives and strategy;
- management and ownership issues;
- personnel objectives and strategy;
- financial objectives and strategy;
- financial data;
- appendices or exhibits.

The plan must be coherent and integrate a range of functional aspects. For example, the core, actual and augmented product strategy must be followed through in the business plan and the promotional campaign must comply with consumer law.

A further challenge for learners is not only managing themselves but also managing and being managed by others in the group. There are significant learning advantages for students working on a business plan in groups rather than as individuals. Learning is a social and collaborative process providing opportunities for interaction and conversation to assist with new learning (Bruffee, 1993). Working and learning collaboratively leads to fulfilment of the basic need for humans to affiliate with each other. The fulfilment of this need leads to higher motivation that in turn creates a greater probability for the learning arising from the preparation of a business plan to be more engaging.

To increase further the motivational potential of the business plan project, learners are in effect self-managing groups. The groups provide opportunities for learners to have control over their learning and development, the kind of empowerment that promotes transformational learning (Harvey and Green, 1993). Moreover, from a learning and development perspective, group members can try out particular group roles, such as co-ordinator or conciliator, and explore different career options by assuming different functional roles (eg marketing, accounting).

The design of the work groups can also maximize learner flexibility to achieve specific ends (ie the business plan). This means allowing as much autonomy as possible to facilitate greater engagement by learners. Thus, learners may be allowed to self-select into groups and groups may be able to reallocate a portion of their final grade based on the results of peer assessment of individual group member contributions. Major conflicts can arise if learners are not equipped with knowledge of group formation processes or peer assessment skills, so these need to be specifically addressed in the curriculum.

In this learning environment, educators act as *provocateurs* rather than as authority figures. They model processes for clarifying problems relevant to learners, such as intragroup conflict, and serve as one source for identifying solution pathways, while at the same time challenging the assumptions in both problem definition and potential solutions. Facilitators must balance the need to create learner autonomy with the exercise of a supportive role. This difficult balance requires significant thought and planning and, more importantly, awareness and constant monitoring of the different roles. To prepare effectively, learning facilitators need to work in self-managing groups themselves and this has its own special challenges for an interdisciplinary course.

Integration

A key curriculum strategy for achieving entrepreneurial outcomes is the creation of an interdisciplinary learning environment. The success of organisations today no longer relies on discrete roles and departments, but on an ability to operate as a cohesive whole, that is to see interrelatedness, to identify impacts and consequences and to work in groups. This means attending to both the complications and the complexity of the situation. Entrepreneurship requires not only good ideas, but also sound financing, the right organisation structure, perceptive market analysis, a vibrant marketing strategy and attention to operational details, including costs, premises and people. Thus, there are significant linkages with other subject areas (see box on page 177).

Exploitation of these linkages through interdisciplinary study within an innovation and entrepreneurship course provides a curriculum platform to develop the kind of broad and cross-functional understanding of business that a fragmented and

Links between innovation and entrepreneurship and other subject areas

- *marketing*, eg marketing mix, segmentation, competitor analysis, pricing;
- *economics*, eg local economic conditions, economic trends;
- *law*, eg contract, employment and company legislation;
- *accounting*, eg cash flow forecast, profit and loss forecast;
- *human resource management*, eg recruitment procedures, codes of practice;
- *research methods*, eg survey methods, statistical analysis.

(Adapted from Macfarlane and Tomlinson, 1993)

subject-oriented curriculum is unable to provide. Interdisciplinarity enables the resolution of more complex problems in the contemporary business environment and is therefore ideally suited for exploration of entrepreneurial issues such as the development and implementation of a new business idea. Learners can compare and contrast the strengths and limitations of the different disciplines in terms of their values, world-views, roles, processes and knowledge-bases. Interdisciplinarity also assists in the development of the ability to analyse, to draw analogies and to synthesize information from a range of perspectives, and creates intellectual coherence for learners (Boyer, 1990). Research indicates that this has widespread effects on cognitive, academic and self-development skills (Austin, 1997). Other noted benefits are a changed world-view (Barnett, 1990), enlarged perspectives, unconventional thinking and sensitivity to bias (Newell and Klein, 1997).

Rigorous interdisciplinarity is dependent on discipline depth. NBD has specific learning outcomes in management, marketing, law, accounting and economics and these are taught by specialists in their fields. Learning and teaching activities focus on both disciplinary and interdisciplinary issues. Examples of interdisciplinary issues include examining the implications of strategies (eg the price of a new product or service, taking into account the cost, the value placed on it by consumers, the state of the market state and the elasticity of demand); the effects of decisions (eg the legal implications of a marketing plan); and the coherence of plans (eg organisational structure and debt financing *vis-à-vis* legal entity and ownership arrangements). Learners need to be made aware of the importance of the respective disciplinary components. Attention to interdisciplinary questions means that less 'traditional' discipline content is covered and this impacts on academic standards and thresholds for discipline competence. Thus, it is important for programme leaders to negotiate a common understanding about traditional discipline expectations and the benefits of a broad and interdisciplinary understanding of entrepreneurship.

An integrated course on entrepreneurship needs a team-based approach to learning facilitation with primacy given to philosophy and outcomes rather than discipline loyalty. This requires the development of a supportive institutional structure;

new cultural frames of reference to develop shared values, norms and beliefs of various coalitions within the teaching team; and new *systemic* frames for institutional policies and procedures relating to communication, quality, teaching, learning and assessment.

Cross-functional teaching teams who are committed to developing an integrated perspective and outcomes are essential to provide an interdisciplinary learning experience. This means developing a new community where team members acknowledge the different socialization processes and consequent norms, beliefs and values of various business professionals, such as accountants, lawyers, strategists and marketers. It also requires the development of a new collegiality based on a mutual understanding of disciplinary contributions and a holistic view of learning outcomes. Interdisciplinary cross-functional teams are fragile in traditional organisational structures where consequent staffing, funding, research and promotion procedures do not support groups that are oriented across disciplines or programmes. New structures that promote the visibility and legitimacy of these groups (Newell and Klein, 1997) are needed to ensure that integrated programmes become institutionalized.

An integrative culture must be modelled in the classroom and this has implications for professional development. In the case of NBD, a rigorous, internally driven and team-based approach has evolved. Regular meetings of new and experienced team members to plan, problem-solve, reflect and evaluate have ensured development. Internal processes are balanced by external assistance (when needed), research and international networks. What has resulted is tacit understanding of integration through practice of the concept and discussion of philosophy rather than a clear definition to which everyone subscribes (Newell and Klein, 1997). Learners also need to embrace the new culture. Initially, some learners moving away from separate discipline pigeon-holes experience a 'grieving' process as they adjust to this new lens with which to view the world. In the long run, to be truly effective the new culture needs to be embedded and communicated through materials, activities and interaction with other learners and to become part of the myths and legends associated with the programme.

Reflection and evaluation

Given the challenging nature of innovation and entrepreneurship, reflective evaluation is critical to ensure that the learning experience retains its cutting edge. With this in mind, NBD uses a reflective model that monitors and evaluates progress both during and at the end of the course. At weekly meetings, team members preview upcoming activities, reflect on events to date and note issues for further consideration. At the end of the course, the team evaluates achievement of the learning outcomes through a review process that includes data from student feedback, assessment and any external input. The review includes an action plan for the next semester. Examples of questions considered during the review are provided in the box on page 179.

> ## Examples of reflective questions for innovation and entrepreneurship educators
>
> - Did the students demonstrate an integrated perspective of entrepreneurial activity?
> - To what extent were the business plans innovative? Did the assessment strategies promote this? If not, why not? If yes, can they be improved?
> - Did the learning, teaching and assessment strategies support and inspire students? Were these strategies sufficiently 'real world'?
> - To what extent have integrative approaches been demonstrated and modelled within the constraints of the programme?
> - What difficulties and problems did students encounter and how effective were the learner support mechanisms in dealing with these?
> - Is the balance between discipline competence and integration right?

Conclusion

The changing environment of business means that more than ever before there is a need for entrepreneurial spirit supported by innovative capabilities. Courses in innovation and entrepreneurship can develop understanding of the entrepreneurial process through learning and assessment activities such as industry analysis, evaluation of business opportunities and preparation of a business plan. In order to motivate students and promote deep learning, assessment needs to be 'real world', problem-focused, interdisciplinary and based on autonomous group working. A core strategy for achieving this is interdisciplinarity. However, this is not without its tensions, particularly with regard to discipline depth and capability development. Success depends on developing new systemic, structural and cultural frames within institutions of HE.

References

Austin, T (1997) What matters in college? Four critical years revisited, in *Advancing Interdisciplinary Studies: Handbook of undergraduate curriculum*, ed W Newell and J Klein, pp 393–415, Jossey-Bass, San Francisco

Barnett, R (1990) *The Idea of Higher Education*, Society for Research into Higher Education/Open University Press, Buckingham

Barnett, R (1999) *Realizing the University in an Age of Supercomplexity*, Society for Research into Higher Education/Open University Press, Buckingham

Bass, B (1990) From transactional to transformational leadership: learning to share the vision, *Organizational Dynamics*, **18** (3), pp 19–33

Beane, J (1997) *Curriculum Integration: Designing the core of a democratic education*, Learning Facilitators College Press, New York

Bechard, J P and Toulouse, J M (1991) Entrepreneurship and education: viewpoint from education, *Journal of Small Business and Entrepreneurship*, **9** (1), pp 3–13

Blagg, N M *et al* (1993) *Development of Transferable Skills in Learners Report No 18*, Employment Department Methods Strategy Unit, Pendragon Press, Cambridge

Boud, D (1995) Assessment and learning: contradictory or complementary?, in *Assessment for Learning in Higher Education*, ed P Knight, pp 35–48, Kogan Page, London

Boyer, E (1990) *Scholarship Reconsidered: Priorities of the professoriate*, Carnegie Foundation for the Advancement of Teaching, Princeton

Brandt, S C (1983) *Entrepreneuring: The ten commandments for building a growth company*, Penguin, New York

Brown, J *et al* (1989) Situated cognition and the culture of learning, *Educational Researcher*, **18** (1), pp 32–41

Brown, S and Knight, P (1994) *Assessing Learners in Higher Education*, Kogan Page, London

Bruffee, K (1993) *Collaborative Learning: Higher education, interdependence and the authority of knowledge*, Johns Hopkins University Press, Baltimore

Chamard, J (1989) Public education: its effect on entrepreneurial characteristics, *Journal of Small Business and Entrepreneurship*, **6** (2), pp 23–30

Dana, L P (1987) Towards a skills model for entrepreneurs, *Journal of Small Business and Entrepreneurship*, **5** (1), pp 27–31

Drucker, P (1990) *Innovation and Entrepreneurship*, Pan Books, London

Eraut, M (1994) *Developing Professional Knowledge and Competence*, Falmer Press, London

Filion, L J (1994) Ten steps to entrepreneurial teaching, *Journal of Small Business and Entrepreneurship*, **11** (3), pp 68–78

Gartner, W B and Vesper, K H (1994) Executive forum: experiments in entrepreneurship education: success and failures, *Journal of Business Venturing*, **9** (3), pp 179–87

Handy, C (1999) *The New Alchemists*, Hutchinson, London

Harvard Business School Press (2000) *Harvard Business Review on Entrepreneurship*, Harvard Business School Press, Boston

Harvey, L and Green, D (1993) Defining quality, *Assessment and Evaluation in Higher Education*, **18** (1), pp 9–35

Harvey, L and Knight, P (1996) *Transforming Higher Education*, Society for Research into Higher Education/Open University Press, Buckingham

Hills, G E (1988) Variations in university entrepreneurship education: an empirical study of an evolving field, *Journal of Business Venturing*, **3**, pp 109–22

Knight, R M (1991) Can business schools produce entrepreneurs? An empirical study, *Frontiers of Entrepreneurial Research*, pp 603–14, Babson College, Wellesley, MA

Macfarlane, B and Tomlinson, K (1993) Reflections on business enterprise projects, *Business Education Today*, June/July, pp 10–12

McMullan, W E and Boberg, A L (1991) The relative effectiveness of projects in teaching entrepreneurship, *Journal of Small Business and Entrepreneurship*, **9** (1), pp 14–24

Merriam, S and Caffarella, R (1991) *Learning in Adulthood*, Jossey-Bass, San Francisco

Newell, W and Klein, J (1997) Advancing interdisciplinary studies, in *Handbook of Undergraduate Curriculum*, ed J Gaff and J Ratcliffe, Jossey-Bass, San Francisco

Osteryoung, J S, Newman, D L and Davies, L G (1997) *Small Firm Finance: An entrepreneurial perspective*, Harcourt Brace, San Diego

Peter, J P and Donnelly, J H (2000) *A Preface to Marketing Management*, 8th edn, Irwin McGraw-Hill, Boston

Ramsden, P (1992) *Learning to Teach in Higher Education*, Routledge, London

Rule, R C and Dickinson, C C (2000) *Rule Book of Business Plans for Startups*, Oasis Press, San Francisco

Schon, D (1983) *The Reflective Practitioner*, Basic Books, New York

Timmons, J A (1999) *New Venture Creation: Entrepreneurship for the 21st century*, McGraw-Hill, Boston

Vesper, K H and McMullan, W E (1988) Entrepreneurship: today courses, tomorrow degrees?, *Entrepreneurship Theory and Practice*, **13** (1), pp 7–13

Zeithaml, C P and Rice, G H (1987) Entrepreneurship/small business education in American universities, *Journal of Small Business Management*, **25** (1), pp 44–50

Part D

The way forward – maintaining the momentum

Given the changes that are currently occurring in HE, in general, and business and management education, in particular, it seemed appropriate to conclude this book by giving some consideration to what may lie ahead and to how those responsible for the learning of others should respond. In Chapter 15, some of the likely future trends are discussed with a view to alerting educators to their probable impact on both learning environments and the resources that they have at their disposal. Many of these trends are global. Thus, although the manner in which they are manifested in individual HE systems may vary, their significance for everyone with responsibility for the learning of others cannot be overstated. Moreover, their implications for professional development, both initial and continuing, are considerable. Hence, the importance of the different approaches to professional development highlighted in Chapter 16. Many of these are predicated on the assumption that, faced with a turbulent and rapidly evolving environment, the way forward for learning facilitators lies in active engagement with the forces of change. To be a passive bystander is no longer a realistic option. Effective learning and teaching in a field like business and management critically depends upon the willingness of educators to respond to change in an informed and shrewd manner. Clearly, this is only possible if they are prepared to invest time and energy in monitoring what is going on and in making a contribution to the shaping of the educational agenda.

15

Anticipating the future

Bruce Macfarlane and Roger Ottewill

Introduction

In looking into the future of business and management education there are plenty of clues to indicate what is likely to happen, to some extent at least. Many of these relate to global trends in HE and include institutional differentiation and diversity; the demand for vocationally relevant programmes from more assertive 'customers', be they students, parents, employers or the state; the growth of online learning; the demands for new skills and knowledge arising from the rapidly changing nature of business practice; and an increasing emphasis on work-based learning. Underlying these trends, there is the shift, highlighted in earlier chapters, from traditional approaches to learning and teaching, often based on didactic methods with limited learner participation, toward a focus on learning as a collaborative and interactive enterprise. Such trends form the basis for discussion in this chapter and serve as a backdrop for the consideration of the professional development of business and management educators in Chapter 16.

Differentiation and diversity

Globalization is both an economic and a social phenomenon connected with 'living in a more interdependent world' (Giddens, 1999: 32). It is also closely associated with the power of the brand. In parallel with globalization, traditional forms of control of HE in many countries, such as Australia and the UK, have been replaced by state supervision of 'quasi-markets', permitting greater competition between HE institutions. This move away from tight control, combined with the impact of a global market for HE, facilitated by technological developments, is likely to encourage greater differentiation and diversity among providers. Popularly, this differentiation has been represented as a split between wealthy institutions, with a strong research basis and a global brand name, such as Harvard or Oxford University, and less 'well-heeled' HE providers lacking either the resources or reputation to compete in the global market. However, these latter institutions will have an important role to play in providing mass HE via a sharper focus on the economic and social needs of local or regional communities. Although the future shape of HE is often represented in dichotomous terms as a straight choice between the 'global' and the 'local', the reality may be a more fine-grained continuum with the rich research elite at one end and tertiary community college-style providers at the other.

Differentiation in the world of HE is likely to be replicated, in microcosm, by a similar trend within business and management education. This means that in the future it is less likely that a business and management provider will try to compete on all fronts: undergraduate, postgraduate, research and management development. Although the mission statements of business schools are currently coy about target customers and specific markets (Stearns and Borna, 1998), there will be a tendency to specialize more in the future (Crainer and Dearlove, 1998). Providers will try to find their niche or basis for competitive advantage.

The 'trickle-down' effect of this trend is likely to produce starkly contrasting roles for business and management educators at either end of what is often termed the global–local continuum. At the global end, those working in prestigious, research-based environments, with a strong focus on postgraduate education, are likely to face a different kind of future in which state control and public funding are less significant, but there is fierce competition in terms of research productivity. A likely consequence of this is that their status will be enhanced, thereby enabling them to enjoy considerable professional autonomy. At the same time, the logic of competitive advantage means that elite providers will not wish to use their expensive, research-active staff as learning facilitators in anything other than an occasional capacity as a 'star turn'. The division of labour will intensify further as part-time facilitators take on the bulk of traditional teaching responsibilities, already a common practice in many institutions. Indeed, some leading business schools now outsource the assessment of student assignments and in the future it is probable that elite providers will franchise more of their courses.

By contrast, those working in local, access-based institutions with large numbers of students may find themselves operating in a 'teaching-only' capacity with diminishing levels of personal autonomy and opportunities for research. Mass student numbers combined with the growing demand for comparable levels of service quality from students and government will result in an increasing 'McDonaldization' of practice. In such an environment, course and teaching materials will be pre-packaged in conformance to a standardized curriculum and often made available online, turning the educator's role into little more than a 'McJob' (Ritzer, 1998). Consequently, there is likely to be very little room, if any, for creativity or professional autonomy in the classroom. Moreover, direct face-to-face contact with learners will almost certainly decrease, thereby providing fewer opportunities for individual contributions to be personalized.

For many involved in business and management education, increasingly the future extends beyond the traditional confines of the publicly funded university campus to, for example, 'think-tanks', management consultancies, as well as corporate and private universities. It is no coincidence that the private, for-profit University of Phoenix is the single largest provider of business and management education worldwide making almost US $13 million a quarter via online and distance learning. There are now over 1,000 corporate universities, a figure that has more than doubled in the space of a decade (Abeles, 1999). Moreover, in the future, it is probable that more countries will follow New Zealand's example in permitting corporations that meet government criteria to award their own degrees. As this consumer-led model of HE takes hold, the monopoly powers of HE institutions are on the wane.

For publicly funded business and management education, this trend points to the need to forge learning partnerships with both corporations and publishers with access to a large portfolio of intellectual property. FT Knowledge, of the Pearson Group, and the Judge Institute of Management at Cambridge University are planning a collaborative e-MBA from September 2001, via a combination of open learning and online materials. Another example is Microsoft designating Paisley University as an 'academic professional development centre', allowing it to offer Microsoft courses and training. Moreover, knowledge consultancy companies are now competing with business schools to leverage intellectual property rights. Thus, the boundary between public and private HE is likely to become increasingly blurred (Giddens, 1999).

In many respects, the preceding analysis offers a somewhat gloomy prognosis of the future, one that will increase the divide between the elite and mass providers of business and management education. It also has serious implications for the extent to which those working in a capacity of reduced professional autonomy will be supported to initiate change through reflective practice. In addition to the barriers facing innovators highlighted in Chapter 7, there are other significant constraints. These include quality assessment procedures that inhibit risk taking, institutional policies that preclude individual initiatives and bureaucratic policies for approval, support and resources (Hannan, 2000). For those working in non-elite institutions, highly dependent on public funding, these factors may militate against the kind of pedagogic creativity advocated in this book.

Vocationalism

While the future may restrict the professional autonomy of those working outside elite institutions, the future demand for business and management education looks strong. HE has become more vocational and this global trend is set to continue (Thorne, 1999). Increasingly learners now regard their study as a preparation for the workplace rather than a retreat into a cloistered world (Winter, 1996). Even the choice of more traditional disciplines by students is often prompted by a belief that successful completion will lead to a particular career opportunity with a prestigious employer (Wellington, 1993). This 'deferred' vocationalism points to a generation of more instrumental students.

Furthermore, the vocabulary and curriculum of business and management are spreading their influence across HE. This development has taken a number of different forms. First, symbolically, the language of HE itself has shifted from an emphasis on the monastic vocabulary of the past to the business jargon of today: 'markets', 'globalization', 'performance indicators', 'quality management' and 'learning organisations' to name but a few. Second, business-related skills are now widely recognized as a key component of every graduate's profile, regardless of the area of study. This implies that nearly everyone working in HE is a *de facto* business and management educator!

Last, business and management is permeating other parts of the HE curriculum, especially degree programmes serving as an academic basis for professional practice or public service. In engineering, education administration, public administration, law and the health sciences, the value of management knowledge and skills is increasingly recognized and looks set to continue to grow in importance. This means that there will be a strong demand for the services of business and management educators across the HE curriculum. However, in responding to this demand, they will need to be adept at meeting the distinctive requirements of their 'clients' and have an understanding and empathy for the concerns of professionals across a variety of fields.

With its long-standing vocational orientation, business and management education is strategically placed to take advantage of the increasing emphasis on work-relatedness in HE. Nonetheless, those engaged in learner support will still need to demonstrate their willingness to fine-tune their offerings with respect to both content and delivery methods, including the application of CIT.

The online future

It is widely predicted that the future of HE will be online with educators working as mediators in an interactive environment based on either Web-supported or Web-delivered approaches to learning, teaching and assessment. However, this vision, with some exceptions, does not reflect the reality of current provision where the response to growing numbers of students and a falling unit of teaching resource in many countries has been what Bourner and Flowers (1997) term the 'default solution'. This involves larger groups of students being taught in traditional ways via mass lectures and impersonal seminars. Nonetheless, in the last few years, some providers, such as the UK's Open University, have made considerable strides towards developing online courses. It is therefore important to consider a number of significant implications of the online future for business and management educators.

First, while it is widely predicted that the Internet and information technology spell the end of the traditional lecture as a means of transmitting knowledge (eg Entwistle, 1992; Bourner and Flowers, 1997), it is essential that online learning is seen as something more than individual learner engagement with print-based material delivered electronically, or in the words of Saunders and Weible 'old wine in new bottles' (1999). Enabling students to download lecture notes does nothing to promote interactive and collaborative learning. Even the UK's Open University, while keen to embrace the new technology and exploit e-learning, still runs on paper. This is because 'people who have to assimilate large quantities of text don't want to do it on the screen' (*The Independent*, 2000: 4). In reality, a great deal of ingenuity and creativity will be required if the potential of online learning is to be maximized.

Second, although online learning is sometimes presented as a more cost-effective means of providing an educational experience, developing and maintaining electronic facilities that secure genuine learner interaction and collaboration is a highly demanding and potentially expensive activity. While synchronous forms of online communication with students may replace traditional time commitments associated with leading seminars, holding workshops or giving lectures, asynchronous activities involving the educator, such as discussion boards and e-mail, make additional demands on time (Postle and Sturman, 2000).

Third, as originally highlighted in Chapter 5, the right question needs to be asked about the use of technology in relation to learning. This is not how pedagogy can be geared to meet the possibilities of technology but, rather, how computers can be used to support a professional vision of effective learning and teaching. In other words, student-centred learning does not solely depend on technologically driven methods, although, if deployed with care, online learning can open up possibilities to achieve this goal (Batson and Bass, 1996).

Last, the demands of an online future may bring about a different kind of division of labour among educators than that previously discussed. Those with a preference for providing creative solutions to educational challenges and utilizing technology may specialize in designing online learning material while those with a stronger interest and ability in personal interaction may spend most of their time facilitating open learning sets and large-group teaching (Bourner and Flowers, 1997). Both groups, however, will need to work closely with Web designers, technicians, information specialists and others, since increasingly learning and teaching will be seen as a collaborative enterprise requiring a much wider diversity of skills and expertise than has traditionally been the case.

There can be little doubt that CIT and online provision will lead to some significant changes in the way that business and management educators relate to both learners and colleagues. While it is important not to overstate these, ignoring them is not really a viable option. Indeed, with their awareness of changes in the business world arising from the growth of e-commerce and e-banking, business and management educators ought to be in the vanguard as far as the development of e-learning, e-universities and the knowledge-based economy are concerned.

Knowledge and the economy

More generally, the fast-moving nature of business brings with it a constantly shifting demand for new knowledge and skills. For business and management educators, the extent and speed with which the curriculum adjusts to these patterns is a key issue (see Chapter 1). Abeles (1999) distinguishes between 'long half-life' knowledge in areas like philosophy, literature and the social and political sciences, and 'short, half-life' skills or knowledge, immediately applicable to the economy. Gibbons *et al* (1994) make a similar differentiation between 'mode 1' or 'traditional' knowledge, generated within a disciplinary, cognitive context, and 'mode 2' knowledge, produced within a broader social and economic 'context of application'.

For business and management educators, getting the balance right within the curriculum between 'short, half-life' and 'long half-life' knowledge is a particular challenge. On the one hand, too great an emphasis on the former may leave learners without a sufficiently robust knowledge-base and as hostages to the latest management fad. On the other hand, failure to update the curriculum runs the risk that students will be perceived as not possessing the skills and knowledge valued in the current market-place. As global trends and the pace at which new business knowledge and skills emerge quicken, this is set to become an increasingly difficult dilemma, which needs to be kept under constant review. The development of new e-business, e-commerce and e-marketing degrees is a response to the rapidly changing nature of business life. However, such programmes need to balance predictions of future change in the way business is conducted with current realities, one that is sometimes referred to as a 'bricks and clicks' economy involving a mix of traditional and Internet trading. This is not easy. Account also has to be taken of the increasing emphasis being placed on learning as an ongoing process, characterized by informality, reflection and flexibility as well as the formality associated with courses and qualifications.

Work-based learning

In many quarters, learning is now seen as a career-long, indeed lifelong, process that does not necessarily incorporate physical attendance at a 'university' or other HE institution. Employee and executive development is now an accepted part of the culture of all enlightened organisations. This has strengthened company support for work-based learning (Crainer and Dearlove, 1998). The commitment of many businesses to organisational learning points to the growth of flexible, work-based approaches. Growth in provision, which is either explicitly or implicitly work-based, is occurring at all levels of business and management provision. This ranges from low-level vocational qualifications, which are assessed or evidenced in conjunction with line managers, to Doctorates of Business Administration, which provide opportunities for undertaking more practically based and work-related managerial research than a traditional PhD. It also encompasses 'in-house' provision of almost infinite diversity, including the development of cross-cultural competency highlighted in Chapter 11.

Significantly, within work-based learning the focus of attention is the learner as opposed to the facilitator. Thus, it reflects the current preoccupation with the effectiveness of learning and how this can best be achieved.

From teaching to learning

This book has self-consciously spoken of 'learning and teaching' rather than 'teaching and learning'. This is more than a pedantic point. It symbolizes a sea change in the focus of HE away from the self-regarding agenda of teaching 'performance' towards an overriding concern for the quality of the student learning experience. Allied to the development of online learning and the increasing emphasis on work-based learning, business and management educators will increasingly require the skills of mentoring, coaching and supervision of learners rather than the more didactic skills of 'lecturing'. Only in this way will effective learning become a reality.

Moreover, references to 'lecturers' or 'professors' have been eschewed for a similar reason. Increasingly, the student learning experience is shaped by a broad range of professionals and specialist support staff. As indicated earlier, the shift to a new learning environment is likely to bring about more collaborative working, especially between 'lecturers' or 'professors' and key support professionals such as software development experts and information specialists (Roberts and Daniel, 1999).

Brave new world

Less...

lecturing;
campus-based learning;
professional autonomy;
formality;
full-time faculty.

More...

mentoring;
coaching;
online tuition;
work-based learning;
action learning;
inter-professional teamwork.

The changes signalled in the box above are as much cultural as procedural or structural (see Chapter 14). Consequently, the difficulties involved in securing them are not to be underestimated. As the literature on the management of change makes clear, long-established norms and values are far harder to change than structures (Dyer, 1985). It requires strong personal commitment and tenacity on the part of the change agents and a willingness to involve all those affected to secure success.

Conclusion

While the impact of the trends highlighted in this chapter will vary considerably from country to country, from institution to institution and from individual to individual, they cannot be ignored. To prosper, educators will need to cultivate the attributes of flexibility and adaptability. They will have to acquire new skills and knowledge and apply existing skills and knowledge in new ways to cope with the changes in working practices and the expectations of learners and other stakeholders. Hence, priority will need to be given to professional and personal development and the application of some, at least, of the approaches considered in Chapter 16.

For business and management educators, in particular, the developments discussed in this chapter should be seen as an opportunity for demonstrating the application of some of the principles and strategies associated with the management of change at both the personal and organisational level (eg Lewin, 1951; Kotter and Schlesinger, 1979). Helping learners to prepare for changes and/or to manage change in the workplace is likely to be a far more credible enterprise if educators can show how they have coped with similar pressures.

References

Abeles, T P (1999) The academy in a wired world, in *Universities in the Future*, ed M Thorne, pp 141–59, Department of Trade and Industry, London

Batson, T and Bass, R (1996) Teaching and learning in the computer age, *Change*, March/April, pp 42–47

Bourner, T and Flowers, S (1997) Teaching and learning methods in higher education: a glimpse of the future, *Reflections on Higher Education*, **9**, pp 77–102

Crainer, S and Dearlove, D (1998) *Gravy Training: Inside the shadowy world of business schools*, Capstone, Oxford

Dyer, W G (1985) The cycle of cultural evolution in organizations, in *Gaining Control of the Corporate Culture*, ed R H Kilmann *et al*, pp 200–29, Jossey-Bass, San Francisco

Entwistle, N (1992) *The Impact of Teaching on Learning Outcomes in Higher Education*, CVCP, Sheffield

Gibbons, M *et al* (1994) *The New Production of Knowledge*, Sage, London

Giddens, A (1999) *The Future of Universities*, Address given at the meeting of University of London Convocation, 9 May

Hannan, A (2000) Innovations in teaching and learning in higher education, Unpublished conference paper, Innovation and Creativity in Teaching and Learning, 12–13 June, University of Stirling

Independent, The (2000), Printing money to the tune of £7m, *Open Eye Supplement*, 1 August, p 4

Kotter, J and Schlesinger, H (1979) Choosing strategies for change, *Harvard Business Review*, **57** (2), pp 106–14

Lewin, K (1951) *Field Theory in Social Science*, Harper & Row, New York

Postle, G D and Sturman, A (2000) Models of learning as a factor in online education: an Australian case study, Unpublished conference paper, Innovation and Creativity in Teaching and Learning, 12–13 June, University of Stirling

Ritzer, G (1998) *The McDonalization Thesis*, Sage, London

Roberts, S and Daniel, J (1999) Changing needs: changing study patterns, in *Universities in the Future*, ed M Thorne, pp 160–71, Department of Trade and Industry, London

Saunders, G and Weible, R (1999) Electronic courses: old wine in new bottles?, *Internet Research: Electronic networking applications and policy*, **9** (5), pp 339–47

Stearns, J M and Borna, S (1998) Mission statements in business higher education, *Higher Education Management*, **10** (1), pp 89–104

Thorne, M (1999) Introduction, in *Universities in the Future*, ed M Thorne, pp 4–16, Department of Trade and Industry, London

Wellington, J J (1993) Fit for work? Recruitment processes and the 'needs of industry', in *The Work-Related Curriculum: Challenging the vocational imperative*, ed J J Wellington, pp 79–97, Kogan Page, London

Winter, R (1996) New liberty, new discipline: academic work in the new higher education, in *Working in Higher Education*, ed R Cuthbert, pp 71–83, Society for Research into Higher Education/Open University Press, Buckingham

16

Professional development

Roger Ottewill and Bruce Macfarlane

Introduction

While some of the future trends in the sphere of business and management education, like those discussed in the previous chapter, are predictable and can therefore be planned for in advance, others are likely to emerge unexpectedly. In either case what in business and management terms is sometimes described as 'environmental scanning' is of particular importance for the professional development of educators. Indeed, a desire to keep abreast of what is happening, not only in their subject area but also with respect to learning, teaching and assessment, is a key attribute of those committed to reflective practice (see Chapter 7). Moreover, such a desire implies not simply a passive or reactive stance to what is going on but a desire to play an active part by contributing to the ongoing debate on how best to respond to changes in the environment of HE and by participating in pedagogic innovation. In other words, it requires educators to adopt a proactive stance and engage with the forces of change rather than ignoring or simply noting them.

Of course, the principle of proaction should be motivated by a desire to improve one's practice, not simply to engage in debate. Thus, in responding to change and reflecting on practice, the key question for learning facilitators should always be, 'How might my students learn better?' In considering this question, it is important to remember Beaty's comments:

> Reflection alone is not sufficient for professional development to occur. The real test is developed practice. Reflection then is a middle ground where theories are brought to bear on the analysis of past action; the really important

stage comes after this and could be thought of as planning. To assess the significance of learning from experience we need to ask 'so what?'
(Beaty, 1997: 9)

Particular attention is given, in this chapter, to a number of ways of applying Beaty's observations, thereby enabling educators to enhance and enrich their professional development. These are mentoring and work shadowing; peer observation; secondments, consultancy and networking; and action research, some of which are applications of methods used to assist business managers in their development. Thus, they have a particular resonance in the context of business and management education. Moreover, they can be viewed as critical ingredients of the learning environment for those with responsibility for the learning of others and as supportive of the principle of continuing professional development.

Here development is seen as extending beyond the definitions of staff development often found in the literature on human resource management, where the emphasis is on 'the improvement of a person's overall career prospects' (Hannagan, 1995: 313). For educators, career prospects might well be enhanced. However, the main priority is that, by participating in development activities, educators are better able to respond to the changing demands of business and management education, in a confident, competent and scholarly manner.

Mentoring and shadowing

These are formalized relationships for enabling a transfer of pedagogic knowledge and skills from business and management educators with particular kinds of experience and expertise to those who do not possess them either wholly or in part. Such arrangements can serve as support mechanisms for those seeking to increase their knowledge and hone their skills in order to respond more effectively to the pressures arising from developments in the educational environment. They can also empower those who seek to play an active part in these developments.

In a mentoring relationship there is a very heavy emphasis on the notion of wisdom. Indeed, mentors are usually selected to act as wise guides and counsellors to their protégés (Harrison, 1997). They have a responsibility for the encouragement and application of learning; guiding; advising; and providing new insights into how to meet challenges faced in the workplace. At best, mentors can also provide what in the business and management literature is sometimes described as a 'stability zone' (Toffler, 1971) for when things go wrong or it becomes difficult to cope with stressful situations, a common enough experience for educators! In addition, if mentoring relationships realize their full potential, then mentors can act as a catalyst or sounding board for new ideas, thereby stimulating and supporting innovation in educational practice. Although mentoring is generally seen as being of particular relevance at the start of an educator's career, there is no reason, in principle, why it should not be used at any stage, especially given the rapidly changing environment of business and management education.

Shadowing, as its title suggests, involves learning facilitators accompanying colleagues as they carry out their normal responsibilities in the classroom and beyond. By watching and listening, a considerable amount can be learnt. However, given the complexity of learning facilitation, opportunities for discussing and analysing what has been witnessed also need to be provided if the full potential of this type of arrangement is to be realized. When it works well, shadowing can be an extremely rewarding experience for the person being shadowed as well as the shadower. Very often in business and management education, it is a short step from shadowing to team teaching. Collaboration of this kind, especially where it brings together the experienced with the less experienced, can be particularly valuable for building confidence. It can also contribute significantly to the realization of inter-disciplinary co-operation and understanding amongst educators from different disciplinary backgrounds (see Chapter 14).

Peer observation

Peer observation schemes within HE are becoming increasingly popular, especially in the UK. This is, in part, a reactive response to external factors, such as quality assurance initiatives from national funding agencies and other benchmarking programmes affecting business schools, such as the European Quality Improvement Scheme (EQUIS) run by the European Foundation for Management Development. It is also due to a recognition that initiatives such as peer observation can make a useful contribution to the personal and professional development of educators. Their value lies in having colleagues observe how classes are conducted and the subsequent provision of informed comment on what has been observed, ideally in a supportive and constructive manner. Thus, to some extent, the observers act as a mirror. They watch what goes on and reflect it back to those who have been observed. Clearly, for such arrangements to be effective, the relationship between the observer and the observed is crucial. It needs to be based on trust and, in some instances, on the principle of reciprocity or mutuality, that is an alternating of roles.

The need for specialists with contemporary business and professional experience means that part-time staff play a significant role as business and management educators. Thus, in establishing peer observation schemes it is essential that all staff have the opportunity to benefit. Programmes also need to be firmly located within a supportive and developmental context and distinguished adequately from more formal appraisal schemes. Failing to maintain this boundary will tend to inhibit innovation in teaching methods and stifle the full learning potential of peer observation schemes. Finally, while peer observation schemes have considerable value, a major limitation is that they tend to focus on only one aspect of an educator's responsibilities, namely what goes on in the classroom. With an increasing amount of learning now taking place elsewhere, arguably peer observation should be extended to embrace other aspects of an educator's role if the educator is to respond to the changing nature of HE.

Secondments, consultancy and networking

Many business and management educators seek to keep in touch with what is going on in the 'real' world by means of full- and part-time secondments with business organisations, consultancy projects and membership of formal and informal networks. Indeed, teaching materials, such as case studies, and the knowledge educators possess can quickly become dated if contact with commerce and industry lapses for any length of time. For those in fast-moving fields, such as international business (see Chapter 11) and innovation and entrepreneurship (see Chapter 14), this is of particular significance. Indeed, awareness of the latest developments can be critical for the sake of credibility with learners and peers. Remaining credible in the eyes of experienced learners, who may also be practising managers, is crucially important (see Chapters 9 and 12).

Significantly, business and management educators are often criticized for failing to update their industrial or commercial experience (eg Department of Education and Science, 1990). In response, some leading business schools allow staff one day per week to carry out private work (Crainer and Dearlove, 1998). Although consultancy of this kind is commonly cited as a means of maintaining appropriate contact with the business world, it has been criticized on the grounds that the relevance of the work is exaggerated, since it often consists of academic pursuits such as teaching and external examining (Cannon, 1992). Nonetheless, through properly organised secondments and placements, incorporating opportunities for shadowing practitioners in a relevant sphere of business, it is possible to generate fresh case study material, to secure consultancy projects and to gain access to valuable networks (Crystal, 1994). Networking can also be more formalized through membership of professional bodies, which in the UK include the Chartered Institute of Marketing (see Chapter 13), the Institute of Personnel and Development and the Institute of Management.

While secondments, consultancy and networking are primarily designed to facilitate the updating of subject-specific knowledge in fields such as marketing or accountancy, there is no reason in principle why they should not be exploited for educational purposes. Given the amount of training and development that takes place within organisations, there are plenty of opportunities for experiencing different approaches to work-based learning, many of which are transferable to HE. Moreover, there is an increasing number of internal and external networks specializing in learning, teaching and assessment. For example, as mentioned in Chapter 3, many HE institutions now have mechanisms for supporting and promoting pedagogic innovation and sharing good practice, including the educational development centres/units and learning and teaching institutes that perform these roles by a variety of means (eg courses, workshops, conferences, newsletters and research projects). In addition, there are a growing number of national and international bodies committed to the enhancement of the student learning experience, such as the Carnegie

Foundation for the Advancement of Teaching in the United States, the UK's ILT and Learning and Teaching Support Network subject centre for Business, Management and Accountancy, the British Academy of Management, the Association of Business Schools, the Association of MBAs and EDINEB. Membership of one or more of these provides educators with a means of keeping abreast of educational developments, sharing ideas and, if necessary, raising concerns.

Action research

McKernan describes action research as a 'form of professional development for the reflective practitioner' (1996: vi). As such, it is a means of giving practical expression to the emphasis placed on reflective practice throughout this book. It is also ideal for those who wish to strengthen their competence with respect to pedagogy and, at the same time, contribute to academic research. By using aspects of their learning, teaching and assessment as the focus for action research projects, educators can genuinely combine the roles of teacher and researcher.

At the heart of action research are the principles of improvement and involvement (Carr and Kemmis, 1986). The prime motivation for undertaking action research is invariably a desire to ease or solve a problem, thereby improving an existing state of affairs. In terms of business and management education, examples of such problems include the failure of students to engage fully with the subject matter because they do not consider it to be relevant from a vocational point of view (see Chapter 2); poor performance in a particular mode of assessment, such as a case study; and mismatches between learning outcomes and assessment instruments (see Chapter 4). For Jin (2000), a discussion with colleagues that took place at a business school 'away-day' served as the catalyst for investigating the expectations of business students and the reasons why they liked some courses but disliked others. Once identified, the problem and the generation and implementation of a possible solution become the focus of the action research project.

In keeping with the principle of involvement, the choice of research tools and methodologies rests with those who own the problem and the solution. Hence, the traditional boundary between researcher and researched is blurred. Critics of action research claim that this can compromise the objectivity of researchers since they are emotionally involved with the problem and the search for a solution. Having been alerted to this potential shortcoming, however, action researchers can take steps to minimize it by asking a mentor or sympathetic colleague to help them maintain a degree of detachment.

Action research has much in common with the case study approach, defined by Johnson as 'an enquiry which uses multiple sources of evidence. It investigates a contemporary phenomenon within its real-life context, when the boundaries between the phenomenon and context are not clearly evident' (1994: 20). In terms of action research, the phenomenon in question is the problem and associated solution, and the context is likely to be the learning, teaching or assessment strategy. Thus, the outputs of action research projects are generally in the form of case studies, the results of which are not generalizable. Nonetheless, they can still be of considerable value, since they are likely to be of interest to educators facing similar problems and may stimulate further investigation elsewhere. As Ghauri, Gronhaug and Kristianslund point out, 'intensive study of selected examples is a very useful method of gaining insight and suggesting hypotheses for further research' (1995: 88).

Towards scholarly teaching

In HE, research and teaching have traditionally been perceived as two very distinct activities where only the former has carried high status and received recognition for achievement. While action research is an important way of bridging this divide there exists a broader debate about the 'scholarship of teaching' in H E Boyer (1990) insists that teaching is properly understood as a 'scholarly' activity with research central to its effectiveness. Scholarly teaching involves not just transmitting knowledge but also transforming and extending it (Boyer, 1990). Being prepared to *problematize* one's own teaching, though, runs counter to the conventions of academic life that treat the classroom as a 'secret garden'. Indeed, announcing an intention to research a problem involving one's own teaching could be interpreted as an admission of incompetence!

> Asking a colleague about a *problem* in his or her research is an invitation; asking about a problem in one's teaching would probably seem like an accusation. Changing the status of the *problem* in teaching from terminal remediation to ongoing investigation is precisely what the movement for a scholarship of teaching is all about. (Bass, 1999: 1)

Changing the status of the problem is also about challenging the traditional mindset that views teaching as a less rewarding and intellectually stimulating activity than research. In achieving a more scholarly approach to teaching in HE a dose of 'intelligent uncertainty' and vulnerability (Mazen, Jones and Sergenian, 2000) should be viewed as a positive step in the right direction. Although the situation is gradually changing, prompted, in part, by the efforts of bodies mentioned earlier in the context of networking, there is still a long way to go in promoting closer links between teaching and research.

Conclusion

Notwithstanding the attention given to methods in this chapter, ultimately effective professional development depends more upon a positive view of its value than finding and applying the 'right' method. In other words, it is essentially an attitude of mind arising from the recognition that in a rapidly changing environment to 'stand still' is in reality to 'move backwards'.

That said, genuine professional development does involve a degree of detachment from the immediate and whatever is in vogue at a particular moment in time. It does not mean accepting every change and embracing every innovation. One of the most important qualities that professional development can foster is discernment. Those responsible for the learning of others need to be clear-sighted and astute in their response to new developments. Thus, in certain circumstances, it may be necessary to resist some of these in the interests of securing or maintaining effective learning and teaching. Such resistance, however, is likely to be more credible if it comes from those who are prepared to make changes to their learning, teaching and assessment strategies where it can be clearly demonstrated that it is in the best interests of learners to do so.

To end on a positive note, professional development should be seen as the essential ingredient of teaching and the support of learning. It serves as an antidote to the routinization and predictability that can easily creep into learning, teaching and assessment, and provides the basis for engaging with the forces of change in a confident and informed manner. This is particularly important in a dynamic sphere of learning, like business and management, where there is considerable emphasis on entrepreneurship, risk taking and innovation. Indeed, the professional development of business and management educators could well be defined solely in these terms. At the same time, it may well be the case that, to coin a phrase, 'educators who are tired of development are tired of life'!

References

Bass, R (1999) The scholarship of teaching: what's the problem?, *Inventio*, **1** (1), pp 1–9

Beaty, L (1997) *Developing your Teaching through Reflective Practice*, Staff and Educational Development Association, Birmingham

Boyer, E L (1990) *Scholarship Reconsidered: Priorities of the professoriate*, Carnegie Foundation for the Advancement of Teaching, Princeton

Cannon, T (1992) Quality assurances, *Times Higher Education Supplement*, 11 September, pp 24–25

Carr, W and Kemmis, S (1986) *Becoming Critical*, Falmer Press, London

Crainer, S and Dearlove, D (1998) *Gravy Training: Inside the shadowy world of business schools*, Capstone, Oxford

Crystal, L (1994) Staff placement programme: keeping in touch, *Education and Training*, **36** (8), pp 32–34

Department of Education and Science (1990) *Higher Education in the Polytechnics and Colleges: Business and management studies*, HMSO, London

Ghauri, P, Gronhaug, K and Kristianslund, I (1995) *Research Methods in Business Studies*, Prentice Hall, London

Hannagan, T (1995) *Management Concepts and Practices*, Pitman Publishing, London

Harrison, R (1997) *Employee Development*, Institute of Personnel and Development, London

Jin, Z (2000) The learning experience of students in Middlesex University Business School (MUBS): why do they enjoy some modules/lectures and dislike others?, *The International Journal of Management Education*, **1** (1), pp 22–36

Johnson, D (1994) *Research Methods in Educational Management*, Longman, Harlow

Mazen, A, Jones, M and Sergenian, G (2000) Transforming the class into a learning organization, *Management Learning*, **31** (2), pp 147–61

McKernan, J (1996) *Curriculum Action Research*, Kogan Page, London

Toffler, A (1971) *Future Shock*, Bodley Head, London

Index